State Investment Companies in Western Europe

Picking Winners or Backing Losers?

State investment companies have become a major instrument of European governments in their pursuit of an "industrial policy." Often able to call upon people with substantial business experience, their grants of public funds are typically rationalized in terms of their ability to find potentially profitable companies overlooked by the private capital market. They pose, in an especially sharp form, the question "Can governments pick winners?"

The studies collected in this volume give brief histories and assessments of the performance of state investment companies in Belgium, France, the Federal Republic of Germany, Italy, the Netherlands, Sweden and the United Kingdom. They disclose that there is little clear evidence of any ability to pick winners. State investment companies apparently spend most of their resources on propping-up losers.

For proponents of industrial policy, a bird in the bush has been worth two in the hand. It has been easier to draw rosy pictures of the benefits to come in the future than to cope with the reality of a "British Leyland" in the present.

If the dearth of evidence for an ability to pick winners continues, then the debate about state investment companies – and industrial policy in general – must shift to the merits of supporting companies that are not going to provide an adequate return on the public funds invested in them. Brian Hindley considers this issue in his introductory chapter.

Also published for the Trade Policy Research Centre

State Investment Companies in Western Europe

Picking Winners or Backing Losers?

Edited by

BRIAN HINDLEY

St. Martin's Press   New York

for the
TRADE POLICY RESEARCH CENTRE
London

ISBN 0–312–75611–9

Library of Congress Cataloging in Publication Data

Main entry under title:

State investment companies in Western Europe.

Includes index.
1. Subsidies—Europe—Addresses, essays, lectures.
2. Industry and state—Europe—Addresses, essays,
lectures. 3. Investment trusts—Europe—Addresses,
essays, lectures. I. Hindley, Brian. II. Trade Policy
Research Centre.
HD3646.E85S72   1983   338.922   83–13968
ISBN 0–312–75611–9

Trade Policy Research Centre

The Trade Policy Research Centre was established in 1968 to promote independent research and public discussion of international economic policy issues. As a non-profit organisation, which is privately sponsored, the institute has been developed to work on an international basis and serves as an entrepreneurial centre for a variety of activities, ranging from the sponsorship of research, the organisation of meetings and a publications programme which includes a quarterly journal, *The World Economy*. In general, the Centre provides a focal point for those in business, the universities and public affairs who are interested in the problems of international economic relations – whether commercial, legal, financial, monetary or diplomatic.

The Centre is managed by a Council, set out above, which represents a wide range of international experience and expertise.

Publications are presented as professionally competent studies worthy of public consideration. The interpretations and conclusions in them are those of their respective authors and should not be attributed to the Council, staff or associates of the Centre which, having general terms of reference, does not represent a consensus of opinion on any particular issue.

Enquiries about membership (individual, corporate or library) of the Centre, about subscriptions to *The World Economy* or about the Centre's publications should be addressed to the Director, Trade Policy Research Centre, 1 Gough Square, London EC4A 3DE, United Kingdom, or to the Centre's Washington office, Suite 640, 1120 20th Street, N.W., Washington, D.C. 20036, United States of America.

Contents

List of Tables

List of Figures

Biographical Notes

BRIAN HINDLEY has been Counsellor for Studies at the Trade Policy Research Centre, London, since 1976. A Senior Lecturer at the London School of Economics and Political Science, Dr Hindley obtained his doctorate from the University of Chicago and subsequently taught at Queen's University, Ontario, Canada, before returning to Britain. Dr Hindley has written many articles and papers on international economics and industrial organisation and was joint editor of, and a contributor to, *Current Issues in Commercial Policy and Diplomacy* (1980).

ENZO PONTAROLLO has been Professor of Industrial Economics at the University of Padua since 1980. Earlier he taught at the University of Trento and then at the Catholic University of Milan. His is author of *Il salvataggio industriale nell'Europa della crisi* (1976), *Struttura dei costi del lavoro e contrattazione* (1978) and *Tendenze della nuova imprenditoria nel Mezzogiorno degli anni '70* (1982).

H. W. DE JONG is Professor of Economics at the University of Amsterdam. He is the author of a number of publications in applied economics including *The Structure of European Industry* (1980). He was also co-editor with A.P. Jacquemin of *Welfare Aspects of Industrial Markets* (1976).

ROBERT JAN SPIERENBURG studied economics at the University of Amsterdam and now works at the Commission of the European Community in Brussels preparing reports.

PAUL DE GRAUWE is currently Professor of Economics at the University of Leuven. He has been a Visiting Professor at the University of Paris (1978), the University of Michigan (1981) and the Free University of Brussels. Earlier, 1973–74, he was an economist at the International Monetary Fund. He has published many articles and is the author of *Monetary Interdependence and International Monetary Reform: a European Case Study* (1976).

GREET VAN DE VELDE studied at the University of Leuven in 1979. She became a research assistant at the Centre of Economic Studies at the University, 1979–80, and currently works in a private company.

RAY RICHARDSON has been a Reader in Industrial Relations at the London School of Economics and Political Science since 1979. He was Special Adviser to the Rt Hon. Harold Lever, MP, as Chancellor of the Duchy of Lancaster, 1974–75. His publications include: R. Richardson and L. Lynch, 'Unemployment of Young Workers in Britain', *British Journal of Industrial Relations*, November 1982; and *Unemployment and the Inner City — the Study of School Leavers*, the Department of the Environment, forthcoming.

GUNNAR ELIASSON has been the President of the Industrial Institute of Economic and Social Research (IUI) in Stockholm since 1976. He obtained his PhD from the University of Uppsala in 1968, before joining the National Institute for Economic Research in Stockholm. Before taking up his present post, he was the Chief Economist of the Federation of Swedish Industries at the IUI.

Dr Eliasson has been a visiting scholar to the Universities of California at Berkeley, of Illinois and of Michigan and to the National Bureau of Economic Research in New York. He has been an expert adviser to and a member of several Swedish Royal Committees, among them the 1979 Committee on Computers and Electronics in Industry, and is author of several books.

BENGT-CHRISTER YSANDER has been an Associate of the Industrial Institute for Economic and Social Research in Stockholm since 1976. He has taught at the Universities of Umeå, Gothenburg and Stockholm and has worked in the Treasury and the Ministry of Defence. He is currently engaged in research on the behaviour and control of Swedish local public authorities.

DIANA M. GREEN has been Deputy Head of the Department of Politics and Government, and Acting Principal Lecturer, at the City of London Polytechnic since 1981. She has been a consultant on French economic and industrial policy to the Department of Industry in London since 1976 and was Hallsworth Fellow of Political Economy at the University of Manchester, 1980–81. Dr Green has lectured and broadcast extensively. Her latest publications include: *French Politics and Public Policy* (1980); *Managing Industrial Change?* (1981); *The Politics of Industry in Britain and France* (forthcoming).

KLAUS-WERNER SCHATZ is Head of the Department of Infrastructure in the World Economy at the Institut für Weltwirtschaft, University of Kiel, Federal Republic of Germany. He is the author of *Wachstumsbedingungen und Strukturwandel der westdeutschen Wirtschaft im internationalen Vergleich* (1974) and co-author of *Trade in Place of Migration* (1979) and *The Second Enlargement of the European Community* (1982).

KARL HEINZ JÜTTEMEIER is Senior Research Fellow in Public Finance at the Institut für Weltwirtschaft, University of Kiel, Federal Republic of Germany. He is co-author of *Konjunkturelle Wirkungen öffentlicher Haushalte* (1978).

Preface

Over the past ten or fifteen years, 'industrial policy' has become a portmanteau term for that broad range of governmental actions which directly affects the structure of production in an economy. Many of the activities included in the portmanteau pre-date the term and its use may suggest more coherence among them than in fact exists. Rather than actual coherence, the development of the term reflects a desire for coherence; and it also reflects, at least as important, a substantial increase in the resources devoted to industrial policy.

These last two facts do much to explain the controversy over industrial policy, especially in Western Europe, where the expansion of such activity has been greatest. The proposal that more resources ought to be devoted to a coherent industrial policy immediately raises the question of why such a policy is needed and what it ought to be doing. In turn this raises issues of principle. To accept as a matter of practical politics that some firms and industries in trouble will receive assistance through the political process is one thing. It is something else altogether to accept as a matter of principle that they *ought* to be assisted in that way (even if the assistance is called 'restructuring' or 'revitalisation'). 'As a matter of practical politics such-and-such an industry will be assisted' is a statement based on a number of suppositions about the working of the political process. Suggesting that such-and-such an industry '*ought* to be assisted' is likely to be based on a different set of suppositions and almost certainly adds yet another set regarding the validity of choices made through the market.

The specifics of the debate over industrial policy have been largely in terms of picking winners and propping up losers. Those opposed to industrial policy argue that it is interest-group politics by another name and that resources devoted to industrial policy will be frittered away in hand-outs to failing companies. Moreover, they suggest that companies which are failing, by and large, ought to be left to fail and, too, that the weakening of market-imposed discipline, which is the inevitable result of automatic access to life-support systems, can only have deleterious consequences for the economy as a whole.

Those in favour of industrial policy tend to dispute that market outcomes have any social merit. They see no presumption that a failing firm or industry should be refused support; and, indeed, they possibly see a presumption in the opposite direction. Moreover, they suggest that imperfections in the operation of the private sector are so great that potentially profitable and socially valuable investments will be overlooked by the market. A primary role of industrial policy, as they see it, therefore lies in the discovery and nurture of such neglected winners (who may have the same identity as the apparent losers, for it is said that restructuring will effect the transfer between categories).

State investment companies are at the centre of this debate. They are the agencies typically charged by governments with the task of discovering the neglected winners. A study of the actual performance of state investment companies in Western Europe can accordingly be said to go to the heart of the issues surrounding industrial policy, which is why the Trade Policy Research Centre embarked on the programme of studies reported in this volume.

What emerges from the studies is that state investment companies, while frequently presented and justified in terms of their ability to pick winners, have in fact spent the bulk of their resources in supporting losers. There is no clear evidence of any special ability to pick winners on the part of any state investment company anywhere.

For proponents of industrial policy, a bird in the bush has been worth two in the hand. It has been easier to draw rosy pictures of the benefits to come in twenty years than to cope with the reality of a British Leyland in the present. But if the dearth of evidence for the ability of state investment companies to pick winners continues, then the defence of industrial policy will have to be conducted solely in terms of the merits of supporting losers.

Moreover, if market choices are good enough that government agencies cannot find neglected winners, there is a strong presumption that there is good economic justification when a company becomes a loser by market tests. Ultimately, what the advocates of industrial policy must defend are the virtues of using the political mechanism to override private choices in the allocation of capital to failing companies. It is not a comfortable ground on which to take a stand. It is difficult to think of cases in which private suppliers of capital have had cause to regret their parsimony with respect to such companies or in which taxpayers have had grounds to be grateful to their government or its agencies.

That state investment companies do not merely correct defects in the operation of capital markets — doing what efficient markets would have done in their absence — but act to maintain output and employment in companies which would contract or disappear if efficient markets held sway, raises a further issue. In the introductory chapter to this volume, Brian Hindley, the Centre's Counsellor for Studies, who supervised the programme, notes that subsidisation of one producer of a good would very likely reduce output and employment in other producers of that good. When the producer whose output is greater as a result of the subsidy is located in one country, however, and the producers whose output and employment are smaller are located in other countries, a new dimension is added.

The problem of subsidisation in international trade, and the grievances caused by actual and putative cases of it, is proving to be one of the least tractable issues in international economic relations. It threatens to cause rifts within the European Community, as well as between the Community and its trading partners and between different pairs of the latter.

State investment companies and industrial policy are at the centre of this issue. The Code on Subsidies and Countervailing Measures, elaborating provisions of the General Agreement on Tariffs and Trade, explicitly mentions as examples of subsidies covered by it the following: 'government financing of commercial enterprises, including grants, loans or guarantees; government provision or government financed provision of utility, supply distribution and other operational or support services or facilities; government financing of research-and-development programmes; fiscal incentives; and government subscription to, or provision of, equity capital'. A question that advocates of state investment companies must address, therefore, is whether the policies serve any domestic end that justifies the creation of international ill-will and the further disruption of the international trading system. On the evidence of the Centre's programme of studies it is hard to see that they could do so.

The type of intervention sponsored by state investment companies probably has been the fastest growing of a rapidly expanding field within Western Europe over the past decade and for that reason alone repays study. But this intervention is different from most other types. First, it is selective, aiding one company in an industry but not another; secondly, it is at the discretion of the members of the state investment company and the controls and checks on their actions are sometimes very weak; and, thirdly, it involves intervention through the capital market rather than product markets. As a result of these differences, state investment companies give rise to novel arguments and propositions and these, in turn, require fresh assessment and study. The programme of studies reported in this volume, covering seven economies in Western Europe, is a contribution to that process.

Unease at the state of affairs which is revealed is evident in all of the papers resulting from the studies. Several of the authors report reassessment of national policies in this respect. This volume should facilitate that process and perhaps will suggest the need for such reassessment where it is not yet contemplated.

The programme of studies leading to the volume was financed by a grant from the Leverhulme Trust Fund in London and the Trade Policy Research Centre has been extremely grateful for this support.

As usual, it is necessary to stress that the views expressed by the contributors to the volume do not necessarily reflect the views of members of the Council or those of staff and associates of the Trade Policy Research Centre which, having general terms of reference, does not represent on any particular issue a consensus of opinion. The purpose of the Centre is to promote independent analysis and public discussion of economic policy issues.

HUGH CORBET
Director
Trade Policy Research Centre

London
Summer 1983

Abbreviations

AGIP	Azienda Generale Italiana Petroli
ANSDER	Association Nationale des Sociétés de Développement Régional (National Association of Societies for Regional Development), France
BL	British Leyland Company
CIASI	Comité Interministériel pour l'Aménagement des Structures Industrielles (Interministerial Committee for Industrial Development and the Promotion of Employment), France
CII	Compagnie Internationale pour l'Informatique (International Information Agency), France
CODIF	Compagnie de Développement Industriel et Financier (Financial and Industrial Development Agency), France
CODIS	Comité d'Orientation pour le Développement des Industries Stratégiques (Interministerial Committee for the Development of Strategic Studies), France
DSM	Dutch State Mines
EFIM	Ente Autonomo di Gestione per il Finanziamento dell' Industria Meccanica (Independent Managing Body for Financing Mechanical Industry), Italy
EGAM	Ente Autonomo di Gestione per le Aziende Minerarie (Independent Managing Body for the Mining Industry), Italy
ENI	Ente Nazionale Idrocarburi (National Hydrocarbon Corporation), Italy
ERP	European Recovery Programme (Fund)
FIM	Fondo Industrie Meccaniche (Mechanical Industry Fund), Italy

FSAI   Fond Special d'Adaptation Industrielle (Special Fund for Industrial Adaptation), France

FTOI   *Financial Times* Ordinary Share Index

GEPI   Gestioni e Partecipazioni Industriali (Industrial Management and Shareholdings), Italy

GNP   Gross national product

IDI   Institut pour le Développement Industriel (Industrial Development Institute), France

IRC   Industrial Reorganisation Corporation, United Kingdom

IRI   Instituto per la Ricostruzione Industriale (Institute for Industrial Reconstruction), Italy

LIOF   Limburgs Instituut voor Ontwikkeling en Financiering (Limburg Institute for Development and Finance), the Netherlands

NEB   National Enterprise Board, United Kingdom

NEHEM   Nederlandse Herstructureringsmaatschappij (Dutch Reconstruction Company)

NIB   Nationale Investeringsbank (Recovery Bank), the Netherlands

NIM   Nationale Investeringsmaatschappij (National Investment Company), Belgium

NOM   Noordelijke Ontwikkelingsmaatschappij (Northern Development Company), the Netherlands

NMKN   Nationale Maatschappij voor Krediet aan de Nijverheid (National Company for Industrial Credit), Belgium

OECD   Organisation for Economic Cooperation and Development

OPEC   Organisation of Petroleum Exporting Countries

R & D   Research and development

SCEO   Société Commerciale pour l'Extrême Orient (Commercial Agency for the Far East), France

SCOA   Société Commerciale de l'Ouest d'Afrique (Commercial Agency for West Africa), France

SDR   Société de Développement Régional (Regional Development Agency), France

SF   Statsföretag (state holding company), Sweden

SIB   State Investment Bank, Sweden

SODI   Société de Développement Internationale (International Development Agency), France

CHAPTER ONE

What is the Case for State Investment Companies?

Brian Hindley

State investment companies are established by governments to use public funds to acquire equity or bond holdings in companies formerly financed through private sources. The outcome of their operations has often been described as 'back-door nationalisation' — a description that has obvious force, particularly when the state investment company buys all the voting shares in a company. But this does not always happen. Indeed, the state investment company may buy no voting shares at all, merely acquiring bonds or non-voting shares. Moreover, the official reasons for establishing a state investment company typically differ from those given for nationalisation. Nevertheless, the existence of a state investment company is likely to tilt the balance of decision-making power between the public and private sectors in much the same way as nationalisation.

Although all West European countries now have some form of state investment company, the timing of their spread across the continent has been irregular. The earliest organisation mentioned in this volume was established in Belgium in 1919. In Italy and Spain, state investment companies have played a major role since the 1930s, when the regimes of Mussolini and of Franco were experimenting with similar types of relationship between the state and private enterprise. In the Netherlands, also, the 1930s saw the establishment of Maatschappij voor Industriefinanciering in the context of a policy of cartelisation of Dutch industry and its protection against foreign competition. In the words of H.W. de Jong and Robert Jan Spierenburg, in Chapter 3 of this volume, its influence was 'slight', although it was followed by a more active post-war organisation. Also, in the aftermath of World War II,

1

a state investment company, Berliner Industriebank, was established by the West German Government (although, as Karl Heinz Jüttemeier and Klaus-Werner Schatz note in Chapter 8, with the benefit of American advice) to deal with the special problems of business investment in West Berlin. Its activities, however, were confined to that beleaguered city.

State investment companies began to appear on a wider scale in the 1960s. In Belgium, the Nationale Investeringsmaatschappij (NIM) was established in 1962 and in Britain the Industrial Reorganisation Corporation (IRC) appeared in 1966. In Sweden, a State Investment Bank (SIB) came into existence in 1967 and was followed by Statsföretag (SF) in 1970. In France, the Institut pour le Développement Industriel (IDI) appeared in 1970, while in West Germany, a projected national state investment company failed to emerge because of a change in government in that year. In Italy, in 1971, the Ente Autonomo di Gestione per le Aziende Minerarie (EGAM) started its short and spectacular career and the Gestioni e Partecipazioni Industriali (GEPI) was added to the already established institutions, which by then included the Ente Autonomo di Gestione per il Finanziamento dell' Industria Meccanica (EFIM), founded in 1962. In the Netherlands, the Nederlandse Herstructureringsmaatschappij (NEHEM) appeared in 1972.

Some of these institutions have since disappeared and others have emerged. Nevertheless, in spite of differences in the details of these national institutions, this concentrated burst of activity, in the 1960s and early 1970s, strongly suggests the possibility of a common cause at work across countries.

Almost invariably, the reason given by a government for the formation of a state investment company is an alleged imperfection in private capital markets. Such putative failings take various forms. Probably the most frequent is that participants in the private capital market are overlooking potentially profitable investment projects (which often, although by no means always, involve new technology). A state investment company, it is said, will be able to discover and exploit these, thereby serving a valuable social function while making a market, or better-than-market, rate of return on the public funds given to it.

An important alternative rationale within the category of capital-market imperfections, however, lies in the contention that the private capital market is under-supplying some particular type of financial instrument — for example, a shortage of equity capital in the Belgian case or of long-term credits in the Dutch; or it is contended that the private capital market is making it unduly difficult for some particular class of company to finance itself adequately — for example, small companies or companies located in particular areas of the country. Obviously, there is a considerable potential overlap between this and the first type of alleged failure, and this overlap includes the proposition that a state investment company will be able to rectify the failure and, at the same time, make a profit. In their pure forms, however, the two rationales raise different issues.

Whatever the original motivation or the precise form of the initial justification for a state investment company, however, a great deal of the energy and resources of state investment companies in Western Europe have been occupied in providing finance for companies that would otherwise fail. The purpose of this has been to maintain employment in the rescued company. In spite of its importance, this is a very much more controversial and contentious reason for establishing a state investment company than is provided by capital-market imperfections and it has accordingly been less prominent as an official rationale.

This rationale is perhaps implicit, however, in the final class of argument for state investment companies. This is that a state investment company is needed to act as an intermediary between the government and government-owned enterprises, supplying them with management expertise and protecting them from political pressure from the government or, in some formulations, protecting the government from the political pressures generated by the enterprises.

This is a rather different type of argument than those just discussed, being concerned not with the merits of intervention, as they are, but rather with how it should be organised, given that it has occurred and will probably continue to occur. Government action to save failing employers is inevitable, it is implied, and the need for a state investment company is deduced from that inevitability which, at the same time, enables exponents of this position to avoid any need to provide justification for such intervention. There is, after all, little point in discussing the desirability of the inevitable.

To summarise, three major functions or objectives of state investment companies can be identified:

(a) to fill perceived gaps in the capital market (i) by spotting investment opportunities not noticed or acted upon by private individuals (picking neglected winners) *or* (ii) by offering or facilitating the offer of specific financial instruments or by directing finance to specific classes of company;

(b) to preserve employment in businesses that would otherwise fail; and

(c) to act as an intermediary between government and government-owned enterprises, buffering political pressures between the two and supplying business expertise to the enterprises.

Needless to say, these functions and objectives are not always so clearly separated in practice. A government or state investment company acting to prevent the closure of a large private enterprise, for example, is very likely to be concerned with the political repercussions of the loss of employment ('b'). It may well argue, however, that the rescued business is basically sound so that, by an appropriate application of managerial expertise ('c'), this apparently costly operation will be made to pay off in commercial terms ('a' and especially, by implication, 'a (i)').

Nevertheless, each rationale raises quite separate issues. In order to maintain a sharp focus on these issues, each rationale will first be discussed in isolation from the others.

ANALYSIS OF THE CASE FOR STATE INVESTMENT COMPANIES

Whether those persons who are appointed to the board of a state investment company can in fact find profitable investments which have been neglected by the private sector (and which would, presumably, have been neglected by themselves if acting in a private capacity) is obviously at bottom an empirical question. Some care is necessary, however, in defining the appropriate form of that question.

Picking Winners

In the first place, it is an easily established fact that private capital markets do not recognise all those companies which will prove to be winners in the future. A sufficiently broad random selection of shares will typically prove in five or ten years to contain some that out-perform the market and, very likely, some that out-perform it to a spectacular extent.

This does not necessarily imply any inefficiency on the part of market participants. The simple fact is that they will have information in five or ten years that they do not have now. To show that the shares of coal-mining companies displayed an abnormal increase in price between 1972 and 1981, for example, is not to convict market participants in 1972 of inefficiency. In common with the rest of mankind, markets failed to predict the massive shift to the Organisation of Petroleum Exporting Countries (OPEC) of power over energy pricing that occurred in 1973. The most that can be asked of market participants is that they make full use of the information that is available to them *now* — not that they are in fact always correct about the future.

This fact has an immediate implication for judging the performance of a state investment company: that a state investment company picks *some* winners is not an adequate test of its special ability to do so. Indeed, with enough chances, it is to be expected that a state investment company will pick some winners just as a selection made with a pin from a list of shares will contain some winners.

Those anecdotal accounts that sometimes appear in newspapers, calling attention to this or that successful company that has at some point been sponsored by a state investment company, therefore, do not bear strongly on the general issue of whether the board members of a state investment company have some special ability to pick winners. Nor, conversely, would a demonstration that their selections included some failures — even disastrous failures — be in itself sufficient to prove a lack of such special ability.

The board of a state investment company can only sensibly be judged by whether it picks enough winners to justify its overall activity. One test would be whether it picks more winners and fewer losers than would have been expected from a similar-sized sample selected randomly. This, however, would be a rather weak test. The board members of a state investment company typically do have business competence and may have access to information which is not generally available — to compare their performance with that of a random sample hardly does justice to these facts.

Of course, a state investment company is not primarily trying to make money in the stock market even though, if it is successful in picking neglected winners, a stock-market selection based on its choices would make money. Once it has selected its potential winners, the function of the state investment company is to supply them with capital and, very likely, with advice and encouragement. To the economy as a whole, the cost of this activity is the return the capital would have yielded in other uses and the value of the time spent in giving advice and encouragement had it been spent elsewhere — usually, in the case of board members, in managing the affairs of other businesses.

The grant of capital resources that might not otherwise have been forthcoming and of free advice and easier access to officials complicates the task of evaluating a state investment company by referring to market outcomes. The problem is captured by conceiving of two sets of companies, the members of one set similar to the members of the other except that they receive assistance from a state investment company, while members of the other set do not. If there is any value in the services of a state investment company, those companies receiving them should, on average, out-perform the others.

It follows that if selections of a state investment company out-perform the market, this does not necessarily demonstrate the ability of a state investment company to choose winners. It may merely show that the services supplied by the state investment company are valuable to the companies receiving them. Moreover, that the services are valuable to those receiving them does not, of itself, give rise to any presumption that the activities of the state investment company have any wider social value. A state investment company diverting capital from other uses and passing it on to selected firms at a subsidised rate will give rise to a gain for the selected firms. Yet there is no reason to suppose that there is a gain to the economy as a whole when account is taken of the use to which the capital could have been put elsewhere. The same is true of other services that a state investment company might supply.

If, therefore, selections of a state investment company can be shown to have out-performed the market, the fact must be treated very cautiously. Before interpreting it as evidence in favour of the proposition that the state investment company has performed a socially worthwhile function, or as evidence of the state investment company's special ability to pick winners, it is necessary to know the value of the services it supplied to its selections. If the market has out-performed the state investment company, on the other hand, that appears, at first glance, to be rather strong evidence against its success.

Even in this last case, however, interpretation is not straightforward. Although a state investment company may claim that its activity is designed to pick winners, it may in fact be doing something else. The constraints on it might be so loose that its board members are able to pursue other objectives, choosing for it a portfolio that they would not choose if their own money were at stake. It might also occur because the incentives to which the board members respond in fact lead them in other directions. Probably the most popular hypothesis in this class is that the choices of a state investment company are dictated by purely political considerations: that although rationalised in terms of finding neglected winners, the state investment company is in fact a means of propping-up losers whose failure would raise political problems for the government. That clients selected by state investment companies on such a basis should fail to out-perform the market is quite likely.

A state investment company rationalised as a potential picker of winners, however, is unlikely to devote all of its energies to propping-up losers. A government may wish to establish a state investment company to prop up losers, but it may not wish to present the issue to the electorate in that light. In order to lend some credibility to the rationalisation, the government is likely to want to appoint to the board of the state investment company well-reputed persons with business experience and competence. But if the state investment company is to have no active hand in choosing its own clients, and if those clients are to be the dead-beats of the private sector, the government might have difficulty in obtaining the services of the kind of people it wants. In order to persuade them to tend the dead-beats, it may have to offer them as well the opportunity of doing something with a more dynamic and creative appearance, for example, picking neglected winners. And since there are, no doubt, businessmen who believe that other companies would perform much better if they themselves had an active role in the management and who wish to be seen to serve the public weal, this is likely to prove an attractive package. If so, the government will get its politically sensitive potential bankrupts tended and financed by a credible state investment company. In exchange, it will allow board members of the state investment company to play an interventionist role elsewhere in the private sector.

Such possibilities blur interpretation of the outcome of the activity of state investment companies. Even with evidence on the outcomes of the activity, some *a priori* assessment of claims to a special ability to pick winners neglected by the private sector is potentially useful.

The central point in any such *a priori* assessment is that the private sector includes numerous persons each of whom has a strong financial incentive to discover winners so far neglected by the rest of the private sector. To discover such opportunities is a route to fame and fortune. Moreover, the board members of a state investment company are often recruited from the private sector, but when they are not, being instead, say, career civil servants with no direct experience of managing companies, the claim to a special ability to discover profitable opportunities missed by the private sector has very low plausibility.

Nevertheless, one ground for the proposition that board members have a special ability to pick winners lies in the claim that politicians and/or civil servants are able to pick from the private sector a group of people who have a special ability to recognise and exploit potentially profitable situations. This is not by itself sufficient to make a case for transferring such people to the state investment company. It also must be argued that their talents are under-utilised in the private sector.

As with companies or shares, so with people. It is very likely that there are people in the private sector whose talents are unrecognised. While this leaves open the *possibility* that the selection of executives of a state investment company will yield people of exceptional — but hitherto not fully recognised — talent, it is an obviously feeble basis on which to attempt to build a *presumption* that it will do so.

An approach more likely to yield such a presumption is *via* the contention that there is some malfunction in the private capital market which will not apply to the state investment company, so that when its executives are transferred from the private sector they will be able to take different and better decisions than they could have taken in a private capacity.

Two possibilities present themselves. One is that, freed from the financial constraints of the private sector, the executives of the state investment company will be able to act in situations which would have been too risky for them to enter in their private-sector capacities. The other possibility is that the executives will have access to more and better information than would have been available to them in the private sector.

Attitudes to risk enforced by activity in the private sector could be used to establish a case that persons transferring from the private sector to a state investment company would take different decisions and could discover neglected profitable opportunities. If the private sector is risk-averse, and requires a higher than average *expected* rate of return to accept risk, then some set of opportunities will exist for the board members of the state investment company, freed from the constraints of the private capital market, that will indeed have an expected better-than-market rate of return.

Three comments are appropriate. The first turns on the evident problem that the board of a state investment company, freed from private capital market constraints, may for a variety of reasons, including a wish to appear dynamic, accept risks even though the expected rate of return is negative: the difficulty of assessing outcomes noted above now acts to limit the constraint on executives of a state investment company that might be implied by their own concern for their future reputations. Second, even if the state investment company does select projects with an expected positive rate of return but with associated risk, such use of public funds will not necessarily increase economic welfare. If the same opportunity was known to the private sector but rejected by it, there is no presumption that members of the private sector will feel better-off when forced to take the rejected risk/rate of return combinations through taxes and the activity of a state investment company. Third, at the time of establishment of many state investment companies, in the late 1960s and early 1970s, most West European governments were expressing concern about the rapid rate of mergers and acquisitions, the so-called merger boom. It was widely held that private-sector managers were being wildly optimistic about the prospects for companies, mergers and reorganisations. It is unlikely, therefore, that widespread risk aversion in the private sector was a primary consideration in establishing state investment companies.

It is less easy to evaluate in general terms the argument that executives of a state investment company have at their disposal better information than could have been available to them in their private-sector capacities. This is because it is difficult to see why it should be so — some specific contention is needed to flesh out the logical possibility. For example, it might be argued that managers of companies will be more willing to provide the staff of state investment companies, bound by codes of official secrecy, with more confidential information than they would be prepared to give to others in the private sector. Yet if such conditions yield valuable information that is otherwise unavailable, it is certainly true that private-sector organisations have an incentive to establish a reputation for maintaining confidences. If they cannot, it may be for legal-institutional reasons, which in turn suggests the possibility that some change in law might be a better means of dealing with the situation than establishing a state investment company.

No strong *a priori* arguments for the special ability of a state investment company to discover neglected winners seem to proceed from these alleged imperfections. Yet where else might such arguments be found?

It is perhaps not fruitful to search too hard for what might not be there. It is not unusual to discover in politicians and civil servants a deep but unresearched belief that the private sector is incompetent (which sometimes boils down to the fact that the private sector does not always, or even usually, do what civil servants and politicians would like it to do). The assertion that state investment companies will be able to discover overlooked profitable opportunities may simply proceed from such views. On the other hand, given that private-sector decisions do not always reflect politicians' wishes, state investment companies may be an additional instrument of political influence, not necessarily associated with any belief that they are capable of making an overall profit, even though the argument for them is made in those terms.

Under-supply of Specific Financial Instruments

This issue can be dealt with quite briefly. In justifying a state investment company, the relevant issue is not whether, or why, the asserted capital-market imperfections exist but whether, if they exist, the discretionary power inherent in a state investment company is needed to correct them.

If a particular financial instrument is insufficiently supplied, it is possible to subsidise its supply through the taxation system (the structure of which, of course, may be responsible for the under-supply in the first place). The same is true of funds for particular kinds of companies or for companies located in particular regions.

The case for a state investment company in this context must be that it is cheaper to provide the subsidies through a state investment company than by generally applicable tax laws. Such a case might be true, for example, if it were not possible to draw up a set of rules that tightly defined the class of transactions to be subsidised. In that event, other transactions, not the subject of the policy, might also receive subsidies so that the policy became unduly expensive. A state investment company might then be employed to choose those applications for subsidy serving the policy goal.

Such a task, however, is one that civil servants should be able to perform: it hardly requires the kind of expertise and business experience displayed by most state investment companies. In so far as a state investment company contains such talent, it is reasonable to conclude that some other objective is more important. Of these, picking winners is perhaps the most likely.

Providing Finance for Companies that Would Otherwise Fail

The objective in keeping an otherwise bankrupt company in operation is, typically, to maintain employment and it is clear that a sufficient supply of official finance can prevent the closure of an enterprise. It is therefore important not to confuse this proposition with the quite different one that *overall* employment will be higher as a result of such action than would otherwise be the case.

Bankruptcy is a change in the *financial* structure of a company. It does not imply the disappearance of the physical capital of the company and it is perfectly possible to conceive that an enterprise becomes bankrupt and that its employment *increases* as a result of the greater managerial efficiency of the new owners of its assets.

Of course, this is unlikely if the causes of the bankruptcy are not removed. In that event, it will be difficult to find a new private buyer for the company as a going concern; and the existing labour force may then lose their current jobs. But even in this case, so long as the firm's assets are not scrapped or removed from the country, new jobs are likely to appear in connection with their new use to offset the effects on aggregate employment.

Even abstracting from such considerations, however, the maintenance of a company that would otherwise be bankrupt clearly has offsetting employment effects elsewhere. For example, if British Leyland ceased production, the demand for the output of Ford (United Kingdom) and of Vauxhall would increase, as would employment in those companies.

No such direct offset would occur if demand formerly directed to British Leyland went to foreign suppliers. Nevertheless, for a country with a flexible exchange rate, and for which, therefore, the balance of payments must balance, an increase in the quantity of imports demanded must lead to a depreciation of the exchange rate until the consequent increase in exports equals the value of the increase in imports (abstracting from any change in capital flows). It follows that the effect of a policy that reduces the demand for imports (for example, by maintaining British Leyland in production) will equivalently reduce overseas demand for the country's exports and hence employment opportunities in the export sector. Maintaining British Leyland means that jobs there are gained at the cost of jobs elsewhere.

To summarise, maintaining a particular company in existence when it would otherwise fail may be to maintain the particular jobs offered by that company. The offsetting effects on aggregate employment, however, suggest that the effect on the number of jobs offered in the economy as a whole is much less than that. The primary effect of such policies is likely to be on the distribution of jobs between persons, companies, areas and industries, not on aggregate employment.

This view contrasts with many official calculations of the effect of such policies on aggregate employment which generally suggest that the overall employment effect of saving lame ducks is much greater than the number of jobs in the lame duck. One element of such calculations is the implicit assumption that there are no offsets whatsoever on employment elsewhere: that if a company becomes bankrupt no one will find it worthwhile to buy and operate within the country *any* of its assets; that if it ceases production, *none* of the demand for its former output will shift to other domestic producers; and that if all of that demand is satisfied by imports, these will be financed *entirely* by some other means than by increasing exports.

The other element in such calculations is to include the employment 'saved' in companies supplying the lame duck with components. This is often assumed to be entirely lost — as if there would be no increase in the demand for components by other firms if the lame duck vanished or as if there was no possibility of those firms supplying the lame duck finding other buyers for their output (which, of course, if true, might explain the duck's lameness).

Such calculations — which are familiar in all West European countries — are analytical nonsense, although they may score higher viewed as an exercise in obfuscation or in public relations. The same is true of those similar calculations of the amount of unemployment compensation 'saved' by the support of lame ducks which is sometimes treated as the 'return' on the funds 'invested' in it. To the extent that the policy merely redistributes employment, no unemployment compensation is saved. At most, the saving is over some transitory period as the labour force adjusts to the shift of employment opportunities between companies. It is not a perpetual return — as is often assumed.

Much of this kind of analysis, however, conceals a set of fundamental assumptions about the functioning of the economy. The basic issue appears in the question of why a company should become bankrupt. If it is performing poorly because it has poor management, it might be expected that it would be taken over before bankruptcy and a better management team put in. This is, after all, a frequently observed event. An explanation of the failure of superior management to appear is that no better team is available; that is, that the company's problems are not the result of the incompetence of its management. If that is the case, the problem may lie in the behaviour of the company's labour force. Its rate of pay may simply be too high for the company's output to be profitably sold, whatever the quality of its management.

The same kind of possibility may lie behind the notion that component suppliers will not be able to find other buyers for their output if a major domestic user is allowed to go out of business; or in the view that the country will not be able to generate more exports to finance an increase in imports. Ultimately, this line of thought boils down to the proposition that any adjustment in the structure of the economy is so difficult, and so costly, that it would be better not to have any adjustment at all, so that economic policy should be directed towards maintaining the *status quo*.

In such extreme form, the notion is so absurd that probably no one would accept it. But then the general question arises: under what circumstances is it sensible for economic policy to intervene in the process of adjustment? And, in particular, if it is the actions of the labour force (or labour unions) that jeopardise otherwise sound companies, or make adjustment to their demise difficult or impossible, is it sensible policy to shield workers and unions from the employment consequences of those actions? For example, if the survival of a company is threatened by high wages (or the low level of effective labour input), should it be kept afloat by injections of public money, thereby possibly suggesting to workers elsewhere that they, too, will be bailed out if they behave similarly?

Two views are possible. One is that the company should be supported essentially in the belief that some process of government-labour-union diplomacy will avoid the consequences of the situation. The other view is that it should not be kept afloat because neither a state investment company nor the government itself have the means at their disposal to restore order to the original situation or to prevent the example from affecting the behaviour of other work-forces in other companies.

In the present context, it is not necessary to take a position on these opposing views. The more important point is that, in the course of supporting employment in particular companies, a state investment company is not only foreclosing employment elsewhere but it may also be helping to create the conditions which called for its first interventions. A state investment company which is energetically saving lame ducks may find itself in a position of being able to point to an evident and increasing need for its services.

Buffer Argument

Obviously, the issue of employment protection bears a high political charge. Recognition of this appears in the frequent argument that a state investment company is a useful buffer between governments and companies dependent upon public funds for their survival. The party needing the protection of a buffer varies between versions of the general argument however. On the one hand, it is said that governments have strong political incentives to interfere in the day-to-day management of their client companies, so that the companies need protection. On the other hand, it is said that governments, aghast at the political consequences of the failure of a large employer, are vulnerable to manipulation by the managements and unions of their clients so that it is the members of governments who need protection against the importuning of their clients and potential clients.

Whichever way the argument is formulated, however, it is, as noted above, of a very different nature than those discussed earlier. It is not concerned with the merits of governmental intervention but with the instrumentality by which it should be arranged and organised, given its political inevitability.

The judgement that intervention is politically inevitable may be correct (although it must be said that political inevitability tends to be judged by a rather lower standard than many other kinds of inevitability). Yet, if the political pressures are so great, it is surely to be doubted that the insertion of a state investment company between government and its client companies will very much change their impact.

Sir Arthur Knight noted in an annual report of the National Enterprise Board (NEB) issued shortly before his resignation as Chairman:

'The magnitude of BL [British Leyland], its problems and its financial requirements means that the Government must inevitably be involved in its major decisions, thus leaving for the NEB only a relatively minor intermediary role. We would gain nothing of substance by having this illusory responsibility.'

Although it is not necessarily the intention of those employing the buffer argument, it is only a short step from that argument to a possible interpretation of state investment companies that emerged earlier in the discussion. This is that state investment companies are merely a prop for dressing political windows — a role possibly sweetened for its executives by the government's permission to do something else, ostensibly more dynamic, creative and useful, such as trying to find and nurture a few neglected winners.

SUMMARIES OF THE COUNTRY STUDIES

The central claim to be assessed in terms of the performance of actual state investment companies is that of a special ability to find or to nurture neglected winners. Remove that claim and the mystique of the state investment company is fundamentally weakened. There is no obvious economic or political advantage in distributing funds to failing enterprises or to backward regions through a specially established organisation that is unable to choose or create successful companies.

This is not to say, of course, that all support for state investment companies comes from those who expect them to be able to choose winners. State investment companies are a means of redistributing income from taxpayers to some other, more narrowly defined, group which might include workers, managers or even shareholders. The precise nature of the beneficiaries of action by state investment companies may vary from country to country; but whoever the beneficiaries are, one would expect them to favour the establishment or continuation of a state investment company regardless of their beliefs about its ability to pick winners. The idea that the state investment company can pick winners, that its activity will return a profit, that there is a pot of gold at the end of the rainbow, is not important in gaining support from this quarter but rather in obtaining support — or defusing opposition — from those who will not benefit but pay.

This observation may be relevant to interpretation of the fact that from the point of view of assessing success in a particular function, the number of functions assigned to a state investment company is a major problem. This is especially true when some of these functions will yield profits if successfully performed while others will give rise to losses. A state investment company that is charged with looking for neglected winners, and also with supporting employment in particular regions, for example, may well be in the fortunate position of being able to decide the justification for a particular intervention *after* the results of the intervention are known. Thus financial successes may be described as the outcome of a process of choosing winners, and financial failures as outcomes of the process of supporting regional employment, whatever the original motivation of the intervention. Even with better information and data than are typically available, the possibilities inherent in such a shell game give to the state investment company substantial protection from outside assessment.

A rather striking illustration of this possibility occurred during the presentation, at a private seminar at the London School of Economics, of an early draft of the Hindley-Richardson paper on the IRC, the final version of which appears as Chapter 5 of this volume. Of all the state investment companies studied, the IRC seems to give the greatest opportunity of assessing the ability of a state investment company to pick winners. This is because the Industrial Reorganisation Corporation Act established a right of the Government to direct the IRC to assist an enterprise. Since such direction was published, it seems possible to separate those interventions desired by the Government but not warranted in the IRC's commercial judgement from those it believed to be justified on commercial grounds.

Examination of the returns to companies subject to IRC intervention reveals, as expected, that the returns to the IRC's 'own' selections were on average much better than those to companies in which the Government directed it to intervene. There were, however, two classes of IRC intervention and some entailed no IRC funds. As the IRC would probably tell the story, it discovered potentially profitable mergers and then, by sheer force of argument, persuaded the potential partners of the virtues of the union. Measured in terms of the post-intervention commercial success, these were the most successful of all IRC actions and a portfolio consisting of shares in such companies has performed very well relative to the market as a whole. Companies that received IRC finance, however, have subsequently, on average, performed worse than the market as a whole, although better than companies that received finance from the IRC at the direct request of the Government.

The interpretation of these observations presented here is that, rather than the IRC picking winners, the winners picked the IRC. The service the IRC could offer such winners, they suggest, is the possibility of steering mergers safely through the administrative machinery — mergers that might otherwise have run foul of the legislation regarding monopolies and mergers. Hence the incentive of the partners in such mergers to seek IRC approval for their plans or to go along with IRC suggestions, even though no IRC finance was given. Where IRC finance was given, possibly to overcome the adverse judgement of the companies involved on the IRC's suggestions, the poor financial results suggest that the IRC was usually wrong. These results, although poor, are better than those from companies in which the IRC intervened at the direction of the government, which suggests to Ray Richardson and myself an ability on the part of the IRC to identify clear losers, even if there is no evidence, on their reading, of any special ability to choose winners.

Not unnaturally, the two former chairmen of the IRC, attending the seminar at the London School of Economics at which these results and interpretations were presented, preferred an alternative explanation. Hindley and Richardson were wrong, they said, in assuming that the existence of interventions openly directed by the British Government meant that all other interventions were backed by the commercial judgement of the IRC. A much better approximation was that all cases in which IRC finance was involved were rescue operations, decided jointly by the IRC and the Government whether or not the decision resulted in a public instruction to the IRC by the Government.

This contention is not incompatible with the Hindley-Richardson conjecture that the IRC's position with those administering the mergers machinery permitted it to associate itself with future winners to which it gave no finance. To judge the extent to which the poor results of companies that received IRC finance should be construed as evidence against the IRC's ability to choose neglected winners, however, now requires information regarding the genesis and motivation of interventions that is not publicly available. In its absence, former members of the IRC can claim actions with good commercial outcomes as monuments to their good judgement and those with poor commercial outcomes as monuments to their benevolence.

The IRC ceased to exist in 1971, before the general increase in unemployment levels of the mid-1970s. Most of the state investment companies discussed in this volume continued to exist through that period and some were founded after it. For them, therefore, publicly financed benevolence has been a dominating theme.

Since the chapters are arranged in order of the date of foundation of the principal organisation discussed, Enzo Pontarollo's chapter on the Italian situation leads. A major theme of Chapter 2, then, is the contrast between the historic performance of the Istituto per la Ricostruzione Industriale (IRI) and Ente Nazionale Idrocarburi (ENI) — efficient and business-like, so that extensive participation by private shareholders was possible — with the very much more confused picture now presented by these two organisations and by EFIM (established in 1962), EGAM (effectively established in 1971 but dissolved in 1977 after an existence as spectacular as it was brief) and GEPI (established 1972).

Professor Pontarollo tells a story which involves the diversion of the Italian state shareholding system from the objective of efficient business operation to such 'social' objectives as industrialising the south, implementing anti-cyclical policy and safeguarding existing employment. In the process, 'fulfilling the demands of the political system ... became the standard by which to appraise managerial abilities'. Indeed, the number and diversity of the objectives thrust upon the system make it difficult to see what criteria other than the satisfaction of powerful politicians might be available. Not surprisingly under these circumstances, the system has lost money consistently since 1970. What are also not surprising, although perhaps more disturbing, are the hints of corruption which accompany the elimination of criteria and means for independent checks of the system's performance.

In Chapter 3, H.W. de Jong and Robert Jan Spierenburg reveal a different background of past achievement in the Netherlands. They note that even in the 1950s and 1960s, when the operations of the Nationale Investeringsbank (NIB) were not distorted by externally imposed employment goals, 'it cannot be said that the NIB was a successful investor'. In the 1970s, however, 'Dutch policy had been oriented mainly towards employment goals... At the end of the 1970s, when this type of policy became visibly a failure, the emphasis shifted towards innovation and modernisation.' Professor de Jong and Mr Spierenburg note that a disproportionate quantity of the funds used by the NIB in rescue operations went to large companies.

Paul de Grauwe and Greet van de Velde, who focus on the NIM in Belgium (Chapter 4), also describe poor rates of return in the period before, as well as after, the 1970s slump. Indeed, their figures suggest that the NIM has made a negative real rate of return on its investments in every year since its formation in 1963 (Table 4.5). Professor de Grauwe and Mrs van de Velde are sceptical of any employment effect of this expenditure. They argue that 'through the NIM, capital provided by society is transformed into consumption by employees in lame duck industries' and they continue:

'Most of the objectives entrusted to the NIM are impossible to realise, given the fact that the NIM has become an instrument of the executive branch of the government... The political decision mechanism channels resources to the best-organised pressure groups... The political pressure exerted on the NIM has become an instrument of protection of failing firms and of preserving the wage incomes of their employees at otherwise unsustainable levels.'

In Sweden, Chapter 6, Gunnar Eliasson, and Bengt-Christer Ysander suggest that this kind of process, although present, has gone less far:

'From official records accompanying the new kind of direct government involvement in business management in the 1970s, we learn that it was originally propelled by high ambitions to improve and innovate. From the records of the 1970s, we can read that such involvement became mostly defensive, supporting declining industries in the hope of getting them back on their feet. Records of success are restricted to a few activities, notably within SF [Statsföretag], where efficiency and profitability have stubbornly been

pushed as the overriding objective, often against the wishes
of the political governing bodies.'

Dr Eliasson and Dr Ysander discuss several means of improving
this situation, or at least of preventing its deterioration. One of
these is to open SF to private participation.

Private capital is, or has been, involved in several state investment companies, for example in Italy. When the Italian companies
were pressed into the pursuit of loss-making social objectives,
Professor Pontarollo observes, private suppliers of capital did
withdraw. But the state simply made good the short-fall in capital
requirements. Obviously, if this can occur, private participation
does not supply a strong constraint on the operations of the state
investment company.

From the point of view of a government establishing a state
investment company, however, the problem with private participation may be precisely that such participation limits the ability
of a state investment company to pursue those loss-making
activities that, for the government, constitute its primary attraction. In the limit, insistence on the participation of private capital
would create a situation similar to that described by Karl Heinz
Jüttemeier and Klaus-Werner Schatz in West Germany (Chapter 8)
which has no state investment company (a fact that weighs against
the proposition that an efficient economy needs such an institution). What it does have is a scheme whereby, under certain
circumstances and conditions, private decisions to invest in a
company can be supplemented from Federal Government sources.
All of the initiative rests with the private investor and there is little
or no encouragement to enter (or remain in) prospectively unprofitable activities. Thus, while the scheme might supplement the
amount of equity capital available to eligible classes of company, it
is not a powerful tool for an active industrial policy. There is an
obvious question as to whether any scheme in which private
participation is important can avoid that outcome.

The tension between private participation and loss-making
social objectives is a major theme of Diana Green's chapter on
state investment companies in France. For the IDI (established in
1970), which provides the main focus of her chapter, it seems
likely that (at least prior to the advent of President Mitterrand,
elected in 1981) the constraint imposed by private participation

has become dominant, so that the IDI responds primarily to commercial criteria. Interestingly, however, even when the French Government established the Comité Interministériel pour l'Aménagement des Structures Industrielles (CIASI) in 1974 its rule of operation was that the state would make only a minority contribution in any intervention. Dr Green comments that 'the chief obstacle to the success of the scheme was the reluctance of private capital to join rescue operations'. In large part, as a response to this, the committee shifted its emphasis to 'accelerating the expansion of efficient firms', while stressing 'the hyper-liberal nature of the procedure as a tool for managing the industrial crisis'.

Dr Eliasson and Dr Ysander are aware, of course, that private participation conflicts with the pursuit of loss-making social objectives. In Chapter 6 they propose (and Professor Pontarollo makes a similar suggestion) a system whereby the government auctions rescues and other operations which cannot be expected to yield profits in the ordinary way of things. Thus the company that is prepared to undertake the specified operation for the lowest payment — whether or not it is a state investment company — should receive the contract for it. In this way, they argue, the costs of interventions for 'social' reasons could be minimised by having them carried out by the least-cost contractor and the cost to the government of achieving the social goal would be known. Moreover, there would then be no reason why a state investment company should not pursue profit-maximising policies (including in its earnings government contract payments for fulfilling social objectives), so that its performance would be very much more subject to independent monitoring and appraisal.

The technical problems of setting-up appropriate and enforceable contracts for the fulfilment of social objectives are formidable. Even if they were soluble, a sceptic might suggest that the assignment of multiple objectives to state investment companies, which makes the monitoring of performance in any one of them difficult or impossible, is not simply an accident or oversight: governments do not necessarily wish the cost of achieving 'social' objectives to be public information.

The penultimate chapter by Drs Hindley and Richardson is on the NEB. The chapter closes with a quote from the *Trades Union Congress Economic Review* for 1981. After arguing for the diversion of £2 billion per annum from the pension and life assurance funds and from North Sea oil revenue into a new National Investment Bank, to be closely connected with a new NEB with a 'stronger initiating role', this document continues:

> 'The NEB and other planning bodies must avoid being over centralized or obsessed with narrow-sighted "rationalisa-tion". These problems can be avoided if economic planning is firmly rooted in industrial democracy, extending the influence and activities of workplace union organisation.'

Presumably in such an approach it is not important to attempt to minimise the costs of 'narrow-sighted rationalisation' and irrelevant or impossible to monitor the performance of a state investment company. That such a system is open to abuse, when viewed from one angle, may from another angle appear as its greatest merit. Whether or not it is technically feasible, the suggestion of Dr Eliasson and Dr Ysander is unlikely to be welcome to the proponents of such a role for state investment companies; or to governments with the satisfaction of such interest groups in view.

Whatever the appropriate interpretation of a state investment company's involvement in loss-making operations, however, the primary point in the present context is that such involvement makes it very much more difficult than would otherwise be the case to assess claims of ability of state investment companies to find neglected winners. It is open to any state investment company to argue that its abilities in that direction are obscured by its obligations to pursue loss-making activities. Whether it is so obscured or not, however, there is certainly no unambiguous evidence of such ability. The papers collected in this volume give no grounds to suppose that the operation of any economy has been improved by a state investment company — although, of course, their activity has benefited particular persons.

NEED FOR A COOL LOOK

State investment companies in Western Europe have been involved in two main types of activity over the past several years:

(i) trying to pick or nurture winners and (ii) propping-up losers. Of these, the second activity has clearly been dominant, especially in the later 1970s. To a considerable extent, therefore, attitudes towards state investment companies are likely to be determined by attitudes towards the support of businesses that would otherwise fail; and these attitudes are, in turn, likely to correlate with opinions on the appropriateness of the transfers of income and wealth implicit in such rescue operations. But the issue should not be allowed to rest there.

It is widely accepted that a well-functioning capital market is essential to the operation of a market economy. Indeed, the establishment of state investment companies to counter putative imperfections in the capital market is a recognition of its importance. The burden of the evidence, however, is that state investment companies have not improved the operation of the capital market but rather have caused misallocation of capital. An institution that makes worse, or even creates, the conditions it was ostensibly intended to correct deserves to be examined with a cold eye.

CHAPTER TWO

Italy: Effects of Substituting Political Objectives for Business Goals

Enzo Pontarollo

State intervention in the private sector of the economy and the existence of a complex system of public shareholding companies are now established features of the Italian economy. They are the outcome of a process which has lasted half a century and the resulting structures are so diversified that no Italian escapes them in the course of daily life. Whoever uses the telephone or the motorway network, drives an Alfa Romeo or buys a Motta cake comes into contact with the state shareholding system.

Among companies with at least twenty employees, the state-controlled companies contributed, in 1977, 44 per cent of the total sales and 48 per cent of employment. In 1961 they accounted for somewhat less than 20 per cent of either. Of course, companies of this size employ only 1.2 million workers in Italy whereas total industrial employment is approximately 7 million. Nevertheless, the relevant fact here is that the state-controlled companies bulk very large among medium-size and large firms. Their importance is even greater in particular sectors, such as services, which are almost entirely provided by state-controlled companies. In manufacturing industry, public enterprises are most active in the mining and metallurgical sector (60 per cent of total sales) and the oil sector (42.2 per cent); while in three other important manufacturing sectors the state-controlled companies account for 20 to 25 per cent of total sales (food, paper manufacturing and mechanical engineering).[1]

The heavy and increasing involvement of the Italian state in business is not primarily due to the thrust of ideologies or parties of a socialist type. Only over the past decade — long after the system had acquired a definite physiognomy and size — have

25

notions which might be defined as socialistic made themselves felt. Even then, this did not occur directly but through the influence of the general political and cultural climate which, between the late 1960s and the second half of the 1970s, affected Italy's entire political system, including those forces most favourable to private enterprise. Only in 1980, twenty years after its creation, did control of the Ministry of State Economic Participation pass from the Christian Democratic Party — Italy's largest party and explicitly in favour of free enterprise — to a representative of the Socialist Party.

The system of state economic participation is presently experiencing a severe economic and financial crisis, coupled with a deep-rooted crisis of identity. Public opinion, the political parties and even the very people who created and shaped the system are questioning the validity of the lines along which it developed.

At the same time, however, there is widespread scepticism about the possibility of reforming it. This is a symptom of the huge difficulties underlying the structure. Given the importance it has acquired, these difficulties cannot be dealt with or solved in any simple way. Moreover, this crisis combines some aspects specific to the Italian situation with the more general problems which have arisen in all countries adopting structures of this kind. What makes the Italian case more complex — and interesting — is the fact that any solution of this crisis will inevitably decisively affect the overall prospects of the country's economy.

The state shareholding system has developed and operated over a considerable time-span and has passed through a number of stages in terms of organisational structure and of managing group philosophy. This means that no synthetic survey of the system's functioning and results can be carried out: what is required is identification of the various stages. Moreover, the system of state participation comprises a large number of bodies each of which presents specific features and peculiarities.

FORMATION OF THE SYSTEM

The origin of the state participation system lies in the 1930s and was an outcome of the close relationships which, from the very start of Italy's industrial development, were established between business and the banking system. Many banks held controlling interests in enterprises, especially in the iron, mechanical and building sectors. The considerable reconversion problems following World War I, and later the 1929 crash, aggravated the troubles of those enterprises and, hence, of the banks controlling them.

In 1933, the Istituto per la Ricostruzione Industriale (IRI) was set up in order to prevent Italy's three prime banks from failing. Its task was to provide for the reconstruction of these banks through the acquisition of all the shares and credit they held in industrial enterprises and to take over the losses which they had accumulated as a result of their industrial shareholdings. By this transfer of shares and losses, the banks regained their economic and financial balance.

The physiognomy of IRI in 1933 was based on the assumed transitoriness of its intervention: on the assumption that the industrial concerns so acquired would be returned to private ownership as soon as conditions favourable to the accomplishment of this operation appeared. Consequently, IRI decided that the concerns under its control should not be invested with a special legal status but should remain limited companies. Shortly afterwards, however, it became clear that the wholesale transfer and restitution of those enterprises to private ownership would not be possible.

The iron and steel and mechanical companies taken over by IRI were among the country's largest: their size was such that none of the remaining Italian private groups had the financial means to buy control of them, an operation which seemed particularly difficult at a time of severe economic crisis. Thus, only foreign capital could have returned them to the private sector and this was incompatible with the autarkic policy followed by the Fascist Government of the time.

Thus, in 1935, IRI was turned into a permanent body whose scope of action was defined by two primary conditions:

(a) the lasting acquisition of manufacturing businesses; and

(b) the preservation for such business of the limited company structure and of the relevant private law regulations.

In addition, IRI was forbidden to use its powers to give companies under its control a monopoly position.

It follows then, that the political justification underlying the establishment of IRI was neither a desire to put an end to private monopoly nor an attempt to foster certain types of industrial production, nor to develop depressed areas. Rather, it was due to the weakness of private enterprise itself and its inability to supply the risk capital required for the control of a rather important group of manufacturing companies. Indeed, one of the attractions of the IRI solution was that it left open the possibility of easily returning businesses to the private sector, although the extent of such transfers since 1936 has been negligible.

On the basis of this rather fortuitous origin, however, IRI's first executive officials erected an ambitious project, namely, the achievement of managerial reorganisation and reconstruction which would turn the businesses they controlled into a model of entrepreneurship and an example and a guide for private industry itself on how to apply technology and business organisation and prosper in the market.[2]

Events connected with World War II struck a terrific blow to IRI concerns. Whole productive sectors, such as iron and building, were destroyed almost entirely. At that stage private industry might have been able to drastically reduce the extent of the state shareholdings; but although private operators were offered the opportunity to take over the destroyed iron plants none were willing to undertake such a task. This caused serious reconstruction and reconversion problems for state shareholdings but it also marked the final consolidation of IRI as a form of state intervention in the economy. The Institute, in fact, succeeded in achieving a leading role in the framework of the country's reconstruction and development plans, thus legitimising its existence in a way that it had not been legitimised by the fortuitous events of its origin.

The state economic participation system broadened its scope in the years immediately after World War II. In 1947, in order to facilitate the conversion from war production of a number of mechanical engineering companies, the Fondo Industrie Mecca-niche (FIM) was established. Its task was to provide financial support to firms which could not obtain credit through the banking system. Many companies resorted to that fund and a large number of them later repaid their loans to FIM. Others, however, proved unable to effect repayment and ended up by being fully financed by the FIM and, in practical terms, owned by it. Nevertheless, IRI refused to take over these companies and, as a result, in 1962 the government decided to turn them into the nucleus of another holding, Ente Autonomo di Gestione per il Finanziamento dell'Industria Meccanica (EFIM).

The above developments were almost simultaneous with the appearance of the Ente Nazionale Idrocarburi (ENI). Its establishment was due to the powerful activity of a particular individual, Enrico Mattei, who asserted, well ahead of his time, the need for public intervention in the field of hydrocarbons and other energy sources and who maintained that such a commitment must take place through a responsible official body. At the end of the War, the Italian Government had entrusted Mr Mattei with the task of winding up Azienda Generale Italiana Petroli (AGIP), a company established during the Fascist period and designed to prospect in the field of natural gas. Mr Mattei was not prepared to liquidate those activities and, having decided to continue the prospecting work autonomously, achieved satisfactory results.

In 1953, these activities were reorganised within the framework of ENI which was entrusted by the Government with the task of promoting and developing nationwide activities in the hydrocarbon and natural gas sectors. Mr Mattei was appointed President of this corporation.

This brief outline gives a picture of the basic framework of the state shareholding system. The process of formation of this system clearly indicates that it was not based on a precise political plan, but was the outcome of a number of interventions, each guided by particular motives. Parallelling this process, however, there was the development of the idea — which progressively gained support among government parties and a considerable portion of public opinion — that Italy's economic reality provided good justification for the existence of state shareholdings. This idea provided the system with its basic legitimacy.

The economic reality which offered the justification for state participation was Italy's late development, compared with the more industrialised countries. Private enterprise, it was said, proved unable to bridge the consequent gap as it exclusively followed the stimuli offered by the market. The basic task of state participation, based on this view, was to supply a portion of the risk capital that was so scarce in Italy. For this purpose, the mixed company, financed from both state and private sources, has many advantages. In order to attract private capital, such companies must make profits comparable with those made in the private sector, so that there is a necessary stimulus towards efficiency. Moreover, the operating businesses are joint-stock companies which possess a flexibility and adaptability, making possible a far greater efficiency than is possible for nationalised industries.

Although these are the basic features of the system, it must be stressed that there are differences in the composition of the various bodies. This applies particularly to IRI and ENI which form the basis of the sytem. A first difference relates more to a matter of style than of substance. On the one hand, IRI views the mixed economy as a peaceful coexistence between private and state capitalism; on the other hand, ENI presents itself in open contrast with the private sector. Both attitudes reflect their developments and histories. IRI, after all, testifies to a failure of Italian capitalism, whereas ENI, in a field where prospects for profit are excellent, denies private firms the possibility of competing. The two corporations share the aim, though, of ensuring domestic autonomy in basic sectors such as iron and steel and energy.

A second difference may be perceived when considering the two organisations' attitude to private monopoly. IRI is not very active in countering this; ENI is much more vigorous and, hence, clashes with private interests in a number of fields such as gas distribution and fertiliser production.

Another difference lies in their relationship with the political system. While IRI strives for the utmost independence from political control, having tested this approach under the Fascist regime, ENI entertains close relationships with politics and the world surrounding it. It is a fact that Mr Mattei never felt that he was dependent upon political power, because he was among the founders of the Christian Democratic Party and had taken a part in shaping the democratic system. Mr Mattei's innovation, however, was that of using political and party conflicts, as well as those between factions within parties, as a means of implementing entrepreneurial strategies. Thus, ENI's links with politics have been numerous. Given his particular ability, Mr Mattei could lead the game. His successors, however, became its victims, unable to escape its webs and traps.[3]

In spite of such differences, the net results of the operations of the state-controlled companies were largely positive up to the early 1960s. The availability of natural gas, steel and services, coupled with massive investment on behalf of the state shareholding system, were undoubtedly among the many factors which led to what has been referred to as 'Italy's economic miracle of the 1950s', that is; the extraordinary growth in investment, income and employment and the transformation of the country's economic structure which took place in those years. The significant fact is that the improvement in macro-economic variables goes hand in hand with highly satisfactory operational results in the state participation sector. The capacity for self-financing was relatively high (50.2 per cent in 1956 and 47.5 per cent in 1961) and, above all, the state's contribution to outside financing was rather limited. During the 1961–63 period, which was characterised by considerable investment, the endowment funds and the other contributions of the state amounted to a mere 11.18 per cent of the system's external financing. The contribution of state shareholdings to the country's total investments in the 1950s may be estimated at about 8.5 per cent of the total, while investments in the industrial sector approximated 15 per cent. Three decisions made in the second half of the 1950s, however, had great influence on the system's further development.

The first decision was the establishment by law in 1956 of the Ministry of State Economic Participation — both a centre of political responsibility and an executive body. The ostensible function of the Ministry is two-fold. First, it is supposed to transmit governmental instructions to the managing bodies. Second, it is supposed to defend the companies' interests within the government structure itself. This law also requires that the companies in whose capital the state participates be organised into managing bodies, operating according to standards of efficiency. Such bodies, then, occupy an extremely delicate position. They act as filters between the government and the companies, transforming government programmes into effective goals to be implemented by the companies and ensuring the working autonomy of the companies, free from government interference.

In fact, however, the formation of the Ministry introduced a whole new element. The Ministry in effect became the bearer of essentially political commands to be imposed upon concerns. In response, the managements of companies started to assess the results of their businesses in terms of the extent to which they met with the political approval of the Ministry. This led managements to replace business logic by an essentially political logic.

A second decision was to remove the state-controlled companies from the Confindustria (the Italian employers' association) which is designed to protect the interests of the industrialists. This change found some justification in the extremely short-sighted and conservative attitudes of private entrepreneurship but it enabled the Government to acquire a further means of influencing the dynamics of bargaining, not only in the public sector but, indirectly, also in the private one. In Italy, agreements between the unions and the employers' associations are made on a national level. From this time onward, the public enterprise organisation (Intersind) almost systematically took a more flexible stand in its relations with the unions than that of the Confindustria. This ultimately weakened the whole entrepreneurial front.

Yet, the main consequence of this decision was more strongly negative. By establishing a different status for private and state-controlled companies, it legitimised union resistance to any possible denationalisation process or any attempt to bring publicly controlled companies under private control. In other words, it triggered off — perhaps unwittingly — a process of differentiation between state-controlled companies and standard private companies, a differentiation which had been strongly opposed throughout the system's first years. These new developments were to have important consequences which would make themselves felt in the course of the 1960s and, particularly, in the 1970s.

A further crucial decision taken in the 1950s related to the economic gap between north and south Italy. As soon as the difficult post-World War II reconstruction period was overcome, the Italian state considered using its highly efficient entrepreneurial organisations (which, being self-financing, did not cut into the Government's budget in any material way) in order to support the industrialisation process in the south. In 1959, a law was passed enjoining all state-controlled companies to make at least 40 per cent of their total investments and 60 per cent of their new investments in the south. This enforced sourthern orientation had several major consequences.

First, the preservation and expansion of the existing state-controlled companies required new investment. The bulk of these companies, however, were located in the north. To be able to authorise such investment in the north while complying with the new rules regarding the south, the managing bodies greatly increased the volume of new investment and the prospective profitability of some of this was not well-judged.

This increased volume of investment could neither be financed internally nor by recourse to the private capital market. As a result, endowment-fund increases became more common. In the 1950s, IRI's endowment funds were increased three times by a total of 110 billion lire. Between 1960 and 1971, five increases occurred, totalling 1,626 billion lire. ENI's development followed a similar course.

The second major consequence, therefore, was a greater recourse to public financing, entailing a dramatic reduction in the independence of the companies. It marked the beginning of a constant political interference which is one of the major causes underlying the deterioration of the system.

The third consequence of the 'southern' orientation of the state-controlled companies directly affected management. The establishment of new plants and the creation of new jobs in the south became a major criterion by which to measure the success of a managing group, regardless of the economic value of the projects involved. Thus, along with some highly valuable efforts, such as the institution and enlargement of Taranto's fourth integral-circuit iron metallurgy centre, and the launching of several enterprises in the petrochemical sector, such as those of Gela and Manfredonia, a number of more controversial initiatives were taken. Examples are the Alfa Sud plant in Naples and investments in the chemical, food, electro-mechanical and electronics, mechanical, textiles and clothing, and tourist sectors. These lacked coordination and were made to cope with specific situations.[4]

As far as the state-controlled industrial complex was concerned, the net result was that employment in the state industries in the south rose from 18.9 per cent in 1958 to 34.6 per cent in 1976. The state-controlled companies were responsible for 72 per cent of the rise in industrial employment in the south during the 1958–76 period and for 95 per cent of the rise in 1968–76.

In spite of such data, it must be noted that the provisions of the 1959 law, and the subsequent 1971 amendment which raised the quota to be devoted to the south to 60 per cent of all investments and to 80 per cent of all new investments, were complied with only up to 1972. After this date, the quotas themselves started to drop. The same applies to industrial investments. This was due to the shortage of large capital-intensive investment possibilities and also to the increasing difficulties of the Italian economic system and of the companies of the public sector.

GROWTH AND CRISIS OF THE SYSTEM

In the 1960s, and especially from 1964, great changes occurred in the environment of the state-controlled enterprises. A powerful thrust towards abandonment of the principle of efficiency became apparent as the momentum which had characterised the Italian economy during the previous decade slowed down for the first time.

Public opinion and the Government both exerted increasing pressure on the state-controlled corporations to spur economic growth. Up to 1966, the investment trend of the state-controlled companies was similar to that of private industry. After 1968, however, the state-controlled companies invested proportionately more. This situation lasted until 1973–4 and contributed to the impairment of the system.

The state, furthermore, assigned to the companies extensive tasks with respect to the implementation of several civil infrastructure programmes. Meanwhile, the general public came to believe that, in the face of business crises and during periods of economic recession, the state-controlled corporations ought to take action at every opportunity so as to safeguard employment levels — even where companies threatened by bankruptcy were concerned and where no return to profitability or productive reconversion was possible. The idea of a 'pre-eminence of politics' gained increasing acceptance. Since public administration proved incapable of developing other more suitable instruments of public intervention, the state-controlled companies were assigned goals foreign to the logic of firms in a market economy.

The 'state-controlled company' formula became some kind of magical incantation to which recourse was had at every stage of the country's politico-economic life. This marked the beginning of a process of progressive bureaucratic degeneration of the state shareholdings' top management, as the latter was led to replace its goals of entrepreneurial success with goals relating to success in fulfilling the demands of the political system. This, indeed, became the standard by which to appraise managerial abilities. To this one must add the unscrupulous use that many executives made of that very pre-eminence of politics to pursue their own personal or career goals and to ensure the leadership of the various productive sectors for certain groups.

A prime example of such a process is provided by ENI's effort, dating from 1968, to gain control over Italy's largest chemical group, Montedison. The ENI sought to eliminate its main competitor in Italy and to achieve a dominant position in Europe. Montedison was then the second largest privately-owned Italian group after Fiat: its 180,000 employees represented 10.8 per cent of the staff employed by the 150 biggest industrial companies in the country; its fixed gross investments were 18.4 per cent of the total; and its turnover was 11.3 per cent of the turnover of this group. ENI, in the same period, accounted for 3.4 per cent of employment, 9.2 per cent of the fixed gross investments and 6.2 per cent of the turnover of the same group of companies.

If attention is limited to Montedison's main sector of activity, chemicals, the disproportion between the two groups was even greater. Montedison accounted for 56.7 per cent of the total turnover of the chemical companies with a turnover of more than 10 billion lira, for 67.6 per cent of the fixed technical assets and for 62.2 per cent of employment. The companies belonging to ENI accounted for 12.8 per cent of the turnover, for 16.4 per cent of the fixed assets and for 10.4 per cent of employment in the same sample of companies.

Montedison was, however, a colossus with feet of clay: it was represented in too many sectors (chemicals, pharmaceuticals, mining, textiles, foodstuffs, publishing, mechanical equipment, electronics and large-scale distribution) and many of its companies were inefficient, burdened by heavy running costs and without valid control structures. Depreciations were insufficient and the overall financial situation was very precarious. Moreover, control of the stock was divided among the main industrial groups and private holding companies, each of which held a very modest share of the capital and thus did not feel directly involved in the running of the group. Clearly, the group was in the hands of an inadequate management.

In this very difficult situation, even if unknown to public opinion and, too, to government forces, ENI began its attempt to gain majority control of Montedison, raking in on the Stock Exchange vast quantities of shares of the private group. The operation succeeded only partially. The political reaction prevented ENI from seizing full control over Montedison: instead, a joint syndicate with private industrialists was established.

But the significance of the incident is that ENI, rather than committing itself wholly to its institutional goals and pursuing them efficiently, which was important in view of the problems which the chemical and the energy sectors posed in Italy in the late 1960s, involved itself in this devious and obscure affair. This weakened both groups and prevented the Italian chemical sector from gaining strength and becoming more compact in the face of the European oligopoly. ENI's biggest mistake was not so much in having under-estimated the political reactions to the attempt, which were easy to foresee in view of the deep implications that the transfer of Montedison to public control would have caused, but in having believed that the problems of the Italian chemical industry could be overcome by concentration and not by the consolidation of technology and management of the chemical concerns operating in Italy.

Furthermore, had ENI's attempt to gain control been successful there would have been dramatic changes in the balances existing between public and private business and evidently this could not have been accepted light-heartedly by the major part of public opinion and by government forces.

The consequences of that affair are still felt — years afterwards — in terms of an increasing penetration into the Italian market of foreign chemical products, a structural weakness of the sector and the loss of huge resources and opportunities.

The ENI-Montedison affair is perhaps the most sensational example of the system's abandonment of its institutional goals, the departure being due to (i) confusion over roles, (ii) changes in strategic orientations and in structural features, (iii) the absence of real controlling devices and (iv) the close relationships between the top management of the corporations and the groups and sub-groups operating in the political system, which protect one another for purposes far removed from those established by law.[5] If that affair constitutes a borderline case — but an extremely important one in view of the sheer size of the corporation involved — it is also the most evident symptom of the strategic and structural changes which affected the state-controlled companies. It may be interesting to recall that, after some years of tension between the two groups, the matter was overcome by, first, the removal, from the top echelons of the above-mentioned groups, of all those who had been involved in the affair and with the disposal, by the state shareholders, of a large part of the Montedison shares which had been acquired and, second, with the arrival of new private shareholders.

IRI, for instance, tends to pursue ever greater development in the sector of infrastructures and services held in concession. These state shareholdings are protected against both domestic and foreign competition by elements of natural monopoly and, with the earnings obtained from such services, IRI makes up for its increasingly large operating losses from enforced investments and rescue operations. All state-controlled corporations reveal a growing tendency to increase (for *social* reasons) their productive capacities through the acquisition from the private sector of unattractive businesses in difficulty rather than by the establishment of new businesses.

During the early 1970s, private investment lagged but the state-controlled companies increased their assets considerably. The growth in investment was accompanied by a sharp increase in employment. During the 1960–69 period, the level of employment for the entire system had risen by 76,000 units (24 per cent): in 1970–74, the total number of employees rose by 270,000, a 64 per cent increase.

In 1974–79, however, the state shareholdings' role as employment-absorbing reservoirs began to fall. For this five-year period, employment rose by 26,000 or 3.8 per cent. From being a leading force in the expansion of employment in 1970–74, the system in 1974–79 acted, at most, as a brake on the total number of lay-offs from industry.[6]

Corresponding to this, investment by the state-controlled corporations began to slow down in 1974: industrial investments (1970 = 100) fell to 60 in 1978 and 1979. Private investments dropped during that period, but the slump was less strong: the index for

1978 was 88, while in 1979 it was 97. As a result, the share of the state-controlled companies in the fixed investments made in the domestic market fell, in 1979, below the 1960–64 level, accounting for merely 8.32 per cent of the total, and their share in industrial investments dropped to 13.2 per cent as compared with 29.6 per cent in 1972. Such a fall in investment involved practically all sectors: the worst off were the iron and steel, the mechanical, the chemical and the motorway-construction sectors, whose levels of investment dropped to half or even one-third of their value at the beginning of this period. The situation in the energy sector was somewhat better though investment remained below the levels of the early 1970s. Telecommunications was the one exception to the general trend, remaining, even after the fall, with double the investment of 1970. Indeed, telecommunications absorbed 70 per cent of investments made in services and 37 per cent of all the system's investments between 1975–79.

The causes of the fall in investment in the state-controlled areas and, particularly, in the manufacturing sector do not lie solely in the difficult economic conditions of the second half of the 1970s. They reflect also the underlying structural problems of the system.

According to data furnished by the Ministry of State Economic Participation, starting from 1970 — and with the sole exception of 1973 — the system recorded negative returns. Moreover, its results tended to deteriorate as time went by. Losses were limited to 100 billion lire up to 1974 and the data for one year even indicate some operating profits. From the 1975 financial year, however, losses increase rapidly, reaching 1,407 billion lire in 1978. The 1979 data, relating to IRI only, indicate further deterioration with losses amounting to 1,500 billion lire. Even telecommunications, which had made the highest profits up to a short time before, suffered a particularly severe decline in 1979.

Even taking the effect of inflation into account, the considerable worsening of the situation is still clear. Thus, the value of the lire being held constant, losses amounted to 33 billion in 1970 and to 483 billion in 1978. The process of progressive deterioration is further confirmed by the loss/turnover ratio, which leapt from −1.4 in 1974 to −7.2 in 1978.

Since 1970, IRI has shown positive returns in only one year and ENI in only two. EFIM has not managed to produce a positive return at all. IRI's greatest losses are in the iron and mechanical engineering sectors, which account for almost 80 per cent of total IRI losses, while 80 per cent of the losses in the mechanical engineering sector are due to Alfa Romeo. ENI's weak sectors include chemicals and textiles as well as the businesses which used to be managed by Ente Autonomo di Gestione per le Aziende Minerarie (EGAM, the independent managing body for the mining industry, to be discussed later on), which in 1978 accounted for more than half of the losses made by ENI. EFIM's 1978 situation is characterised by generalised losses, although on a more limited scale than the other corporations due to its smaller size.[7] Thus, the data relating to the single companies show the bulk of the losses concentrated in particular areas although it is also true that almost all sectors show losses.

All of this suggests that the early 1970s had a decisive influence on the following five-year period. Even though the roots of the profitability crisis are to be sought in earlier periods — probably in the mid-1960s — this period was characterised by a number of specific facts: on the one hand, a considerable increase in investment coupled with an equally considerable increase in the number of the employed and, on the other, economic results which were already deteriorating. Violent crisis was to break out in the following years, during which investment was low and the rate of growth of employment slow but during which, also, the deficit grew out of all proportion.

Thus, the large growth of the state-controlled companies, in terms of investment and of employment, failed to fulfil expectations. This phenomenon can be perceived more easily by comparing the data for public companies with those relating to private companies. In 1979, the state-controlled companies included in the Mediobanca (Credit Bank) sample had 2,106 billion lire losses as compared with 1,808 billion in 1978. During the same period, the private companies managed to turn losses of 2.4 billion into an 85 billion lire profit. During the same two-year period, there is evidence that funds derived from inside sources for the financing of new fixed assets increased for both groups of companies. But it must also be pointed out that during the 1968–79 period, this proportion was highly unfavourable to the state-controlled companies (26.4 per cent of the increment in all fixed assets for technical purposes as compared with 74.4 per cent relative to the sample of private companies and with as much as 105.3 per cent for the sample of medium-size enterprises). This cannot be imputed merely to the fact that the state-controlled companies accomplished a‚larger volume of investments during the earlier years; rather, it is a result of the gross profitability gap between the two types of enterprise. In 1979 public companies obtained a 2.1 per cent gross profit margin on their turnover, as compared with 4.4 per cent for private companies. This is the main cause underlying the deterioration of the financial structure. The Mediobanca survey indicates that for every lira of their equity, the state-controlled companies were indebted for 13.2 lire, whereas the figure for private companies was 3.5 lire.

The constant and progressive worsening of the results of business management led to a severe crisis in one of the essential features of state participation as it had formerly been known in Italy, namely, the presence of private shareholders. The crisis was to be perceived in two distinct ways. First, the number and proportion of companies in which the managing bodies had controlling or sole interest increased. Similarly, in a considerable number of companies which were already characterised by a controlling public interest, that interest went further still. Hence, many state-controlled companies in which the public interest exceeded 50 per cent became entirely state-owned.[8] Second, there was a dramatic fall in the number of individual savers holding shares in companies where only a minority interest was possible. Above all, the contribution of new capital on behalf of minority shareholders became insignificant. In the case of IRI — the corporation which, from its very beginning, had based its philosophy on the shareholding interest of private capital — the contribution of other shareholders to the group's businesses, banks being excluded, fell from 61 billion lire in 1978 to 7 billion lire in 1979. The financial requirements of the group in both years exceeded 4 thousand billion lire.

Throughout the 1950s and during the first half of the 1960s, in the greater part of those companies in which the private shareholders had minority interest, this proportion had been considerably higher, with an average of 12.7 per cent and peaks of up to 18.3 per cent. Subsequently, this proportion deteriorated progressively as private shareholders withdrew from IRI enterprises. ENI's case was similar.

It thus appears obvious that far-reaching changes are affecting the very institutional framework of the system. These changes imply the abandonment of the profit motive as a fundamental stimulus for the activity of the companies. As a result, even though the law still ranks private and state-controlled companies together, the state-controlled companies today look, not like private firms, but more like nationalised companies, where the main goal is not the attainment of good business results, but the pursuit of social objectives.

The crisis in the state-controlled segment of the economy is, undoubtedly, part of the general crisis which affected all of Italy's large businesses. The degree of inflexibility in all the industrialised economies increased considerably over the last years. On the one hand, there was an increase in the size of the investments to be made and in the time required for their implementation; on the other, the flexibility necessary to correct past mistakes diminished considerably. Any attempt to put investments back into perspective or to effect productive reconversion seems to meet with increasing difficulty, due to the social tension caused by these phenomena. In large companies, such tension and lack of flexibility constitute, naturally, a stronger constraint and the pressures exerted by the various groups within and without the structure itself are also perceived in a more powerful way.

The data relative to the performance of the large corporations indicate, however, that the crisis in the public sector is more severe than that experienced in the private sector, company size being equal. A first element explaining this result is, without doubt, represented by the greater weight of some sectors, such as iron and steel, chemicals and shipbuilding, in the state shareholding complex. These sectors, in fact, are undergoing a period of crisis in almost all industrialised countries. Consider the crisis in the iron and steel sector, which absorbed 20 per cent of all investments in fixed assets made by the state-controlled companies in the last twenty years and 40 per cent of all industrial investments. As such a large portion of the economy enters a period of crisis, its repercussions are bound to affect the entire system.

The chemical and fibre industry is also in general crisis, made worse in Italy by the excess productive capacity installed during the 1960s and the early 1970s. Such excess is a consequence of the attempt to gain predominance in the sector, a goal pursued both by private operators and state ones, which led both of them to build new plants without taking market potential properly into account.

Hence, not all of the losses borne by the state-controlled companies can be imputed to system deficiencies.

A second explanation may be found in the rapid development of the state shareholding interests between 1968–74. During this period, the state-controlled companies share of the total turnover of Italy's large corporations boomed, rising from 35 to 44 per cent, and it is exactly at this time that operating deficits began to appear. There is no doubt that this must be imputed to a slackening in the pace of development during the early 1970s and must have affected the profitability of businesses. An even more important reason was that the state-controlled corporations were weighed down by excess employment and by financial burdens caused by the investments made in the preceding years. The new financial contributions obtained through increases in the endowment funds or through bank loans had to be used to finance losses rather than new investments. This led to the well-known spiral by which new debts are incurred in order to pay back old ones.

The financial crisis which followed the investment boom entailed a further reduction of the independence of the state-controlled companies *vis-à-vis* political power, as the system became totally dependent upon such power for the supply of its financial resources. This dependence caused, in its turn, the goal of employment to prevail over any other business goal. As noted earlier, employment grew most during the 1969–74 period. Part of this rise in the employment figures must be traced back to the internal strategy of development of the existing corporations and of the relevant managing bodies. A considerable part, however, is due to the establishment, in 1971, of two new corporations, the Ente Autonomo di Gestione per le Aziende Minerarie (EGAM), and Gestioni e Partecipazioni Industriali (GEPI, industrial management and shareholdings) which absorbed a considerable number of employees. It appears necessary, therefore, for attention to turn to the origins and respective histories of these two bodies.

EGAM: Origins, Development and Dissolution

EGAM was formally established in May 1958 together with two other less important managing bodies (the Thermal Baths Managing Body and the Cinema Managing Body). The object of this measure was to organise — on the basis of the model tried out in earlier years with IRI and, especially, ENI — the management of the state shareholding interests in the mining sector.

At the time of its first establishment, EGAM was provided with the relevant administrative and control boards but was left idle for a rather long time because the state shareholdings were not conveyed to it but were managed directly by the various ministries.

The state, in fact, had direct control over a group of mining companies acquired at various times. These included Nazionale Cogne, Monte Amiata and AMMI. The idea behind the establishment of EGAM was to apply the mixed-company form to the management of these companies which currently was being handled in a rather bureaucratic way by state employees.

It was not until June 1971 that the Ministry of State Economic Participation decided to put an end to the merely formal existence of EGAM, thus providing for its 'reactivation' and the appointment of the organisation's President, Board of Directors and Boards of Auditors. EGAM was to manage Cogne and its associated companies and Silea, which at the time was under the control of the Ministry of State Shareholding.

The timing of this decision is interesting. The economic presence of the state in the mining sector may have required the aid of some rationalising structure but such a requirement had made itself felt for many years without anything being done, even at times when the economy was booming. Perhaps the main reason lay in the need to contribute to the reorganisation of Montedison, an important share of which had been taken over by ENI in that same period and which was overloaded with many diversified, but rather unbalanced, businesses. Some of these businesses were taken over by other state-controlled bodies. EFIM, for instance, which already operated in that field, took over shareholdings in the aluminium sector and IRI acquired a large company in the food-processing sector. Nevertheless, there were still several companies in the mining and metallurgical sectors which were hard to allocate to existing state companies but which none of the parties involved was prepared to wind up.

In March 1972, EGAM extended its scope beyond the mining sector so as to encompass the metallurgical one as well and all the sectors 'connected to the latter by instrumentality, accessoriness and complementarity' and was therefore able to relieve Montedison of a considerable burden, as 25,000 of its 150,000 total employees were attributable to such companies. Moreover, they were employed in areas subject to heavy losses and which, in any case, had no connection with Montedison's main focus in the chemical sector.[9]

In addition, EGAM acquired other mining and metallurgical businesses formerly belonging to other state-controlled corporations and making very heavy losses. Particularly important operations included the take-over, from IRI, of Breda Siderurgica, a company with almost 4,000 employees active in the field of special steel production, and of SBE, an industrial nut and bolt factory with 250 employees. Other acquisitions related to the following companies: Sogersa (2,200 employees), a company established in 1971 and located in Sardinia, its purpose being the survey of Montedison's mines on the island; Sadea, a company established as a result of rescuing the Brambilla Company of Verres in 1972 (150 employees); Tematex, located in Vergiate, a company operating in the mechanico-textile field, having 240 employees; Nuova S. Giorgio (800 employees), another enterprise operating in the mechanico-textile sector, taken over from IRI; Officine Savio of Pordenone (1,800 employees), taken over in 1971, a company which produced textile machinery and performed the final stages of the spinning cycle, and Acciaierie di Modena (500 employees), a steel-producing concern which developed out of Pages, which in turn belonged to IMI.

Subsequently, EGAM gained control of AMMI and the companies connected to it: this operation concerned 3,200 employees. AMMI, in its turn, had taken over a number of businesses prior to its acquisition on behalf of EGAM: these included metallurgical plants as well as enterprises dealing in the barium, abrasives and galvanising fields, and even a furniture factory.

Thus, the organisation's entire first year of activity was devoted to the implementation of these acquisition plans, even though EGAM had not yet received any financial endowment from the State. The various political parties, therefore, put forward a number of proposals to the effect of granting an endowment fund to it: the Italian Communist Party suggested a 450 billion lire fund, the Italian Socialist Party a 400 billion lire one — and so did the Christian Democratic Party. The Government suggested a 192 billion lire endowment fund. After a lengthy and difficult course through Parliament, during which several political groups tried to outdo each other in assigning all kinds of tasks to EGAM, a law was passed establishing for it a 330 billion lire endowment fund.

In the meantime, EGAM pursued its acquisition policy which gathered fresh momentum after the conferment of the endowment fund and, especially, during 1974. The annual budget report for that year emphasised that 'the process of integration underlying our purchasing decisions over the last two years developed especially in the direction of activities connected with the metallurgical sector, in order to ensure the supply of raw materials and of basic consumer items for our companies'.

The following companies thus became part of the EGAM group: Solmine, which enabled the organisation to gain possession of Italy's most important iron ore deposits — since they exist in the form of iron pyrites, they can be employed also for the production of sulphuric acid (2,000 employees); Nuova Fornicoke (500 employees); Vetrocoke Cokapuania and Cokitalia (1,500 employees). The latter company is 50 per cent EGAM. Furthermore, shareholdings were obtained in Rivoira, in Promedo and in Fluormine, companies operating in the fields of technical gas production, insulating material production and fluorite mining respectively.

Apart from these acquisitions, the organisation had to deal, upon specific government instructions, with solutions to important problems concerning the maintenance of production and of employment levels of a number of companies, all of which suffer from serious financial and economic situations — such companies as Mercurifera Monte Amiata (1,000 employees); Billi (400 employees); Moncenisio (600 employees); IMFG and Apuana Marmi (each having 200 employees).

By the end of 1974, the group had attained a well defined appearance and was focussed on three basic areas: the mining and metallurgical sector, the textile machinery sector and the iron and steel sector.

The first of these areas accounted for more than 14,000 employees and the second for approximately 5,000 and the iron and steel sector for more than 14,700. That is to say, in the course of only four years, EGAM had taken over a total of more than 100 companies with over 33,000 employees. It is interesting to note that during the period from 1 January 1973 to 31 July 1975, it took over 29 companies with 9,631 employees, 5,441 of whom were derived from Montedison, 1,333 from IRI, 2,264 from private companies and 593 from the ENI group. These data do not take into account acquisitions made prior to 1973, where the bodies conveying companies to EGAM were practically the same groups mentioned earlier. It is also interesting to observe that, besides Montedison and the private sector, IRI and ENI also took the opportunity to shift some of their more troubled businesses onto EGAM.

The net result of this acquisition policy was that EGAM put itself into a situation of having to manage a group of marginal companies, technologically obsolete and financially precarious, with a random management and no goal other than mere survival. Given the overall picture, it is no wonder that the economic results were disastrous, with substantial operating losses and negative results for all operations.

It should be noted, however, that the actual crisis within EGAM did not break out for economic/financial reasons but because of strictly political ones relating to the acquisition, in spring 1975, of the Compagnia di Navigazione Villain e Fassio on behalf of one of the companies of the group. EGAM's justification for this acquisition was that it needed to carry the coke it produced by sea but both the political parties and public opinion opposed this decision most vehemently. The frantic expansion of EGAM had, in effect, a negative impression on public opinion, which was unable to understand the advantages of uniting in a sole management body such diversified activities, especially as they were considered in almost every case to be 'lame ducks' which should have been wound-up.

In the light of these facts, the acquisition of a shipping company seemed to be entirely unjustified and extremely dubious. What is more, Villain & Fassio also owned a daily newspaper, so that the overall target of the operation appeared to be to purchase the newspaper in order to influence public opinion rather than to actually transport coke.

In addition to these specific motives EGAM became the scapegoat of the growing lack of confidence of the Italians towards the way state holdings were run and the Villain & Fassio affair was the straw which broke the camel's back. The outcry resulted in the appointment of a committee of inquiry. And, as the President of

EGAM resigned, a new president was appointed. The latter held office for about one year, during which the situation worsened, particularly because of financial burdens which reached a peak value of 22 per cent of turnover. In October 1976, a provisional administrator was appointed who initially tried to reorganise EGAM by requesting Parliament to grant new funds amounting to approximately 1,600 billion lire. His proposal was rejected so in December of that year he decided to wind up a number of companies employing a total of 18,000 people — about half the employees of the group. In order to avoid such a drastic solution, both the Government and Parliament decided to pay 90 billion lire (i) for salaries and wages to employees until February 1977 and (ii) to cover accounts payable to major suppliers. Possible ways of restructuring the group, within the wider framework of a reorganisation of the state-controlled corporations, were studied.

In March 1977, the Minister of State Shareholding presented a bill in Parliament with the object of dissolving the organisation and assigning the management of EGAM's iron and steel businesses to IRI and the mining and textile machinery ones to ENI. The government bill met with strong opposition in Parliament: a group of highly influential senators and members of the same party to which the relevant Minister belonged (the Christian Democratic Party), spoke against a solution, the only outcome of which would have been to shift the EGAM companies onto other managing bodies, thus contributing to their further deterioration. They seized the opportunity to discuss publicly the operations of the state-controlled companies and the propensity of such companies to safeguard the current number of jobs for their respective employees under all circumstances. These senators suggested the liquidation of all businesses where losses exceeded a given peak, the dismissal of relevant staff and the return to the private sector of all sound businesses or those for which reorganisation was thought to be possible. In order to win acceptance of these measures, which entailed the lay-off of a considerable number of workers, the promoters of the plan suggested the adoption of a number of social welfare measures for those eventually made redundant, such measures being planned in accordance with the geographical distribution of the personnel concerned. Another original feature of the proposal was to force banks to accept the principle that the state is not entirely responsible for debts incurred by state-controlled companies.[10]

As might have been foreseen, Parliament approved the Government's bill. Thus, the EGAM group was dismembered: the iron and steel companies were taken over by IRI, while the mining and mechanico-textile ones became part of ENI. Nevertheless, the EGAM affair and the battle fought in Parliament regarding that affair had an extraordinary impact on the state shareholding system. Indeed, that discussion pointed out very clearly that the degeneration of the system had reached such a degree that its very survival was jeopardised. The only solution seemed to entail a drastic change of course, so as to lead the managing bodies back to their original philosophy — that the state-controlled companies do not have the task of undertaking rescue operations (in this context, we shall soon analyse the case of GEPI) or of ensuring present employment levels at all costs and that the state is not always obliged to pay the debts of the state-controlled companies. In other words, a mixed economy has meaning only in so far as state interests are capable of performing their institutional tasks with the same degree of efficiency as company owners in the private sector. Otherwise, the state may run the risk of having to rescue its own shareholding system.

It is not surprising that a therapy as strict as the one suggested was bound to meet with fierce opposition from the left-wing parties, the unions and all those who thrived on the system; nevertheless, it undoubtedly had considerable impact on the country's public opinion. The parliamentary debate contributed to the restatement of a specific kind of awareness that had been lost, namely, that even where state interests are concerned, the market constitutes an important and, indeed, an indispensable sifter of good and bad enterprises. The public perceived that the future of the state-controlled corporations lay in a firm return to their original premises, to the philosophy of efficiency which accounted for the system's success during the first twenty-five years of its existence.

It was considered that any attempt to rescue the system must be based upon the allocation of definite responsibilities to management, by appraising its performance against precise, measurable parameters rather than political results which can hardly be quantified. This trend also cleared a path away from the theory of 'improper burdens' which prevailed within IRI during the early

1970s. According to this theory, the state-controlled companies were entitled to receive from the state resources to match additional costs imposed upon them by external social and political structures. Such burdens might include installation of businesses in areas which proved unsuitable for their specific activities or the need to bear additional labour costs due to a surplus of employment over personnel actually required and so on. The theory of 'improper burdens' was not just an attempt to rescue the budgets of the relevant bodies for it also aimed at preserving the professionalism and independence of the executives. The attempt failed since it proved impossible to define the nature of these burdens or to measure their costs. Moreover, acceptance of this doctrine *per se* entails the acceptance of the principle that enterprises must relinquish such goals as business efficiency and competitiveness — and this contradicts the very philosophy of the Italian state-controlled company. In which case, it would have been better to recognise the end of the mixed-economy system and, perhaps, turn those companies into nationalised enterprises.[11]

Whatever view one takes on these issues, it is a fact that the consequences of the public rescue operation of EGAM still weigh heavily on the state shareholding system. For instance, approximately 50 per cent of ENI's losses are due to former EGAM companies. Banking was also affected by the repercussions of the EGAM affair. Banks, in fact, have since become much more careful when granting loans to state-controlled companies because they are no longer certain that they will be completely reimbursed should difficulties arise. As a result, public companies presently have more limited recourse to credit and must, therefore, appeal to Parliament in order to obtain increases in their endowment funds out of Treasury funds. On the other hand the situation of public finance is such as to make any increase in the endowment funds a rather complex matter. The combination of all these factors has led companies to develop more cautious business policies, to slow down their rate of growth and to weigh prospective investment more thoroughly. The net result may be said to be positive, since companies have become extremely careful in their behaviour. Moreover, the EGAM affair engendered a highly critical attitude among the public where state control is concerned, in contrast to the general feeling of many years that state participation in the economy was a kind of panacea to the problems of the

Italian economy as a whole. The affair had a further impact on another important aspect of the operation of an industrial system — namely, rescue policy.

Public rescue interventions are a constant feature of Italy's history. From the foundation of IRI up to the present day, the history of Italian industry has been characterised by state intervention designed to rescue businesses in difficulty and this has occurred in many and varying forms, the most common of which is the incorporation of these businesses into the broad and diversified state shareholding system.

This process has undergone periods of acceleration or slowing down, depending on the phase of the trade cycle. The phenomenon was very strong during the post-World War II period but was then interrupted during the period from 1955 to the late 1960s. It enjoyed a dramatic revival in the first half of the 1970s — particularly in 1975 and 1976 — and finally slowed down in conjunction with economic recovery. It was, in fact, in the early 1970s that a special body was established whose specific task was the implementation of industrial rescue projects.

GEPI and the Rescue Policy

It was in the Ministry of Economic Planning that the idea first developed that the 1969 crisis showed that the old mode of development was finished. It had been based on low labour costs, internal migration and the rather unique propensity to work of the Italian working class. Its putative demise was held to give rise to a need for a thorough restructuring effort which had to be guided in one way or another by the public authorities.

An important aspect of these views must be emphasised. During the years which constitute the focus of this discussion, widespread mistrust of the market as the leading criterion for industrial reorganisation processes was expressed. The general trend was to foster a process of structural reorganisation guided, not by the 'blind forces' of the market but by the state or, to be more precise, by state shareholding bodies on its behalf. This was, perhaps, the first time that such views on the appropriate aims of the state shareholding bodies were explicitly stated in Italy.

The birth of Gestioni e Partecipazioni Industriali (GEPI) was accompanied by an awareness that efficient structural reorganisation could not be accomplished by traditional means of intervention such as state subsidiaries or the intervention in weak companies of the state shareholding managing bodies. The state, it was therefore thought, must play a more positive and vigorous role, itself replacing those entrepreneurs who were incapable of accomplishing the necessary structural changes. One way of achieving that goal was thought to lie in the establishment of a new body in which the financial expertise of IMI (a public investment bank) could be combined with the industrial experience of the state-controlled corporations.

In spite of the resistance offered by these bodies and continual governmental and ministerial changes, the idea gained increasing support and was ratified as Law No. 184 on 22 March 1971. Under this law, IMI and the other three large state-controlled bodies (EFIM, ENI and IRI) were assigned the task of setting up a *holding* company. This organisation would act to safeguard and raise the current employment levels, in accordance with definite structural reorganisation plans, in companies in *temporary* difficulty. IMI and the other three large state-controlled bodies were supplied with financial means (50 per cent going to IMI and the other half to the other three corporations). GEPI was permitted to acquire interests in companies and to grant loans, if necessary on very favourable terms.

The law, in other words, emphasised the managerial aspect. It thus recognised that unfavourable business situations are, in the majority of cases, due to a lack of entrepreneurial abilities. Hence, the holding company was permitted to intervene by establishing managing companies to take over the plant and equipment of other businesses.

GEPI was entitled to take such action provided it did not exceed a maximum level of expenditure set at 9 billion lire for the south and the depressed areas of central and northern Italy, and at 6 billion lire for all other cases. It was not, however, entitled to undertake rescue operations in companies with less than 100 employees.[12]

From the outset the new company developed along lines other than those generally expected. In the first place, the state shareholding bodies stressed the distance separating them from GEPI by appointing minor figures to the board of directors. This meant that the new company was deprived of that basic managerial skill upon which it was supposed to rely. IMI took a similar attitude as soon as it discovered that the political pressures exerted on GEPI were so strong that genuine restructuring of the businesses taken over by it could not possibly take place.

F.A. Grassini, Managing Director of GEPI during its first years of activity, noted: 'Shutting down a factory was a deadly sin for public enterprise in the Italian society of the 1970s'. In order to prevent factory shut-downs and employment cuts, the unions and the political parties resorted to all kinds of pressures on management. These ranged from demonstrations to strikes on various levels (local, provincial, national and on the level of the individual productive sectors) and from personal pressures exerted by influential politicians on the management of specific holding companies to even more explicit pressures — such as the more or less significant or swift increase in the body's endowment fund — intended as a means of bribing the management to intervene in one company rather than another. Professor Grassini explicitly admitted to one such case where this practice was followed to rescue a Tuscan hat factory. In the face of such pressures, GEPI's activity was bound to meet with growing difficulties and an inability to comply with the procedures established for it.[13]

Faced with the progressive withdrawal of the other state-controlled corporations, the management of GEPI decided to turn to the market for the entrepreneurial resources denied it by the public sector. The original idea behind GEPI, according to which the state and its managers reorganised failing businesses and then returned them to the market, thus, was replaced by another notion. This was that the state agency identified a private sector partner to whom the restructuring task could be assigned and who, eventually, took over the failing business, financially aided by the state. Undoubtedly, this reliance on private enterprise is one of the GEPI's contributions to Italy's recent industrial history.

This first aspect of GEPI's activity was supplemented by another. In all GEPI partnerships, the prospective partner was required to introduce a certain amount of risk capital into the business as evidence of his conviction that the business at issue could actually be reorganised. Hence, it was possible to identify and deter prospective partners whose only aim was to make personal gains from the state and from companies in serious difficulties.

A second far-reaching transformation was brought about by the facts themselves. While the original plans referred to a relatively small financial structure (GEPI's capital was not to exceed 60 billion lire), the severe 1974–75 crisis produced strong pressures on the company to multiply the number of its interventions, and this development was paralleled by the actions of the Government, which forced GEPI to take over an increasing number of businesses.

In 1976 a certain number of companies (for example, Leyland-Innocenti) threatened to close down and, in consequence, cause some thousands of dismissals. In the event of dismissal, *the worker is deprived of his salary*. If, on the other hand, the company does not close but is taken over by GEPI, the workers, although suspended from work, are placed in the 'Earnings Integration Fund' which permits them to maintain 95 per cent of their wages. In view of the large number of concerns involved and the impossibility of saving so many jobs, GEPI refused to intervene. Therefore the Government, in order to avoid the dismissals and the explosion of even more serious social tension, compelled GEPI to create IPO, a company formally independent from GEPI, whose purpose was simply to hire the above-mentioned workers so as to permit them to benefit from the 'Earnings Integration Fund' and to receive 95 per cent of their wages. The creation of IPO was, therefore, the most symbolic example of the fact that GEPI is not free to operate according to the criteria set forth by the law, but is subject to the obligations imposed by the Government.

This has had dramatic repercussions on GEPI's accounts. It was forced to take over too great a number of bankrupt enterprises while the state was opening its purse-strings. Since the day of its establishment, GEPI has executed 105 interventions in firms employing a total of 58,000 people. It has so far received about 1,600 billion lire from the state but its losses average 160 billion lire per year. As from 1973, the year in which re-sales to the private sector were started, GEPI has sold forty-five concerns, totalling almost 11,000 employees: this means 6.7 companies a year, with a yearly average of 1,500 employees. Thus, for every employee moving out, the company has burdened itself with another four. As a result, reconstruction proves extremely difficult and complex — and so do the opportunities for reconversion. In order to find a way out of this situation and to prevent each and every bankrupt company from ending up as part of GEPI, steps were taken at the beginning of 1977 to render rescue operations less haphazard, more serious and not so subject to abuses of political power.[14]

The first basic issue raised related to the geographical range of the rescue operations. It was pointed out that the various areas of the country could not be compared in any meaningful way as long as similar standards were applied to quite different regions, the more industrialised and the less developed. Due to the uneven distribution of industry over Italy, rescue operations were more frequent in the north than in the south, although a business crisis could be a much more serious matter in the latter region. Hence, one proposal was to concentrate resources for rescue operations in the south and in the country's more backward areas while avoiding further interventions in the north. The relevant bill was carried in Parliament (Law No. 675 of 1977). This law represented an important innovation within the framework of the rescue policies. It had the effect, however, of making the management of GEPI more vulnerable to pressure when it dealt with southern companies facing a crisis. Because its range of intervention was narrower, it did not have the same ability to balance those pressures upon it.

A further important effort to rationalise rescue policy was made by an attempt to reduce considerably GEPI's shareholdings in northern companies. Many northern companies had been aided by GEPI, some for several years, and it seemed clear that many of these enterprises would never again be able to stand on their own feet. Consequently the Government tried to induce GEPI to wind up those northern companies for which no favourable prospects seem to exist. A first attempt was made in autumn 1979 but failed. A second was made at the beginning of 1981. The answer may lie in setting definite time limits for reconstruction operations so as to avoid an endless drain on public resources.

This latter proposal is based on the assumption that rescue ought to be a transitory phenomenon: a period of hospitalisation, not permanent admission to an institute for chronic diseases. This criterion would particularly affect those businesses which have no prospects of being returned to the private sector. Such a policy, however, is bound to come up against considerable obstacles. Whenever reconstruction measures requiring a price to be paid in terms of employment are suggested, they are inevitably opposed by a coalition of trade union and other interests. Thus their implementation is delayed and efficiency of the responsible state organisation is jeopardised.[15]

CONCLUDING COMMENTS

The available data on performance testify to the fact that state-controlled corporations in Italy employ resources less efficiently than their private competitors. The ratio between gross or net operating margins, on the one hand, and net assets, on the other, is lower for state-controlled companies than for private ones and has been for the last few years.

In individual sectors, moreover, depreciations in the public sector cover a small share of fixed assets after depreciation and the size of cash-flow relative to total sales is systematically smaller. This suggests that public companies use resources less efficiently than private ones within particular industries.

The existence of such a situation, affecting so large a portion of the industry, has called forth many proposals to reform the system itself. Some of these aim at rationalising the presence of the managing bodies in the various sectors in an effort to group public companies together on a sectoral basis. Others assert the need to remove those businesses that cannot be fitted in any rational way into the framework of the state shareholdings (such as RAI, the television and radio broadcasting corporation). Still others maintain that it is necessary to introduce and apply throughout the system strict external auditing procedures, so that it is possible to know exactly how companies are being managed and how public resources are being employed.

Much attention has been paid also to fostering decentralisation within the bodies themselves through the creation of new internal organisational structures. And, along similar lines, efforts have been made to re-establish the direct accountability of management for company performance — a requirement of efficiency that has been lost sight of in recent years as a result of political pressures and constraints imposed from outside the system.

The White Paper on state shareholding, drawn up in 1980 on behalf of the newly appointed Socialist Minister of State Economic

Participation, provides for massive recapitalisation (13,000 billion lire over the next four years). This reflects the belief that financial elements are basic in the crisis of the system. Important as such measures may be, however, they cannot provide a complete solution to the problems affecting this part of the Italian industrial system.

The point is that state-controlled companies are undergoing several highly ambiguous internal processes and this makes any proposal of a technical reform — even of the most serious type — extremely difficult. Two conflicting views of the nature, operations and, indeed, the very substance of these bodies are now clashing within the system, dividing political and governmental bodies and Italian public opinion itself.

On the one side, there is the idea that, in an industrial system, the state ought to act as an entrepreneur. Hence, it should follow the rules of the market and ensure the overall efficiency of the system and, therefore, the best allocation of resources from the point of view of the collective interest. On the other side, it is believed that the 'social responsibility of the state' ought to be the fundamental value. Thus, public companies become a tool through which the state supports economic policy. Those who support this approach are convinced that certain specific objectives (such as safeguarding existing employment levels, industrialising in the south, implementing certain anti-cyclic policies) should be pursued through the state-controlled companies.

Neither philosophy has emerged suddenly during the last few years: they have existed side by side from the very beginning of the system. Until 1965, the state-controlled companies were managed on the basis of the philosophy that the state should act as an entrepreneur. Thus, private shareholders were able to participate in the capital of the public companies. In 1965 the opposite view became dominant.

Through both stages, some influence of the 'opposite' philosophy could be perceived. Thus, during the first period, state-subsidised companies certainly did exist. Similarly, since 1965, rescue operations have sometimes been carried out very efficiently. From the point of view of the overall framework, however, one approach has prevailed at specific times.

The new aspect which emerged in 1977–78, in the face of the crisis of the system, was the rediscovery of the market as the standard by which to appraise the degree of efficiency of the public corporations. The then existing conditions revived the idea that the state must act in industry as an entrepreneur and this might, once again, change the overall orientation of the system. For, if the state-controlled companies revert to the market as an external criterion for measuring efficiency, it is highly probable that the system will regain its ability to attract private capital and to fulfil a strictly entrepreneurial role.

In the balance is the very nature of the Italian industrial system. If the state-controlled sector reverts to its original, entrepreneurial, philosophy then it is possible that Italian industry will be able to recover the fierce dynamic character that its larger organisations, at least, have now lost. Adoption of the social responsibility perspective would produce a quite different result.

The outcome of this conflict will not be clear for some time and will be influenced by developments in the political sphere. The performance of private industry is important here: if it provides growth and better employment opportunities, pressure in the direction of a 'social function' of public enterprise will ease off and state-controlled companies will be able to act as entrepreneurs. If, on the other hand, private industry rests on its laurels, enormous pressure will be exerted on the state — and, consequently, on the companies under its control — to compel them to compensate for this. It is a significant fact that the switch in the philosophy of the state-controlled corporations occurred in the mid-1960s and during the first half of the 1970s: at a time when private industry simply preserved the position it had previously gained and proved incapable of leading economic growth.

NOTES AND REFERENCES

1. Gianluigi Alzona, 'Il vertice dell' industria in Italia nel periodo 1971–77', *Rivista di Economia e Politica Industriale*, Bologna, May-August 1979, pp. 163–72.

2. Pasquale Saraceno, *Il sistema delle imprese e partecipazione statale nell'esperienza italiana* (Milan: Giuffré Editore, 1975) pp. 7–13.

3. Beppe Gatti, *La crisi delle partecipazioni statali: motivi e prospettive* (Milan: CIRIEC, 1980) pp. 2–4.

4.   Pietro Armani, 'I problemi economici', in P. Armani and F.A. Roversi-Monaco (eds), *Le partecipazioni statali: un'analisi critica* (Milan: Franco Angeli, 1977) pp. 24–30.

5.   Eugenio Scalfari and Giuseppe Turani, *Razza padrona* (Milan: Feltrinelli Editore, 1974) pp. 153–253.

6.   Enrico Filippi, 'Un Contributo al dibattito sull' impresa pubblica in Italia', *Rivista di Economia e Politica Industriale*, January-June 1975, pp. 121–43.

7.   Giuseppe Bognetti, *La crisi delle partecipazioni statali: motivi e prospettive* (Milan: CIRIEC, 1980) pp. 5–8.

8.   Francesco Cesarini, 'La situazione finanziaria delle partecipazioni statali', *Banche e Banchieri,* Rome, March 1981, pp. 187–204.

9.   Gaetano M. Golinelli, *Vita, crisi e ristrutturazione di un gruppo industriale pubblico* (Milan: Giuffré Editore, 1980) pp. 27–49.

10.   AREL, *Rapporto sul gruppo EGAM*, Rome, April 1977, pp. 2–34.

11.   Romano Prodi, 'La crisi delle partecipazioni statali conseguenze economiche di faticosi processi di decisione', *L'Industria*, Bologna, January-March 1981, pp. 5–20.

12.   FLM Milano e Bergamo, *La politica della GEPI* (Milan: Franco Angeli, 1981) pp. 15–55.

13.   Franco A. Grassini, 'Vincoli politici e direzione delle imprese pubbliche nell'esperienza italiana', *L'Industria*, July–September 1980, pp. 343–68.

14.   Grassini, 'Le imprese pubbliche', in AREL, *Stato e Industria in Europa: l'Italia* (Bologna: Il Mulino, 1979) pp. 79–115.

15.   Pontarollo. *Il Salvataggio industriale nell'Europa della crisi* (Bologna: Il Mulino, 1976) pp. 7–46.

CHAPTER THREE

The Netherlands: Maintenance of Employment as a Primary Objective

H.W. de Jong and Robert Jan Spierenburg

Shortly after World War I there emerged among the political parties and the socialist movement in the Netherlands a broad consensus on the desirability of industrial regulation. Both the Christian Democratic Parties (Roman Catholics as well as Protestants) and the Socialists, in their programmes of 1923, embodied proposals for a semi-planned economy with sectoral councils. These parties aimed at some degree of *ordening* (the specific Dutch world for cartelisation and the regulation of industries under government guidance) although the Catholics, with a strong membership amongst businessmen and farmers, respected the freedom of enterprise more than the Socialists.

During the severe crisis of the 1930s these plans were realised, to some extent, under the auspices of the Department of Economic Affairs. In 1931, to implement an industrial policy, the General Directorate of Commerce and Manufacturing Industry was set up as part of the Ministry of Economic Affairs and, during the 1930s, the Dutch Government developed policy instruments designed to regulate private industry — such as protection against foreign competitors, the use of the law to impose privately concluded cartel agreements on unwilling industrialists and the closing of some branches of industry to new entrants.

At the same time, a movement aiming at accelerated industrialisation appeared. This movement achieved its first result on a regional level: in 1935 the Industriebank in Limburg was founded. A year later Maatschappij voor Industriefinanciering, a national state investment bank, started operations with the objective of combatting the severe unemployment. The influence of these banks, however, was slight.

After World War II the Minister of Economic Affairs, the Social Democrat H. Vos, strove for a planned economy but, faced with

59

strong opposition, he could not achieve his objectives. While the idea of regulating industries survived (although it was hardly put into practice), the idea of speeding up industrialisation got the upper hand in practical politics. The Nationale Investeringsbank, the recovery bank (which became the NIB in 1963) was founded to pursue this goal. This state investment bank played a much more important role than its predecessors, especially during the recovery period of the 1940s and the early years of post-war industrialisation, in helping companies to start and/or expand. But, increasingly during the 1950s, with the freeing and integration of Western European markets and the acceleration of economic growth, the Government relied on market forces — except in labour, housing and a very few basic food markets which remained under their control. The overriding goal was to industrialise, in order to provide employment for a rapidly rising population and to compensate for the loss of the former colonies. In particular, it was deemed necessary to round off the earlier industrialisation, which had been mainly confined to the textile, food and metal working industries, as well as shipbuilding, and to promote new sectors such as chemicals and petro-chemicals, pharmaceuticals, electronics and aircraft.

This policy of industrialisation, on the basis of a low wages standard and within the context of a free and expanding European market, was rather successful. Indeed, too successful, for in 1963 there was the so-called 'wage explosion' which came unexpectedly after a number of years of large balance-of-payments surpluses, which had resulted in the virtual disappearance of unemployment and a large increase in unfilled vacancies.

The second round of industrialisation established a structure of industry with the following generalised characteristics.

    (a) A basic processing industry in the west, situated at the mouth of the rivers Rhine, Meuse and Schelde, consisting of oil refineries, petro-chemical and basic chemical installations, metallurgical industry, breweries and drinks production and food processing. This type of industry is capital intensive, employs skilled and highly skilled labour, imports many raw materials and exports a good deal of its output. This processing industry was not hurt by the 'wage explosion'. Indeed, it benefited from rising foreign and domestic demand during the 1960s and 1970s until the recession of 1974–75.

(b) The assembly type of industry (textiles and clothing, furniture making, shoe production, radio and television making *et cetera*) prevails in the eastern and southern provinces. It is wage intensive, employs lesser skilled people, is open to international competition and not based on natural comparative advantage. In addition, there is the shipbuilding industry, with several sub-sectors (tanker-building, repair, specialised building of small ships) mainly located in the west and north. These assembly type of industries were badly hurt by the wage explosion and increasingly came into difficulties during the late 1960s and throughout the 1970s. For example, in 1978, employment in the textiles, shoe, clothing and leather industries had declined to nearly one third of its 1963 volume: 76,500 in the latter year, in comparison with 219,700 in 1963. In the food, drinks and tobacco industries, employment fell some 30,000 during the same period to 169,200 in 1978, while the oil and chemical industries' employment actually rose 9,000 to nearly 100,000.

(c) Machine building, in the broadest sense, is — and has always been — a relatively weak sector in the Netherlands as neither a large-scale motor car industry nor a durable consumer goods industry existed nor were there strong companies in either mechanical or electrical engineering. The wage explosion, which could have provided good prospects for strong and innovative companies in labour-saving equipment if a sufficiently large market had existed, instead only hurt companies by increasing their costs.

The results of these developments were two-fold:

(a) a general decline in industrial employment, even though this was compensated to a large extent by the strong growth of the private and the public service sectors; and

(b) a pronounced concentration of employment problems in particular industries and regions: the assembly-type of industries located in northern, eastern and southern areas and the shipbuilding and machinery activities in a few cities in the west and east.

In addition, the southern area of Limburg, where coal mining had been important, was hit by the penetration of natural gas and oil in energy markets which is reflected, together with the declining importance of agriculture in the halving of employment between 1963 and 1978 (see Table 3.1).

Table 3.1
Employment in the Main Sectors of the Dutch Economy, 1963–78 ('000, excluding military, maids and employment less than 15 hours per week)

	1963	1978
Agriculture, fishing and mining	143	75
Manufacturing industry	1 269	1 114
Building and construction	391	386
Commercial services	974	1 318
Other services (government, defence, education, medical, social insurance etc.)	675	1 134
Total	3 452	4 027

Source: Centraal Bureau voor de Statistich, The Hague.

Since the mid-1960s, as a reaction to the difficulties in the textile, shoe-making and shipbuilding industries, the idea of regulation has been revived. Sectoral policies were tried in these and other industries beset with problems and, in 1972, the Nederlandse Herstructureringsmaatschappij, the Dutch Reconstruction Company (NEHEM) was founded to further such a policy.

In more recent years, business failures have spread like an epidemic. In the period 1973–78, more companies began asking for financial support from the Ministry of Economic Affairs. Salvage actions were started and successive governments increasingly subscribed to such policies during the 1970s. The state made funds available to the NIB and asked the bank to invest these funds in companies which were close to bankruptcy. At the same time the existing development companies were reorganised. The Limburgs Instituut voor Ontwikkeling en Financiering, the Limburg Institution for Development and Finance (LIOF), was set up in 1975.

LIOF is the continuation of the Industriebank in Limburg. The Noordelijke Ontwikkelingsmaatschappij, the Northern Development Company (NOM) was founded in 1974.

This chapter primarily focuses on the role of the NIB but the activities of this bank are discussed within the broader framework of Dutch industrial policies. NEHEM, whose poor performance illuminates the changing role of the NIB, is also discussed.

From this introduction it should already be clear that Dutch policy has been oriented mainly towards employment goals. To a large extent this was seen as complementary to macro-economic employment policies. At the end of the 1970s, when this type of policy became visibly a failure, the emphasis shifted towards innovation and modernisation.

National Investment Bank

Dutch commercial banks have never been enthusiastic about industrial projects. They rarely provide long-term credits and only issue new shares in exceptional cases — industrial capitalists are largely self-financing. The banks changed their practices during World War I but, after the economic crisis of 1921–23, they returned to their traditional policy.[1]

After 1945, business prospects were favourable and the conditions of international trade improved rapidly. Under these circumstances the need for long-term credit was very great and the Government thought it necessary to improve the Dutch institutional framework in this respect. In 1945 the Minister of Financial Affairs, P. Lieftinck, founded the Reconstruction Bank which was transformed into the NIB in 1963. The Bank provided long-term credits for manufacturing industry but was not allowed to compete with the commercial banks, which became shareholders of the investment bank, together with institutional lenders and the state. On the occasion of the tenth anniversary of the Bank, the Mayor of Amsterdam, an ex-chairman of the Dutch Bank, wrote: 'By providing long-term credit — commercial banks were not enthusiastic about industrial financing — the Dutch Recovery Bank was able to participate on a large scale in the economic resurgence of our country, but — as a matter of fact — this happened in close contact with the existing bank relations.'[2]

The connection between the state and the National Investment Bank is that the state acquired a 50.3 per cent participation in the Bank in which commercial banks and institutional investors also took a share. The Dutch Crown nominates the chairman and secretary of the board of management, while the supervisory board nominates the other two members of this board. The Minister of Financial Affairs appoints three of the fifteen members of the supervisory board and the old members themselves appoint the other members. Four members of the supervisory board have the task of looking after the credit policy of the management but the state controls the general policy of the bank (although this control can only be formally exercised during the shareholders' meeting).

When an industrial company asks for financial support, the NIB sends its own experts to that company for a financial and economic investigation. After the examination, there is a decision as to which financial instrument is to be used. The following instruments are available:

(a) Guarantees, credits and participations at the Bank's own risk. The provision of such support depends on commercial criteria.

(b) Guarantees, credits and participations to enterprises which are guaranteed to the Bank by the state. The state accepts the risk and the National Investment Bank recovers any losses. In this case, commercial criteria are weaker.

(c) Guarantees, credits and participations on request of the state and at the state's risk. The Bank allocates and administers funds available within the framework of government policy. These funds are to assist companies in difficulties and, in these cases, the application of commercial criteria is even weaker. These funds are provided via the instrument of employment money (to be discussed below).

In Appendix 3.1 the number of contracts concluded by the NIB between 1976 and 1979 are given, together with the amounts involved.

Only a small amount of assistance is provided by means of equity capital. The shareholdings of the Bank at the risk of the state are relatively restricted, but rose in 1978 and 1979. (See

Table 3.7, below.) Participations at the Bank's own risk are even less important. The Bank has indirect shareholdings mediated by its subsidiaries, the Dutch Participation Company (Nederlandse Participatiemaatschappij) and the Industrial Guarantee Fund (Industrieel Garantiefonds), which again are relatively unimportant.

The activities of the Bank are financed by the issue of bonds on the private capital market, by loans from institutional lenders, by sundry creditors and by a small amount of loans from the state. From Appendix 3.2 it follows that there has been a big increase in the financial means available to the National Investment Bank during the second half of the 1970s.

Because the NIB is also used to allocate and administer funds provided as an outcome of the economic policy of the Dutch Government, its activities have changed significantly. During the 1950s and 1960s the Bank gave, at its own risk, long-term credit mostly to fast growing industries; in particular, the metallurgical and chemical industries received large amounts of financial support. In 1957, the outstanding loans of the Bank amounted to 77 million guilders to companies in the chemical industry and to 80 million guilders to companies in the metallurgical industry.[3]

During the 1950s and 1960s the Bank realised only a very moderate rate of return. As a percentage of equity capital, the rate of return was in 1957, 1963 and 1967 slightly more than 3 per cent.[4] This was rather low in comparison with the earnings of private enterprise companies. In the ten-year period 1957–66 (inclusive), the average rate of return of all Dutch limited corporations, both quoted and non-quoted on the Amsterdam stock exchange, was 14.7 per cent on equity capital. Excluding the profits resulting from the participation in domestic and foreign companies (because the large Dutch multinational companies, having many foreign participations, might distort the picture), the average rate of return was still 8.5 per cent for Dutch corporations, the number of which rose from 22,900 in 1957 to 36,100 in 1966.[5] Thus, it cannot be maintained that the NIB was a successful investor, the more so as employment goals were irrelevant in view of the continuous full and overfull employment during the 1950s and 1960s. The total amount of outstanding loans amounted in 1963 to 522 million guilders, of which only 49.2 million was backed by the state.

During the 1970s, activity on the bank's own account slowed down. At the same time, operations in which the state accepted risk increased from 50 per cent of the total amount of outstanding loans and guarantees in 1975 to 75 per cent in 1979. Obviously, this shift was related to the slowing down of economic growth and the increasing problems with companies and employment.

Dutch Reconstruction Company

The Dutch Reconstruction Company, NEHEM, founded in 1972, pursues a different policy from that of the NIB. Instead of financing individual companies, which is the major part of the activities of the NIB, the objective of this company is to improve the structure of sectors: NEHEM prepares sector structure studies and puts them into effect.

At first, Pieter Langman, Minister of Economic Affairs, intended to create a type of organisation similar to the Industrial Reorganisation Corporation in Britain, which pursued its policy independently and relied on its own financial means. The type of organisation finally chosen, however, fitted better the tradition of the Netherlands. It had the following characteristics: (i) whole sectors were to be considered (not individual companies); (ii) the organisation was created as a foundation and did not have its own financial reserves; (iii) companies should only participate in a sector project on a voluntary basis; and (iv) its legal structure reflected the tripartite system in which government, employer and employee were all represented.

As a whole the foundation fitted very well into the policy which the corporative movement in the Netherlands pursued. The board of directors was composed of three groups of representatives: the Ministers of Economic and Social Affairs each nominated a member, while the other members of the board represented employers and employees. The Minister of Economic Affairs is given the ultimate right to cancel decisions of the board and to nominate the chairman. The NIB is represented by its chairman.

Improvement of the structure of Dutch industry is attempted by: (i) promoting sector structure studies; (ii) controlling and guiding these studies; and (iii) initiating a 'follow-up': advising the Government on the use of assistance and acting as an intermediary between firms and financial institutions. For each project a research team and a structure commission are installed. The team makes a sector structure study. The research may be done by civil servants of NEHEM, by a private consulting organisation or by an academic institution. The implementation of a sector project is subject to the approval of the structure commission which retains ultimate responsibility for the policy conclusions.

Not having financial means, the Dutch Reconstruction Company can function only as an intermediate negotiating body. Most financial support for sector projects is given by the National Investment Bank under the guarantee of the state.

Regional Development Companies

As we have seen, before World War II, it was thought to be the task of the government to speed up industrialisation. In 1935 the Industry Bank in Limburg was founded with the objective of improving the industrial development of this province. In The Hague a central commission was set up to supervise the credit policy of the Bank.[6] The Bank was not allowed to support companies with poor commercial prospects. The loans of this bank were insignificant.

As mentioned above, in May 1975 LIOF was founded as a successor to the Industry Bank. The activities of the Bank are subject to the approval of the Government. The central authority is exercised by a group (De Haagse Contact Groep) comprising representatives of NIB and NEHEM. These civil servants are responsible for the allocation of funds within the framework of national economic policy. Moreover, these officials implement the rules of the Government concerning: (i) the establishment of new companies; (ii) the provision of advice, information and subsidies; and (iii) support to companies in difficulties. The LIOF can only give advice on these matters. The state took a 36 per cent interest in the Bank, the other shareholders being the Province of Limburg, chambers of commerce and others. The state is represented in the supervisory board by the Ministers of Economic and Social Affairs. Employers and employees are also represented.

The nature of NOM very much resembles that of LIOF. This company was founded in 1974 with the objective of improving the social and economic development of the northern regions. The activities of the company are in acquisition, merger stimulation, joint ventures and promotion. Primarily, though, the company is an investment company for regional development. The NOM provides risk-bearing capital for new or established companies with the ultimate objective of selling the participations if the prospects for the companies are promising. This still remains a pious hope, however, as NOM has not been successful in this respect (see below).

The Bank first investigates a project. The management board then asks the board of directors to judge a proposal to participate in a company and, after getting the approval of this board and the Minister of Economic Affairs, the proposal is implemented. Depending on the number of shares, the NOM appoints some members to the board of directors of the failing company. The board of the NOM consists of representatives of the central and regional governments and of employers' organisations and trade unions. The National Investment Bank is also represented in this company. The state owns all NOM shares. The activities of the company have to fit within the goals of the national economic and social policy. Like the Industry Bank in Limburg, the activities of NOM are subject to the approval of the Government. The Government fixes the amount of capital that NOM can borrow on the capital market guaranteed by the state. In the years 1975–80, this amounted to 300 million guilders.

FINANCIAL INSTRUMENTS OF INDUSTRIAL POLICY

The NIB is the major agent of the Dutch Government in the execution of industrial policy. In most cases LIOF and NOM only give advice to the NIB and the Department of Economic Affairs. As a result of the failure of the sectoral structure policy, the same holds for the NEHEM. Financial assistance to failing companies is granted under the Special Credit Scheme and Employment Money. The NIB concludes an agreement with the Government (Special Credit Scheme) or acts as the Government's representative (Employment Money). The development companies and the NEHEM provide small amounts under the Special Credit Scheme and employment money.

Special Credit Scheme

The Special Credit Scheme (Regeling Bijzondere Financiering) was set up at the end of World War II. Since that time the NIB has been allowed to grant long-term credit, guaranteed by the state, to private industry. The official philosophy behind these grants is that distortion of competition must be avoided: the future prospects of the company should be promising and only short-term problems are to be met. There is of course a difficulty here: if the state grants to companies financial assistance which these firms lacked because commercial banks considered these credits too risky, then there is an alteration in the conditions under which competition between companies takes place.

To qualify for assistance a company must meet three conditions: (i) the company has to offer employment in the Netherlands; (ii) there should be no alternative financial sources; and (iii) the future prospects of the company should be promising.

Under the influence of current economic problems the Special Credit Scheme has been extended. The following types of credit can be distinguished:

(a) The 'normal' Special Credit Scheme as it existed from 1945 onwards. If a company asks the NIB for assistance the Bank investigates the prospects of the firm. If the credit is too risky, the Bank asks the Work Commission Special Credit Scheme to make a decision. This commission consists of representatives of the Ministries of Finance, Economic Affairs, Agriculture and the NIB. Approval of a credit guaranteed by the state must be unanimous and depends on the above-mentioned criteria.

(b) General Credit Scheme (Kaderregelingen). This type of credit was the first extension of the Scheme with the objective of stimulating restructuring projects. The Work Commission Special Credit Scheme makes the decisions, the NIB and the NEHEM mediate between the industry and the Commission and advise the latter. LIOF and NOM advise the Commission about companies in the south and north of the country.

(c) The so-called 'improper' Special Credit Scheme (Oneigenlijke Bijzondere Financiering) was created in 1974 as a result of the economic crisis. In this case commercial criteria for the company under consideration are weaker. These weaker criteria are coupled to the objective 'to avoid sudden large dismissals and the destruction of productive capacity'.[7] Here again LIOF and NOM give the Commission advice.

(d) Subordinated loans (Achtergestelde leningen). The subordinated loan is designed to reinforce the financial structure of companies. The loan anticipates an enlargement of the company's risk capital. This instrument was established as a result of the increasing debt/equity ratio of most firms during the last years of the 1960s and 1970s. These loans also are available to companies in difficulties. Their purpose is to safeguard the continuation and expansion of the activities of such companies.

In 1975 the Minister fixed a maximum amount of 500 million guilders. In 1980 this maximum was reached and was increased to 750 million guilders.

The character of the Special Credit Scheme has changed significantly. More and more failing companies have benefited from funds provided under this scheme. These losses increased from 6 million in 1974 to 111 million guilders in 1978.[8] The losses are chargeable by the NIB in the Ministry of Financial Affairs.

Employment Money

In 1973 and 1974 a rapidly growing number of failing companies asked for assistance. As a result, funds were set aside with the objective of safeguarding employment levels. The commercial criteria for assistance from these funds are even weaker than the criteria for the 'improper' Special Credit Scheme. The general criteria which have to be met are as follows:[9]

(a) there should be no adequate alternative means of safeguarding employment;

(b) the region under consideration should be in severe social distress;

(c) there are reasonable prospects for the restoration of profitability;

(d) distortion of competition is to be avoided; and

(e) obstruction of the sector structure policy by assistance to individual firms must be avoided.

These general criteria were given a concrete form by the Minister of Economic Affairs in a statement to Parliament.[10] First of all, unemployment levels in the area of operation should be at least 8 per cent, or would rise to 8 per cent after the closing of the company under consideration. Second, the amount of assistance needed should be no more than 10,000 guilders per employee. Third, if the unemployment level in the area under consideration exceeds 8 per cent, for every percentage point the employment level exceeds 8 per cent, 3,000 guilders more per employee is provided with a maximum of 30,000 guilders.

In April 1977, Rudolph Lubbers, the Minister of Economic Affairs, adjusted these specified criteria. The required level of unemployment was diminished to 7 per cent. The maximum amount of assistance at this unemployment level was raised to 15,000 guilders per employee, with a maximum of 30,000 guilders per employee at any level of unemployment.

When a company asks for assistance the request is handled by the Office for Special Company Problems at the Ministry of Economic Affairs. Depending on the area of operation, the company is investigated by one of the investment banks, by NEHEM or the Office for Special Company Problems. The outcome of this investigation is subject to the approval of the Employment Commission to which the Ministers of Economic, Social, Agricultural and Financial Affairs each appoint a representative. NEHEM also participates in the sessions of the Commission. There is no formal arrangement for the decision-making process.

The NIB acts as an intermediary for most of the assistance financed from Employment Money and provides guarantees and credits. The state grants subsidies and participations under this scheme. The funds are chargeable to the budget of the Ministry of Economic Affairs. If a company receives assistance, the state can make the following requests:

(a) that the Government demands a suspension of payment to its suppliers to be sure that the company has pursued all alternatives;

(b) that a complete plan to save the company exists;

(c) that the management of the firm negotiates the details of this plan with the supervisory board, the workers' council and the organised employees; and

(d) that the state is allowed to nominate a government observer and a representative to the board of directors. An accountant supervises the financial structure of the firm.

SECTORAL STRUCTURE POLICY AND STATE INTERVENTION IN COMPANIES

As more companies faced difficulties and asked for assistance from the Ministry of Economic Affairs, the amount of support given grew rapidly. The amounts of assistance financed from the Special Credit Scheme are given in Table 3.2. The fall in 1979 occurred because of an attempt by the Minister, G.M.V. van Aardenne, to reduce support to failing companies.

Table 3.2
Financial Support Provided Under the Special Credit Scheme (million guilders)

	1973	1975	1977	1978	1979
'Normal' Special Credit Scheme	47	351	587	579	221
'Improper' Special Credit Scheme	3	201	187	172	216
Total	50	552	774	751	437

Sources: 'Steunverlening Individuele Bedrijven', *Rapport Commissie Van Dijk*, Tweede Kamer, Zitting 1979–90 (The Hague: Staatsuitgeverij, 1980) 15306, Nos. 2–3, p. 14; *Annual Report* (The Hague: NIB, various issues).

The great majority of this support is mediated by the NIB. Only a small amount is mediated by NEHEM, whose activities are in practice almost restricted to the promotion of sectoral structure studies (for example, in the foundry and footwear industries). It is an advisory body and does not have the power to implement its recommendations. The projects of NEHEM are now restricted to small domestic branches. Moreover, its activities are almost entirely limited to the first stages of the projects: 'follow-ups' hardly ever take place.

The failure of the sectoral structure policy is illustrated by the figures. In the period 1975–78, the sector aid controlled by NEHEM amounted to 132 million guilders: only 2 per cent of the total amount of assistance financed from the Special Credit Scheme and 'employment money' in the period under consideration. The clothing, textile and shoe industry benefited from this support but NEHEM projects in these industries are still in the first stages. During the years 1975–78, the amount of support by the NIB to improve the structure of sectors controlled by it amounted to 320 million guilders.[11] The distribution of these loans is given in Table 3.3.

Table 3.3
Sector Aid by the NIB to Various Branches (million guilders)

Cotton, rayon and linen industry	119
Fishery	18
Inland shipping	3
Shipping industry	166
Foundries	1
Clothing industry	13
Total	320

Source: *Rapport Commissie Van Dijk, op. cit.*, p. 17.

Including individual assistance mediated by the NIB to these sectors, the textile, the ready-to-wear clothing and shipping industries received most assistance. Even before 1973, the textile industry received, by means of investment premiums, 98 million guilders, financed from the Special Credit Scheme. In spite of this assistance the position of the industry has declined steadily. The clothing industry also remains in severe crisis for a number of reasons: (i) as a result of conservative management, labour costs have grown significantly; (ii) in many companies family owners have not invested in modern machinery;[12] (iii) imports from Third World countries and the European Community grew steadily during the 1960s and 1970s; and (iv) in order to reduce wage costs the family owners have shifted the labour-intensive activities to low-wage countries. As a result of this 'run away' policy and the closing down of factories, employment in this sector declined from 60,000 in 1960 to 26,000 in 1975.

Assistance to the shipping industry is provided both in the form of premiums (not listed in Table 3.3) and under the Special Credit Scheme. Premiums granted by the Dutch Government amount to 20.5 per cent of total investments. With the help of this support, the Government is attempting to modernise the old-fashioned Dutch merchant fleet. As a result of technological developments, shipowners identified new commercial opportunities neglected by them during the 1960s and invested in more specialised ships. After the restructuring of the Dutch (merchant) fleet the share of the conventional line and tramp navigation activities decreased from 54 per cent in 1968 to 27 per cent in 1975.[13] During the same period, the share in world trade of ships carrying the Dutch flag declined, although the number of Dutch ships carrying a foreign flag increased vastly.

A large amount of sector aid was also granted to the wool industry. The support given to this industry amounted to 100 million guilders. During the 1960s and 1970s imports from Italy grew steadily. In 1974 NEHEM promoted the restructuring of this industry and a foundation, named Wolcon, consisting of representatives of the Government, employers and employees, was set up. Wolcon was to control the implementation of the restructuring of the industry in Tilburg. The holding Sigmacon, founded by three firms, led the total restructuring operation. The company AaBb had the most important position within this group. Its director, who was also the director of Sigmacon, supervised the entry of other companies into Sigmacon. Only the promising parts of firms that went bankrupt were allowed to enter the holding. Some companies were even reorganised with the financial support of the Government, preceding entry into Sigmacon. Thus, the idea was to set up a viable large-scale woollen company. But in 1977 Sigmacon was already facing problems and the minister responsible postponed the restructuring of the wool industry. Instead of the projected 1,200 employees, in 1978 Sigmacon only employed 400 people. The restructuring of the wool industry had nearly come to an end: of the sixty-five companies concentrated in the

Tilburg area in 1958, only five were left in 1978. During that period, employment declined from 18,000 to 1,200.[14]

The 1970s were characterised by two opposite phenomena. On the one hand there was stagnation of sectoral aid provided *via* institutions like NEHEM. On the other hand, assistance to failing companies rose rapidly. The amount of employment money granted is shown in Table 3.4. During 1979–80 less funds were raised but as noted earlier, Minister van Aardenne by 1982 was attempting to reduce financial support to failing companies. At the same time, more funds were given as general financial instruments for the improvement of business (Wet Investerings Rekening and Loonkostensubsidies) and in order to stimulate innovation in private industry.[15]

By 1982 more than 6,000 million guilders annually were provided under these schemes. It is too early to evaluate the impact of these changes but it has to be noted that large amounts are still made available to failing companies. For example, the stagnating shipbuilding industry received 392 million guilders in 1980.[16] That these amounts were given under general financing schemes has no effect on the consequences.

Table 3.4
Employment Money (million guilders)

1974	1975	1976	1977	1978	1979
90	450	600	926	1004	512

Source: *Rapport Commissie Van Dijk, op. cit.*, p. 14.

A substantial amount of assistance, financed from the Special Credit Scheme and Employment Money, was used to support large companies. During the 1970s those companies listed in Table 3.5 benefited from support which amounted to more than 100 million guilders per company (Wet Investerings Rekening excluded).[17]

In spite of this support, some of these large companies went bankrupt and the remaining firms still face problems. Nederhorst and Koninklijke Scholten Honig went bankrupt and the Volvo Car

BV remained shaky. In the latter company the state took a shareholding of 45 per cent mediated by the National Investment Bank and Dutch State Mines (DSM). The divisions of VMF — mechanical engineering, plastic processing machinery and in the jobbing industry — all face problems despite being reorganised with government aid. Prospects for the shipbuilding industry (RSV, Van der Giessen-de Noord, IHC-Holland) are not promising. During 1974–79, this industry alone received public assistance of 900 million Dutch guilders.[18]

In order to save these large companies, the state had to provide risk-bearing capital. The state took, for example, a 40 per cent direct shareholding in RSV. Most risk-bearing capital, however, is

Table 3.5
Support to Large Companies (million guilders)

Rijn Schelde Verolme (RSV)	1550[a]
Volvo Car BV	680
Nederhorst	600
VMF (Verenigde Machine Fabrieken)	235
Van der Giessen de Noord	280
Koninklijke Scholten Honig	150
IHC-Holland	180
Vredestein	158

Source: *Rapport Commissie Van Dijk, op. cit.,* p. 14.
[a] Including support from 1969 onwards.

provided by means of subordinated loans which also applies to the support offered by the state to other companies. The state refuses, though, to take responsibility for the company concerned and provides minority participations mediated by the NIB, with only a few exceptions. Such direct state shareholdings are financed from Employment Money. From 1974–78, only 1 per cent of the support was provided by means of direct shareholdings. Table 3.6 reveals the direction and amount of government investment in equity capital. Thus, the total amount of assistance by means of direct shareholdings adds up to only 30 million guilders. Indirect shareholdings mediated by the NIB are more important. These participations are financed from the Special Credit Scheme. Table 3.7 lists the NIB's investment in equity capital.

Table 3.6
Direct State Participation

	1976		1977		1978	
	million guilders	%	million guilders	%	million guilders	%
Vredestein	9.0	49	9.0	49	9.0	49
Tealtronic	1.4	67	bankrupt		—	—
De Vries Robbé (steel windows)	—	—	3.5	100	3.5	100
ASW-App. BV	—	—	0.8	25	0.8	25
UDEC	—	—	0.3	14	0.3	14
Mercon Steel Struct. BV	—	—	3.5	26	3.5	26
Daisy Systems Holland (continuation Tealtronic)	—	—	10.0	100	10.0	100
Gero	—	—	2.8	76	2.8	76

Source: Ministry of Financial Affairs, The Hague.

Table 3.7
Participations Concluded by NIB (million guilders)

	1975	1976	1977	1978	1979
Participations at Bank's own risk	24	28	28	32	31
Participations guaranteed to Bank by state	10	10	10	96	117
Participations at request and risk of the state	3	52	53	155	268
Total	37	90	91	283	416

Source: *Annual Report* (The Hague: NIB, various issues).

The most important shareholdings of the NIB in companies which went bankrupt were the following: OGEM Nederhorst Bouw (50 per cent), bankrupt in 1979; KSH, bankrupt in 1978; and Amsterdamsche Droogdok Maatschappij (47 per cent), nearly bankrupt in 1980. The other important companies in which the state took an indirect shareholding were Volvo Car BV (45 per cent), RSV (40 per cent), Giessen-De Noord (22 per cent), Baggerwerk IHC-Holland (48 per cent), Stork-Werkspoor Diesel

(49 per cent), Spinnerij Nederland (48 per cent) and DAF-Trucks (25 per cent).

The participation of the NIB amounted in 1979 to 416 million guilders. This was equivalent to 15 per cent of the Bank's outstanding loans at the risk of the state. The bulk of the assistance is provided by means of credits and guarantees.

Sometimes a limited corporation was transformed into a foundation in order to get government assistance. This solution was chosen if the capital of the firm was nil or negative and if the company was family-owned. The shareholders then had to sell their shares for one guilder. As a result of the setting up of such a 'one guilder foundation', shareholders would no longer benefit from the possible survival of the firm and the new management was able to take a strong line. In 1977 there were twenty-one one-guilder foundations. This instrument is no longer important.

Finally, the state participated — mediated by LIOF and NOM — in the equity of companies. The investments made by LIOF are relatively unimportant compared with those made by NOM: in 1979 these investments amounted to 16 million guilders.[19] The Bank is mainly used to allocate and administer funds made available by the NIB and the Ministry of Economic Affairs: the NIB concludes contracts and LIOF mediates between NIB and the company under consideration. In the period 1975–79, these contracts amounted to 209 million guilders.[20]

The NOM, on the other hand, provided larger amounts of risk-bearing capital — these participations are even the main activity of the Bank. Six new participations were begun in 1979, bringing the total to twenty-eight (see Appendix 3.3). The Bank has not been very successful, however — the annual report stated that the performance of the majority of the companies was worse than expected. During the last year four companies went bankrupt. Not one of the firms was able to continue its activities without further help from the NOM, bringing the value of NOM's shares to 209 million guilders in 1979.[21]

It is possible to summarise government aid with the help of the figures presented by the NIB. These figures are given in Table 3.8.

Thus, the share of the activities at the NIB's own risk decreased from 50 per cent in 1975 to 25 per cent in 1979 (as a percentage of total loans and guarantees). At the same time, the involvement of the state with companies in difficulties mediated by the NIB and

Table 3.8
Outstanding Loans and Guarantees of the NIB (million guilders)

	1975	1976	1977	1978	1979
Loans at Bank's own risk	1 158	1 018	1 023	1 045	1 084
Loans at risk of state:					
'Normal' Special Credit Scheme	499	754	1 031	1 183	1 274
Subordinated loans	—	213	311	407	457
General Credit Scheme	255	256	390	420	426
'Improper' Credit Scheme	233	294	459	454	516
Credits and guarantees at					
risk and request of state	202	578	832	1 032	1 349

Source: *Annual Report* (The Hague: NIB, various issues).

financed from the Special Credit Scheme and Employment Money grew to nearly 4,000 million guilders.

Formal Competence of Audit Office and Parliament

In the Government's White Paper on Selective Growth (1976), the Minister of Economic Affairs mentioned three problems connected with support to individual companies in difficulties. These were (i) the use of the assistance by the company, (ii) the relation between the industrial structural policy and individual company support and (iii) the criteria for assistance.[22]

It is only possible to formulate criteria (and to test the usefulness of the policy) when the objectives of the assistance are clear. In spite of the fact that the Minister considered these problems to be important, the Government has not formulated clear objectives.

In 1976, support was provided with the objective of safeguarding employment in regions where the labour market was thought to be defective. One year later, it was stressed that the future prospects of the firm should be promising and that profitability of the company had to be restored in the near future. It is not clear, however, what exactly is meant by safeguarding employment and restoring profitability in the near future. Which objective is the more important and what is the foreseeable future? If this is not clear, how should the criteria be interpreted?

In practice, the Minister diverged from the more specific criteria that the amount of assistance needed should be no more than 30,000 guilders per employee and that the unemployment level in the area of operations should be at least 7 per cent. The criterion of the amount needed per employee is coupled with the requirement that profitability should be restored in the near future. This objective is difficult to interpret and can easily lead to strong deviations from the more specific criteria. In the case of Tealtronic, for example, the assistance given by the state reached the level of 142,000 guilders per employee.[23] In 1975 the state took a 40 per cent shareholding. In 1976 this participation became 100 per cent, although the state expressly did not want majority participations. The following year Tealtronic went bankrupt.

In this case it was clear that the Minister had deviated from his own stipulated criteria. It is often stressed, however, that it is difficult to monitor an assistance policy because there are generally no clear objectives and criteria on which the allocation of assistance depends. This situation did not change with the reorientation of industrial policy which took place in March 1980. The specific criteria were almost the same and there were still no clear objectives. What was excusable because of the unexpected recession in the mid-1970s was no longer acceptable when it was known that many restructurings had to take place.

Parliament and the Algemene Rekenkamer — the State Audit Office, which has to examine public expenditure — cannot check financial assistance provided to support companies. Only in exceptional cases, when the state has taken a 100 per cent shareholding (for example, in the Northern Development Company), is the Algemene Rekenkamer able to ask the company under consideration for information and to make its own investigation. If the state has a majority participation, the Algemene Rekenkamer is only permitted to ask the Minister for more detailed information. Minority interests and the indirect shareholdings of the state are outside the scope of the Algemene Rekenkamer. This means that the Audit Office is not allowed to supervise a shareholding of the state which is mediated by the National Investment Bank and financed from the Special Credit Scheme. Finally, if the state provides gifts, subsidies or guarantees, the Algemene Rekenkamer is permitted to examine only when a special arrangement exists between the state and the company which benefits from the assistance.

In practice, the Algemene Rekenkamer restricts supervision to direct majority interests in the state financed from Employment Money. This leads us to the conclusion that the policy of the state of avoiding direct majority interests restricts the auditing task of the Algemene Rekenkamer while at the same time strengthening the hand of the departmental bureaucrats: they can provide money to private interests without having the responsibility and without being controlled.

According to the Van Dijk Commission, the Dutch Parliament has made insufficient use of its right to change the budget of the Ministry of Economic Affairs.[24] In particular, Parliament has approved too easily the Ministry's budgets and alterations of budgets without clear insight as to how the finance is used: it has not controlled government policy. This is especially true regarding Employment Money (which is a part of the budget of the Ministry of Economic Affairs whereas funds provided from the Special Credit Scheme are financed by the operations of the NIB). If the Investment Bank suffers losses, these losses are financed out of the budget of the Ministry of Finance but, in general, the operations of the NIB fall outside the scope of Parliament. State policies of support by means of indirect shareholdings also restrict, therefore, the competence of Parliament.

SECTORAL POLICY AND FINANCIAL SUPPORT TO INDIVIDUAL COMPANIES

During the 1960s and 1970s successive Dutch governments devised a system of financial instruments in order to implement a so-called sectoral structure policy and to support individual companies in difficulties. The institutional framework followed suit. During the 1960s the state's aim was to improve the structure of industries which faced problems. In order to promote sectoral structure studies and to 'follow-up' on them, NEHEM was founded in 1972. Since the economic crisis of 1974–75, however, many large firms faced financial problems and asked the Ministry of Economic Affairs for individual assitance. As a result, the sectoral structure policy was to a large extent replaced by individual assistance. 'Follow-up' hardly ever took place in branches in which NEHEM operated. The question may therefore be posed: was the starting point of the state policy correct?

Sectoral Restructuring Policy

The possibility of pursuing a sectoral policy on the basis of a free participation of entrepreneurs depends on the character of the problems in the industry under consideration.

Entrepreneurs will only be willing to cooperate if they face the same kind of problems. The existence of such problems depends first of all on market growth and on market structure. Because entrepreneurs have to cooperate, the factors which condition cartelisation are relevant — that is, relative stagnation, inelastic demand, a homogeneous product and restrictions on entry. Indeed, NEHEM operated to a large extent in branches where cartelisation had often occurred in the past. Even in these industries, though, the conditions were not met during the 1970s and most of NEHEM's projects stagnated in the first phase. The main reason for this is the existence of an open international economy which makes entrepreneurs unwilling to abandon competition and means that the Government is not able to pursue a sectoral policy on a voluntary basis. The problem is well illustrated by a comparison of economic policies during the 1930s and the 1970s.

Before World War II conditions were relatively favourable for cartelisation. Under the influence of the severe crisis, the representatives of domestic industries had a major influence on the formulation of state policy. As a result, the state took protectionist measures which facilitated the cartelisation of the Dutch manufacturing industry. Moroever, the state stimulated regulation by the imposition of privately concluded cartel agreements on unwilling industrialists and the closing of industries for new entrants. So the *ordening* was implemented by means of cartelisation and the state had only to sanction the sectoral policy pursued by the entrepreneurs themselves. In industries in which cartelisation did not succeed, the state gave individual assistance or support with the objective of stimulating mergers.[25] This happened, for example, in the metallurgic and shipbuilding industries. So, even under comparatively favourable circumstances, voluntary cartelisation often failed.

During the 1960s and 1970s conditions were much less favourable for cartelisation. As a result of the open market policy of the European Community, competition increased. Moreover, other factors affecting the implementation of sectoral policies became more important, particularly differences between the interests of firms. First, there was the difference between companies which make profits and companies which make losses; second, large and small companies often face different problems; and, finally, in some industries there were integrated companies and producers operating on an international scale.

Empirical evidence shows that, in industries having problems of restructuring, there are almost always profitable companies. These companies are not interested in a general approach to the problems of the industry — in the foundry industry, for example, the profitable Lovink group of companies was not interested in a general arrangement to diminish over-capacity. In industries in which large and small companies operate, one cannot presume that both types of companies are facing the same kind of problems. For example, the small firms are not likely to be interested in the problems which follow from mass production; and moreover, large companies are likely to have a better opportunity to benefit from government support. In the chemical engineering industry the big companies RSV and VMF received large amounts of government assistance, which the small companies were denied.

Moreover, large firms often cross national boundaries. The decisions of international concerns and integrated companies are different from decisions of domestic companies which often operate in only one stage of the production process. Multinational corporations occupy a very important position in the Dutch economy; and in case of difficulties an international concern is able to shift its activities to foreign countries. Moreover, in open markets, sectoral policies are hampered because the reactions of foreign companies are important. For success, almost every producer who operates on the market has to participate.

As a result of these factors, the *ordening* by means of cartelisation stood no chance during the 1960s and 1970s. It was questionable whether a forced sector policy would be more successful. It is very difficult to predict how the market will develop and a forced reduction of sectoral capacity in the Netherlands has to be agreed at the level of European Community producers otherwise there is a good chance that Dutch industry only will lose its market share.

Finally, it is often difficult to predict market prospects. This has an important consequence. The effectiveness of cartelisation depends on the realisation of an intended strategy. If this strategy is based on wrong predictions, serious problems can arise. The cement industry was one of the very few branches in which a 'follow-up' was implemented. However, at the moment the reorganisation was completed, the market proved to be larger than expected and producers could not satisfy demand. Another example is the shipbuilding industry. In 1965, the Commissie Nederlandse Scheepsbouw started an investigation which eventually resulted in the foundation of the Beledscommissie Scheepsbouw — a kind of cartel office. With the aid of the Commission, which consists of representatives of employers, employees and the Government, producers had to coordinate their investment decisions and to control their capacity. During the 1960s, sector projects had already been started, aiming at adaptations of individual wharves. During the years which followed, though, demand was larger than expected and the producers, following an independent strategy, expanded their capacity.

Support to Failing Companies and the Position of the State

The independent strategy of companies caused the downfall of sectoral policies. When large companies faced problems, they asked the Ministry of Economic Affairs for individual support. As individual assistance grew, the implementation of the sectoral structure policy was further weakened. In consequence, even though the Government expressed its intention of pursuing a sectoral policy and of reducing support to individual companies, the opposite happened. The amount of support controlled by NEHEM in order to improve the structure of industries ceased to expand. At the same time individual assistance grew rapidly as Table 3.9 shows.

The main reason for this was the influence of the economic crisis: the state's objective of safeguarding employment levels, in particular in regions with high unemployment levels, became more important. Most assistance is provided under pressure of growing unemployment in the area under consideration. The companies use this argument when they ask for financial support. If the Government decides to provide assistance, it becomes involved in the restructuring process of the industry under consideration and the state faces major dilemmas if it takes a shareholding in a failing company — for example, the Government is probably forced to take responsibility for future problems in the industry and competitors are likely to ask for more support if the growing danger of over-capacity as a result of the survival of the supported company (which is now a state company) causes prolonged problems. So a condition which has to be met in order to receive assistance is that other companies should not face problems as a result of assistance to failing companies. To avoid such problems the Minister attempts to limit the amount of support and prefers to aid companies in difficulties by means of loans and guarantees instead of participations. In this way the state tries to restrict its responsibility for restructuring industry. At the same time, however, the

Table 3.9
Government Financial Support to Companies
(million guilders)

	Employment money	Sector projects
1974	90	—
1975	450	45.3
1976	600	72.4
1977	926	40.6
1978	1 004	5.0
1979	512	54.0

Sources: *Rapport Commissie Van Dijk, op. cit.,* p. 14; and H. Vrolijk, in C. Weijk, R. de Klerk, G. Reuten and B. Thio (eds), *Economisch Beleid uit de Klem* (Amsterdam: Socialistiche Uitgeverij, 1980) p. 111.

Government tries to avoid rising unemployment levels. These objectives are difficult to reconcile because the Government simultaneously tries to persuade private companies to take over the ailing company and may ask private research institutes for solutions. This means that the responsibility is handed back to private organisations with commercial interests. These organisations therefore have a great influence on the solutions chosen.

The weaknesses of this policy of the state are well illustrated by three examples. The first concerns the construction company Nederhorst United NV which grew very fast during the 1960s and the beginning of the 1970s, taking over many other firms, but which, however, faced problems in 1975.[26] The state provided 100 million guilders assistance, nominated a supervisor and the Ministry of Economic Affairs negotiated with private companies interested in the take-over of parts of Nederhorst. As the international construction company OGEM seemed to be the most promising candidate, the Minister asked this concern for solutions. After an investigation, OGEM was only interested in the building division and suggested that this division should be separated from the steel construction divisions.

The state accepted the solution proposed by the OGEM and, after the sale of some parts of the steel construction division, a new holding company was founded in which the state and OGEM each took a 50 per cent shareholding. In 1979, however, market prospects became less favourable than expected and OGEM withdrew from the cooperation with the state — a course open to it because the cooperation was based merely on a letter of intent and no formal agreement had ever been signed. The state was now the exclusive owner of Nederhorst and could exercise complete control. It chose, however, to hand formal ownership back to the original managers.

Another illuminating example is Tealtronic. In 1963, the American multinational corporation, Singer, took over the company Friden. One of the plants of Friden is in Nijmegen, near the German border. In 1974, after some unsuccessful reorganisations, serious problems arose with this plant. During the second half of 1974, in the interest of those employed there, the Ministry of Economic Affairs started looking for a private company that might take over the failing company and, eventually, with the aid of financial inducements, succeeded in interesting the British company Tealtronic, a subsidiary of the British AML Distributors Ltd. In March 1975 the state took a shareholding of 40 per cent in a new holding company in which Tealtronic held the remaining 60 per cent. The state acquired the right to nominate three members of the board but, after nine months, had nominated only two of them during which time some irregularities occurred. The new company was not successful and in 1977 went bankrupt. Finally, Daisy Systems NV (100 per cent owned by the state) was founded as a continuation of Tealtronic in Nijmegen, employing 160 of the 500 employed at the plant in 1974.

Similar problems beset the policy of the state with respect to the restructuring of industries. Entrepreneurs tend to be interested in general measures which favour the financial position of their particular company. Hence their primary interest in joining a restructuring project will be in the use of the general financial facilities offered and they will wish to withdraw as soon as a 'follow-up' takes place. Indeed, a survey undertaken into a number of restructuring projects makes clear that companies, in industries in which NEHEM operates, benefit from the use of financial instruments but a 'follow-up' hardly ever takes place.[27] Entrepreneurs will often participate in the first stage of a restructuring project because they are only interested in financial support or they want to be informed about developments or they may hope to promote their own particular goals. But, when business has to be done in the follow-up of a restructuring project, they tend to back out. An instance of this, already noted above, was signalled by the Algemene Rekenkamer with reference to the restructuring of the wool industry. In this industry Wolcon was established in order to safeguard employment levels in the Tilburg area. On the other hand, the restructuring took place under the leadership of Sigmacon, a private company for which commercial criteria prevailed. As a result of these different objectives the Chairman of Sigmacon and members of Wolcon disagreed about the policy to be pursued. The Algemene Rekenkamer remarked: 'When the results of the company failed to improve, reorganisations were inevitable and as the Government, by means of subsidies and guarantees, became more and more involved in the project, it was finally decided that Sigmacon had to pursue a commercial policy.[28]

The examples of Nederhorst, Tealtronic and Wolcon show clearly that the Government tends to become more and more deeply involved in the reorganisations it attempts. As a result, the amount of public support increases and the Government diverges from its own criteria. In less than two years the state provided 61 million guilders' support to Tealtronic.[29] This meant that, per employee, 42,000 guilders was provided instead of the maximum amount of 15,000 guilders per employee. Daisy Systems, which was set up by the Government to replace Tealtronic received 25 million guilders for 160 employees, which is 156,000 guilders per employee.[30]

The number of companies which received a second, or further, amount of support from Employment Money increased fast. The figures are listed in Table 3.10. Furthermore, most support is given to large companies. These companies are better placed to obtain government assistance because many workers are involved. In 1976, for example, support was given to 160 companies. The seven largest each employed over 500 people and received 60 per cent of the funds available. In 1979, five companies, each employing over 1,000 people, received 90 per cent of the amount of support.[31] In several of these cases the criteria supposedly governing aid could not be met. As a result, the Government also deviated from its criterion that support has to be restricted to areas where the unemployment levels were highest.

Table 3.10
Projects Receiving Repeated Support

	1975	1976	1977	1978	1979
Percentage of the number of companies	8	30	60	62	78
Percentage of the amount of assistance	28	55	77	88	97

Sources: *Rapport Commissie Van Dijk, op. cit.*, p. 37; Memorandum of the Ministry of Economic Affairs, The Hague, 25 March 1980, No. 160.

The geographical subdivision of the amounts of assistance and the amount of support per employee is given in Table 3.11. The percentage of 25.7, which is not subdivided, includes the support given to the metallurgical industry and the construction concern Nederhorst. Including this amount the percentages for North Holland and South Holland probably add up to more than 30 per cent. Hence, the largest amounts of support went to the western and southern regions of the country. But, during the 1970s, unemployment in the western provinces, Holland, Utrecht and Zeeland, was lower than elsewhere in the country. The large amount of support to the south was caused by assistance to Volvo Car BV. More than 15 per cent of the 21 per cent for Limburg went to this company which is considered of vital importance by the state since the closing down of the Dutch State Mines in the south of Limburg.

Table 3.11
Direction of Government Aid to Failing Companies

	Special Credit Scheme 1973–78	Funds set aside to fight unemployment 1975–78		Amount per employee (guilders)
	% of amount of support	% of amount of support	Number of employees involved	
Groningen	13.8	7.3	5 731	28 000
Friesland	0.5	1.3	1 528	14 000
Drenthe	0.3	4.1	3 130	29 000
Overijssel	5.9	11.3	7 971	31 000
Gelderland	5.8	9.7	10 679	20 000
Utrecht	0.4	2.1	2 780	16 000
Noord-Holland	12.9	4.0	2 222	39 000
Zuid-Holland	36.6	3.4	5 849	13 000
Zeeland	0.4	0.6	1 172	10 500
Noord-Brabant	18.9	9.7	18 960	11 000
Limburg	4.4	21.0	12 267	37 000
Not subdivided	—	25.7	54 500	10 000
Total	100.0	100.0	126 789	258 500

Source: *Rapport Commissie Van Dijk, op. cit.*, p. 36.

As long as there are no simple and clear objectives which fit in with an industrial policy, it is difficult to formulate clear criteria. It is still more difficult when the Ministry of Economic Affairs explicitly reserves the right to deviate from once-stated guidelines. So the Minister answered the Algemene Rekenkamer with reference to support to the textile industry as follows: 'The criteria are a guideline for the decisions about the amounts and the direction of financial support. However, the Minister for Economic Affairs explicitly has the right to diverge from these criteria. A deviation is the result of a consideration of economic and social aspects.'[32] This point of view was repeated in the general debate on industrial policy matters in Parliament in March 1981. It showed that government aid to industry often is not only uneconomic and contrary to the market system, but also has a tendency to degenerate into undemocratic handouts.

SUMMARY AND CONCLUSIONS

Dutch industrial policies have, up until now, not been of a systematic and consistent type. In fact, governments have not had it as their policy goal to pursue industrial policies at all, let alone a particular type of industrial policy. So, in periods of economic difficulties, they have been *ad hoc*. As a result, successive governments diverged from their own criteria and lately have begun to say openly that that is what they want to do if 'circumstances' require it.

In the Netherlands, the institutions are not allowed to pursue policies independently on the basis of their own financial means. So NEHEM became a foundation dependent on the state and its legal structure reflects the tripartite system. Furthermore, financial support provided by the development companies is subject to the approval of the Minister of Economic Affairs. Thus activities on NIB's own account are not directly subject to the approval of the Minister, but the Bank was not allowed to compete with commercial banks. During the 1950s and 1960s NIB promoted new ventures with only meagre results. During the 1970s support grew strongly.

The responsible minister decides the amount and direction of the support but the salvage operations are mainly entrusted to institutions like NIB, NOM and LIOF. So the state authority is restricted to deciding whether financial support will be made available to companies in difficulties. Control, if any, is restricted by the limited formal competence of Parliament and the Algemene Rekenkamer.

In conclusion, it is clear that industrial policies in the Netherlands leave much to be desired. If the government wants to make a contribution towards the strengthening of the Dutch industrial structure, this policy is in need of total remodelling, if not total abolition.

NOTES AND REFERENCES

1. P. E. de Hen, *Actieve en re-actieve industriepolitiek in Nederland* (Amsterdam: De Arbeiderspers, 1980) pp. 130–34.

2. J. F. Posthuma *et al.*, *Tien jaar economisch lefen in Nederland* (The Hague: Recovery Bank, 1955) p. VII. The ex-chairman was Mr A. J. d'Ailly.

3. *Recovery Bank* (the NIB since 1963) *Annual Report* (The Hague: Recovery Bank, 1957) p. 19.-

4. *Ibid.;* and *NIB Annual Report* (The Hague: NIB, 1963 and 1967).

5. *Zeventig jaren statistiek in Tijdreeksen* (The Hague: Centraal Bureau voor de Statistich, 1970) Tables S 17, 19, 20 and 21.

6. De Hen, *op. cit.*, p. 159.

7. *Special Credit Scheme* (The Hague: NIB, 1971) Article 8.

8. 'Steunverlening Individuele Bedrijven' (Support to Individual Companies), *Rapport Commissie Van Dijk*, Tweede Kamer, Zitting 1979–1980 (The Hague: Staatsuitgeverij, 1980) 15306, Nos 2–3, p. 13.

9. 'Nota Selectieve Groei', *Government White Paper on Selective Growth* (The Hague: Staatsuitgeverij, for the Ministry of Economic Affairs, 1976) pp. 301–2.

10. *Memorandum from the Minister of Economic Affairs to the Lower Chamber of Parliament* (The Hague: Staatsuitgeverij, 6 April 1977) p. 6.

11. *Rapport Commissie Van Dijk*, p. 17.

12. M. van Klaveren, in A. W. M. Tuelings (ed.), *Herstructurering van de Nederlandse Industrie* (Alphen aan den Rijn: Samsorn, 1978) pp. 174–9.

13. K. Schoenmaker, 'Analyse van de Nederlandse Scheepvaartindustrie', unpublished paper of the University of Amsterdam, 1978, p. 26.

14. *Memorandum from the Minister of Economic Affairs, op. cit.*, p. 9.

15. The wage subsidies amount to 25 per cent of wage costs. The maximum subsidies on new investments (Wet Investeringsrekening) amount to 20 per cent of new investments. These subsidies are available to every company.

16. 'Sectornota', *Memorandum of the Ministry of Economic Affairs* (The Hague: Staatsuitgeverij, 3 October 1980) p. 1.

17. D. J. Haank and R. de Lange, *De Uitvaart van Nederhorst* (Gorinchem: De Mandarijn, 1979) pp. 174–5; *Vredestein Annual Report* (The Hague: Vredestein, 1979) p. 9; *Het Financieele Dagblad*, Amsterdam, 30 August 1979 and 26 June 1980; *Memorandum of the Ministry of Economic Affairs* (The Hague: Staatsuitgeverij, 21 March 1978) No. 121.

18. *Rapport Commissie Van Dijk*, p. 19; *Memorandum*,

Tweede Kamer, Zitting 1979–80 (The Hague: Staatsuitgeverij, 1980) 15818, No. 4, p. 16.

19.   *LIOF Annual Report* (Maastricht: LIOF, 1979).

20.   *LIOF Annual Report* (Maastricht: LIOF, 1976, 1977 and 1978).

21.   *NOM Annual Report* (Groningen: NOM, 1979).

22.   *Government White Paper on Selective Growth, op. cit.*, p. 300.

23.   *Algemene Rekenkamer Annual Report* (The Hague: Staatsuitgeverij, 1977) p. 133.

24.   The *Rapport Commissie Van Dijk* represented the second Chamber of Parliament. In 1978 this Commission investigated salvation policies.

25.   De Hen, *op. cit.*, pp. 292–300.

26.   This example is based on the study of Haank and de Lange, *op. cit.*

27.   H. Vrolijk, *Strutuurbeleid, een terreinverkenning*, Research Memorandum No. 7803 (Amsterdam: University of Amsterdam, 1978).

28.   *Algemene Rekenkamer Investigation into the Restructuring of the Wool Industry* (The Hague: Staatsuitgeverij, 1978).

29.   *Algemene Rekenkamer Annual Report, op. cit.*, p. 133.

30.   *Ibid.*, p. 137.

31.   *Memorandum of the Ministry of Economic Affairs* (The Hague: Staatsuitgeverij, 25 March 1980) No. 160.

32.   *Algemene Rekenkamer Annual Report* (The Hague: Staatsuitgeverij, 1978) p. 136.

Appendix 3.1
Contracts Concluded by the NIB (million guilders)

I. Contracts Negotiated in the Name of the Bank (on the Bank's own
   Account and Granted under the 'Normal' Special Credit Scheme)

	Loans		Guarantees	
	Number	Amount	Number	Amount
1976	153	460	20	235
1977	170	765	11	196
1978	157	545	11	192
1979	139	331	17	151

II. Contracts Negotiated at the Government's Request and Risk
    ('Improper' Special Credit Scheme)

	Loans		Guarantees	
	Number	Amount	Number	Amount
1976	9	49	1	23
1977	15	96	2	90
1978	5	67	1	1
1979	5	45	4	57

III. Contracts Negotiated on Behalf of the Government
     (Employment Money)

	Loans		Guarantees	
	Number	Amount	Number	Amount
1976	46	160	53	275
1977	74	260	37	151
1978	31	212	19	129
1979	16	377	20	244

Source: *Annual Report* (The Hague: NIB, 1979).
Note: As a result of the time lag between the formal arrangement and the
implementation of the contract, figures published by the NIB and the Ministry of
Economic Affairs are not the same.

Appendix 3.2
NIB Liabilities (million guilders)

Liabilities	1975	1976	1977	1978	1979
Share capital	100	100	100	100	100
Reserves	164	168	172	177	182
Netherlands government loan	61	57	53	48	43
Bonds issued	451	500	514	743	884
Loans from institutional lenders	675	913	929	1266	1250
Sundry creditors	278	371	382	429	477
Dividend payable	4.5	4.5	4.5	4.5	4.5
Guarantees at own risk	90	81	87	78	90
Government backed guarantees	177	355	400	466	544
Guarantees provided at government's request and risk	179	190	258	255	208
Guarantees provided on behalf of the government	87	310	271	297	96

Source: *Annual Report* (The Hague: NIB, various issues).

Appendix 3.3
Participations of NOM, 1979

Name	Area of operation	Type of industry	% of equity capital	Number of people employed, end 1979
Okto BV	Winschoten	Cardboard	49	256
SMD-Holding BV	Leeuwarden	Boilers	100	60
Delamine BV	Delfzijl	Ethylene-diamine	30	90
Holvrieka Holding BV	Emmen	Stainless-steel products	50	377
Prins NV	Dokkum	Metal construction, prefabricated houses	53	442

Appendix 3.3 cont'd

Name	Area of operation	Type of industry	% of equity capital	Number of people employed, end 1979
Steenfabriek Schenkens-chans BV	Leeuwarden	Bricks	11	25
Wm ten Cate & Zn BV	Heerenveen	Foundry products	100	61
Heuga Bonaparte BV	Steenwijk	Carpet printing	33	339
Silenka BV	Hoogezand	Glass fibre	33	763
Halbertsma BV	Grouw	Pallets, doors, scaffolding	100	771
Noord Nederlandsche Machinefabriek BV	Winschoten	Metal products, engineering	100	140
Machinefabriek Werkland BV	Nieuw Weerdinge	Metal products, engineering	100	139
Kipp Analytica BV	Emmen	Analytical and de-ntal equipment	34	95
Rademakers Gieterij BV	Klazienaveen	Foundry products	100	213
Wilten Instrumenten Noord Nederland BV (WINN)	Leek	Laboratory equip-ment	40	5
Lignostone Ter Apel BV	Ter Apel	Pressed-wood pro-ducts	49	35
Brons Industrie BV	Appingedam	Diesel engines, hydraulic foundry	97	245
Vastgoedmaatschappij Friesland BV (Casolith)	Leeuwarden	Acrylate sheets, casolith	100	122
Drenta Radiatoren BV	Emmen	Central-heating radiators	49	70
Markomark BV	Veendam	School furniture, heaters	33	325
Laadtechniek BV	Emmen	Waste compact-ing, hydro-motors	50	10
Van Poppel BV	Assen	Lighters	100	170
Warrior Insulation Com-pany BV	Emmen	Insulation material	75	35
Staalbouw Bergum BV	Bergum	Metal products	60	143
Magnesia International BV	Veendam	Processing magne-sium oxide	50 ⎫	
Noordelijke Zoutwinning BV	Veendam	Exploration: mag-nesia salts	50 ⎭	150
Parley BV	Dokkum	Woollen yarns	31	135
Kaufeldt Inter BV	Drachten	Industrial robots	50	20

Source: *Annual Report* (Groningen: NOM, 1979).

CHAPTER FOUR

Belgium: Politics and the Protection of Failing Companies

Paul De Grauwe and Greet van de Velde

The Belgian National Investment Company, Nationale Investeringsmaatschappij (NIM) was set up in 1962.[1] The explicit aim of the NIM was spelled out in its charter. According to the charter the NIM should stimulate the renewal and the expansion of industrial and commercial firms by taking temporary participations in the capital of companies incorporated in Belgium.[2]

The aims of the NIM were deliberately left vague and its role was initially quite limited. Limitations on the activities of the NIM were imposed by stipulating that participations had to be temporary and by the restriction limiting these participations to 80 per cent of equity. Over the years, however, these restrictions were relaxed.

The factors, in the early 1960s, which led to the institution of the NIM are complex, being both political and economic. Here we focus on the economic arguments which were put forward by proponents of the NIM and which are still used by those who favour an expanded role for state investment companies. These arguments rested on the existence of market failures which were widely perceived to exist on two levels.

First, there was a general consensus among economists and policy makers that the private investment companies had failed to detect profitable investment opportunities in dynamic and high-growth industries. Given the importance of these private holding companies in the Belgian economy, it was widely believed that their conservative investment policies explained the low growth of the Belgian industry in traditional sectors such as basic steel making.[3]

The second market failure was seen to be the inability of private firms to attract equity capital. In fact, many firms, especially small ones, were compelled to finance their operations using bank credit. As a result, the financial structure of private firms tended to deteriorate. It was, of course, realised that this feature of the financial structure of private firms has much to do with government-induced incentives, that is, the existence of interest subsidies and a tax structure which favours debt financing. The incentive to rely more on debt financing than equity financing is due to the fact that interest payments are tax-deductible whereas dividends are treated as profits and taxed at the corporate profit tax rates.

Whatever the reason for these market failures, the NIM was (and still is) seen by its proponents as the answer to the problem. The public investment company would create new companies, induce the development of new products and stimulate reorganisations and the restructuring of production *et cetera*. In short, what

Table 4.1
Investments by the NIM and Total Equity Financed Industrial Investment in Belgium (BF '000 million)

Year	NIM investment (1)	Total equity financed industrial investment in Belgium (2)	(1)/(2) %
1963	214.5	—	—
1964	554.9	29 700	3.22
1965	333.8	38 248	1.42
1966	82.9	38 553	0.33
1967	617.1	41 873	
1968		38 505	
1969	271.8	42 889	0.63
1970	331.0	52 678	0.63
1971	604.0	55 424	1.09
1972	847.0	58 112	1.46
1973	381.0	63 608	0.60
1974	1 113.6	81 972	1.40
1975	1 534.1	78 501	1.95
1976	1 491.9	73 619	2.03
1977	1 711.5	—	—
1978	2 365.5	—	—

Sources: *Annual Report* (Brussels: NIM, various issues); *Statistisch Tijdschrift* (Brussels: NIS, March 1979) p. 257.

private entrepreneurs have failed to achieve would be realised by civil servants. How the latter would effectively be stimulated to achieve these objectives was never seriously discussed.

The purpose of this chapter is to evaluate these ambitious objectives. From the outset, however, it should be stressed that, until recently, the opponents of the NIM have effectively been able to limit the role of the NIM in the Belgian economy. This is illustrated by Table 4.1 which gives the evolution of the size of equity investments made by the NIM since 1963. It can be seen that NIM investments have never exceeded 3 per cent of total (equity-financed) investment in Belgium. In addition, there is no discernible increase of NIM activities, at least until the mid-1970s. The role of the NIM can be said to have been marginal over this time span.

Because of its minor role, public debate about the merits of a public investment company has not progressed markedly since the early 1960s. Opponents stress the limited impact of the NIM whereas proponents argue that the beneficial effects of public investment policies can only be realised if substantially more funds are made available to the NIM.

EXPANDED ROLE OF THE NIM

Over the years pressure was built up to expand the role of the NIM. Major changes occurred in 1970 and during the second half of the 1970s.[4]

First, the initial restriction limiting the size of the NIM participations to 80 per cent of equity capital was abolished as was the temporary nature of these participations. As a result, the NIM can now set up public firms with 100 per cent state control. In addition, the number of objectives vested in the NIM was drastically increased. The NIM now is supposed to aim at: (i) the dynamic pursuit of good projects; (ii) finding skilled and specialised managers; (iii) diversifying risk; (iv) stimulating innovations; (v) sectoral and regional diversification of investment; (vi) support of small and medium-size firms; (vii) support of export-oriented firms;[5] and (viii) reorganisation of weak firms. On top of these (often inconsistent) objectives the major objective of the NIM investment policy has become the safeguarding of employment levels. In trying to achieve these objectives the NIM is supposed 'to apply rules of good industrial, financial and commercial management; and to realise normal rates of return'.[6]

A second major change has occurred since 1970. The Belgian Government regularly provides funds to the NIM and obliges it to invest these funds in firms which are close to bankruptcy. Given the substantial increase in the number of bankruptcies in the Belgian economy, this government policy of bailing out Belgian companies has increased substantially. As a result, the portfolio of the NIM tied to these operations has increased substantially. This is shown in Table 4.2. It should be noted here that the NIM does not normally use its own financial resources (its so-called 'normal' portfolio) for such bailing-out operations. This distinction, however, between the normal portfolio and the portfolio owned by the Government is an artificial one, for the Government also indirectly controls the operations of the NIM in its normal activities. The third major change, which occurred in 1978, is that the NIM became the agent of the Government to execute 'industrial policy'.[7]

Table 4.2
Composition of the NIM Portfolio (BF '000 million)

Year	Total portfolio	Normal portfolio	Portfolio for bailing-out operations
1970–71	1.9	1.9	0.02
1971–72	2.4	2.4	0.07
1972–73	3.3	3.2	0.09
1973–74	4.0	3.9	0.1
1974–75	5.1	4.3	0.8
1975–76	6.4	4.8	1.6
1976–77	7.8	5.6	2.2
1977–78	7.5	5.6	2.0
1978–79	8.0	6.0	2.0

Source: *Annual Report* (Brussels: NIM, various issues).

It is still too early to evaluate the effects of these changes. The funds available to the NIM can now increase much faster. The counterpart of this, however, is that the relative independence of the NIM *vis-à-vis* the Government is drastically reduced. These trends will be discussed later when the crucial issue of the effectiveness of the NIM in achieving its goals is discussed.[8]

ALTERNATIVE POLICY TOOLS FOR ATTAINING THE AIMS OF THE NIM

Belgium has a wide variety of public institutions which have broadly similar objectives to those of the NIM. In this section these different public institutions are described briefly.

National Company for Industrial Credit

Nationale Maatschappij voor Krediet aan de Nijverheid, the National Company for Industrial Credit (NMKN),[9] was set up in 1919. It has evolved as one of the major credit institutions in Belgium. Its objectives are similar to the objectives of the NIM in that it was intended to promote the restructuring and the development of Belgian industrial and commercial firms and to stimulate the development of new products and new technologies.

Table 4.3
Outstanding Credit of the NMKN and of the Whole Belgian Banking Sector (BF '000 million)

Year	Credits of the NMKN (1)	Total bank credit (2)	Share of NMKN credit in total bank credit (3) = (1)/(2)
1965	56.2	151.2	0.37
1970	118.9	316.2	0.37
1971	128.4	370.4	0.34
1972	131.6	423.3	0.31
1973	142.5	509.6	0.27
1974	160.9	589.9	0.27
1975	172.5	707.6	0.24
1976	199.8	814.0	0.25
1977	209.0	965.5	0.28
1978	231.5	1 068.1	0.22
1979	262.0	1 272.5	0.21

Sources: *Annual Report* (Brussels: NMKN, various issues); Bankcommissie, *Annual Report,* Brussels, 1978, p. 283, and 1979, p. 274.

The major difference between the NIM and the NMKN is that the latter provides medium-term and long-term credit. It does not take participations in the equity of companies, however, and therefore has no direct control on the internal operations of the firms, as does the NIM.[10] The relative importance of the NMKN is shown in Table 4.3.

It can be seen that the NMKN takes a substantial share of total bank credit in Belgium. Over time, however, this share has been eroded and the Belgian banks have been able to increase their shares in the medium- and long-term credit market. In spite of the reduced importance of the NMKN, however, it is fair to say that it has had a more important place in the Belgian economy than the NIM.

Regional Investment Companies

These public institutions were set up during 1979–80 and have been allocated capital allowing them to operate in much the same way as the NIM. There are three regional investment companies, one for Flanders, one for Wallonia and one for Brussels. These companies have exactly the same objectives as their national counterpart and can take shares in any company within their regional jurisdiction. It is clear that this situation can lead to conflicts between the national and the regional investment companies. It is too early to determine how important the latter are going to be as they only started operating at the beginning of 1980.

Regional Development Companies

These were instituted in 1970 and became operative in 1975. Seven exist in Antwerp, Limburg, East Flanders, West Flanders, Flemish Brabant, Brussels and Wallonia. The tasks and the objectives of these companies are quite extensive. Some are similar to the tasks and objectives of the NIM — in particular, the task of executing the industrial policy of the Government. Up until 1979 development companies could also invest in equity capital of private enterprises but in 1979 this faculty was transferred to the regional investment companies. The other areas of competence of the regional development companies are the study and the promotion of regional economic development.

Fund for Industrial Renewal

This fund, which was instituted in 1978 as the main instrument of the 'new' industrial policy of the Government, has been endowed with a relatively large capital (BF 9.2 billion; increase up to BF 21 billion is foreseen). Its main objective is to stimulate and to promote the industrial renewal of Belgium and as such, shares one of the main objectives of the NIM. Again, it is too early to evaluate the effectiveness of this institution.

LEGISLATIVE AND PARLIAMENTARY CONTROLS

The organisational structure of the NIM can be described as follows: the board of directors determines the general policy of the NIM and controls the day-to-day operations of the management council. The council consists of twenty-five members, the president and the vice-president of which are appointed by the Government.[11] The board of directors consists of eleven members and the president is appointed by the Government whereas the other members are appointed by the council. Six of these are selected from a list drawn up by the Minister of Finance and the Minister of Economic Affairs.

Apart from the important governmental influence of the appointment of the members of the council and the board, the Government also directly controls the operations of the NIM by the presence of government officials during the meetings of the council. These officials have the right to discard decisions made by the council when these decisions are deemed to be in contradiction with the law. There is a total absence of direct parliamentary control, however, on the operations of the NIM: parliamentary control, if any, could only be exerted indirectly through the control the Parliament has over the Government by the use of its power to topple the Government.

SOURCES OF FINANCE

The NIM can attract funds by issuing equity or by issuing debt.

Equity Financing

When the NIM was instituted, its equity was fixed at BF 2 billion. An amount of BF 491 million was subscribed by the state, BF 1.1 billion by the NMKN and public savings institutions, and the rest was subscribed by private banks and insurance companies. Since 1976, however, these latter were compelled to convert their share into government bonds. As a result the NIM became a fully state-owned company, partly through direct state participation and partly through participation of public financial institutions. The National Bank became a share-holder in 1971 and subscribed BF 50 million. In 1979 the equity of the NIM amounted to BF 9 billion. The evolution of equity issued by the NIM is shown in Figure 4.1.

Debt Financing

The NIM is allowed to attract funds by issuing bonds with maturity of at least five years. It can also obtain funds in limited amounts from the public saving institutions. The reorganisation in 1978 opened the door for a potentially very large source of financing. As indicated earlier, in 1978 the NIM was made one of the major instruments of the state's industrial policy. As a result, substantial funds can now be channelled to the NIM by the state. The discretionary power of the NIM over these funds, however, is severely limited. Table 4.4 provides some statistical information on the different sources of funds of the NIM.

HOW WELL DOES THE NIM FULFIL ITS OBJECTIVES?

The objectives of the NIM were spelled out above. As pointed out, many of these objectives are so vague as to make their evaluation, let alone their quantification, extremely difficult. For

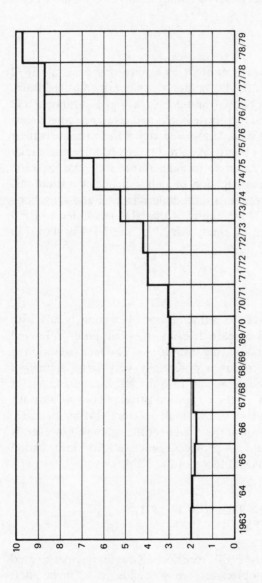

Source: *Annual Report* (Brussels: NIM, 1979) p. 9.

Figure 4.1
Equity Issued by the NIM, 1963–79 (BF '000 million)

example, whether NIM investment policy has contributed to more innovation in industry or to more rapid growth.

In what follows, those NIM objectives that have a precise and quantifiable content are evaluated. These are (i) the rate of return on the equity of the NIM, (ii) the employment effect of NIM policy, (iii) the degree to which the NIM has increased the

Table 4.4
Source of Funds of the NIM, 9 September 1979
(BF '000 million)

Capital	8.5
Reserves	0.5
Long-term debt	1.9
Short-term debt	0.2
Other	0.2
Total	11.3

Source: *Annual Report* (Brussels: NIM, various issues).

provision of capital to private firms and (iv) the financial performance of the firms in which the NIM has a participation. Investment policy which the NIM pursues with its own financial resources (its equity) is analysed — the investment activity of the NIM using financial resources provided directly by the state is disregarded. In a later section both types of investment activities are considered.

Rate of Return on the Equity of the NIM

A first explicit objective of the NIM is the attainment of a reasonable rate of return on its portfolio. Table 4.5 gives the evolution of the net rate of return on the equity of the NIM since 1963. It can be seen that the rates of return on the equity of the NIM hover around 1–3 per cent per year. As a proxy for the real rates of return the rate of inflation is subtracted from the nominal rate of return.[12] It can be seen that these real rates of return are negative in all years and that they are especially low during the period 1974–78.

In order to give a better idea of what a 'reasonable' rate of return might be, the rate of return of the NIM in 1979 (a relatively

Table 4.5
Rate of Return on Equity of the NIM

Year	Nominal rate of return (%)[a]	Inflation rate[b]	Real rate of return[c]
1963	1.18	2.2	− 1.0
1964	−0.58	4.0	− 4.6
1965	−5.54	4.1	− 9.6
1966	−1.25	4.3	− 5.5
1967–68	1.16	2.9	− 1.7
1968–69	−1.08	2.6	− 3.7
1969–70	2.93	3.9	− 1.0
1970–71	2.04	3.9	− 1.9
1971–72	0.30	4.3	− 4.0
1972–73	1.52	5.4	− 3.9
1973–74	2.35	6.9	− 4.6
1974–75	1.72	12.7	−11.0
1975–76	3.38	12.7	− 9.3
1976–77	1.16	9.2	− 8.0
1977–78	−1.38	7.1	− 8.5
1978–79	1.12	4.5	− 3.4

Source: *Annual Report* (Brussels: NIM various issues). Note that the figures relate to the rate of return on the capital of the NIM: it does not include the funds provided by the state to bail out firms.
[a] Nominal rate of return relates to net profit (after tax and depreciation) over equity plus reserves.
[b] The inflation rate is the yearly percentage increase in the consumer price index.
[c] The real rate of return is the nominal rate minus the inflation rate (see Chapter 4, Notes and References no. 12).

Table 4.6
Rate of Return on Equity of the NIM and of Private Belgian Investment Companies, 1979

	Nominal rate of return[a]	Real rate of return[b]
BLM (Bruxelles-Lambert)	10.7	6.2
Cobepa	8.9	4.4
Société Générale	7.2	2.7
NIM	1.1	−3.4

Sources: Annual reports of these institutions
[a] Nominal rate of return relates to net profit (after tax and depreciation) over equity plus reserves.
[b] The real rate of return is the nominal rate minus the inflation rate (see Chapter 4, Notes and References no. 12).

successful year for the NIM) is compared with the rate of return realised by the largest private investment companies in Belgium. This is shown in Table 4.6.

In comparison with other major Belgian investment companies the rate of return of the NIM is dismally low. Table 4.7 shows the rates of return in the stock market of a number of private investment companies during 1975–79. Here, too, the rates of return of the private investment companies are relatively high. The fact that during its whole existence the NIM has operated at a negative real rate of return should not be under-estimated. Over the period 1963–79 the average yearly real rate of return was −5 per cent. Another way to look at this figure is that the NIM

Table 4.7
Yearly Rate of Return (Stock Price + Dividend)
Average Over 1975–79

Company	Nominal rate of return	Real rate of return
BLM	7.4	−0.6
Cobepa	5.2	−2.8
Electrobel	10.0	2.0

Source: Parisbas, *Economische Berichten*, Brussels, June 1980. Note that NIM shares are not traded so no market rates of return can be computed.

manages to lose half of the real value of the capital entrusted into it every sixteen years. In principle, there is nothing wrong with this if it can be shown that this destruction of capital enables the NIM to achieve worthwhile objectives. The difference in the rate of return achieved by the NIM and by the private investment companies, however, is such that in order to justify the continuing investment of equity capital in the NIM, the social benefits elsewhere should be large and identifiable.

The findings reported here are in agreement with those of a recent study by S. Beckers *et al.*, who find that during 1972–79 the equity of the NIM declined in value (after correction for inflation) by 30 per cent.[13]

NIM and the Employment Objective

Over the years the employment objective has increased in importance in formulating official NIM policy. Every year the NIM publishes favourable reports about the employment effect of its participations. These favourable effects are calculated by adding up the number of jobs 'saved' due to a NIM participation in individual firms. As an illustration, Table 4.8 shows the number of jobs the NIM considers it has saved every year by taking participations in private firms. These numbers are obtained by simply adding the existing employment of the firms in which the NIM has taken a participation during the year.

Table 4.8
Job Effects

1974–75	1975–76	1976–77	1977–78	1978–79
17,500	21,200	21,800	19,900	22,250

Source: *Annual Report* (Brussels: NIM, various issues).

It is clear that this is not a valid test of the employment effect of NIM policies. In order to create such a test one has to follow, over time, the employment levels of firms in which the NIM has taken a participation. Such an analysis was performed recently by Beckers *et al.*[14] These researchers computed indices of employment in NIM-controlled firms during the period 1972–79. The problem is that the number of firms in which the NIM has invested does not remain constant over time because failing firms disappear from the sample and others are added. An employment index designed to avoid this problem was constructed.

The result of the calculations made by Beckers *et al.* is given in Table 4.9. We have also added the index of total employment in the Belgian manufacturing sector during the same period. The striking thing about this table is that the employment in firms in which the NIM is a shareholder declines faster than total dependent employment in Belgium, even if the adjusted employment series is taken.[15] It is, therefore, doubtful that, in spite of claims to the contrary,[16] the NIM has been effective in promoting

Table 4.9
Employment in Belgium and in NIM Firms

Year	Total Belgian industrial employment	Total employment in Belgium (excl. self-empl'd)	Employment in NIM firms	
			Total	Adjusted[a]
1972	100	100	100	100
1973	100.5	102	98	97
1974	101.5	104.2	95	100
1975	96.8	103.0	97	99
1976	93.9	102.6	93	99
1977	91.0	102.4	89	96
1978	87.8	102.3	80	96
1979	86.0	103.5	78	96

Sources: S. Beckers, P. Sercu and J. Fabry, 'Een Evaluatie van die NIM als Autonome Investeringsmaatschappij', in *Vijftiende Vlaams Wetenschappelijk Economisch Congres* (Louvain: Louvain University Press, 1981) pp. 161–78; and National Institute of Statistics information.
[a] The corrected series excludes two large firms (Cockerill and UCB) in which the NIM has relatively small participations.

employment. Note that the question of whether the safeguard of employment should be an important objective of a state investment company is not discussed here. The above evidence indicates that the NIM has been ineffective in realising the objective which constitutes its official *raison d'être*.

NIM and Financial Intermediation

A second objective of the NIM is facilitating the access of private firms to equity capital. As mentioned above Belgian firms tend to neglect this source of financing because of the unfavourable tax treatment it attracts. The question then again is how effective has the NIM been in achieving this objective?

In order to give a preliminary answer to this question we compared the balance sheet of the NIM to the balance sheet of the largest private Belgian investment company (Société Générale). This is shown in Table 4.10. A comparison of the balance sheet of the NIM and the Société Générale allows the following conclu-

Table 4.10
Balance Sheet of the NIM and the Société Générale, 1979 (BF '000 million)

Assets	NIM	Société Générale	Liabilities	NIM	Sociéte Générale
Participation in equity	5.9	14.5	Capital	8.5	7.5
			Reserves	0.5	2.4
Other long-term financial assets	2.2	3.3	Long-term debt	1.8	5.3
Short-term financial assets	3.0	6.0	Short-term debt	0.2	8.8
			Other	0.3	0.8
Other assets	0.2	1.0			
Total	11.3	24.8	Total	11.3	24.8

Source: National Bank of Belgium's Balanscentrale (databank).

sions. First, the ratio of participation in equity to capital is completely different in the two financial institutions. For every franc of equity attracted by the NIM only BF 0.67 has a counterpart in equity investments in private firms (5.7/8.5). The Société Générale, however, invests BF 1.93 in equity for every franc it attracts by issuing its own equity.

The comparison of these ratios probably exaggerates the favourable performance of the Société Générale. As a private company, the Société Générale has a tax incentive to issue debt instead of equity whereas the NIM, as a state company, has no such incentive. It is more useful, therefore, to compare the ratio of participations in equity with total long-term liabilities. One then obtains for the NIM a ratio of 0.53 and for the Société Générale 0.95. Thus, in 1979, for every franc attracted by the NIM (either by the issuing of equity or of long-term debt) the NIM invested only half a franc in the form of equity. On the other hand, during the same year, the Société Générale transformed every franc of long-term debt or equity into approximately one franc of equity participation.

A second conclusion can be drawn from Table 4.10. The degree of maturity transformation of both institutions is indicated more fully in Table 4.11: again, the difference is striking. On the short side, the Société Générale tends to have less assets than liabilities, whereas, on the long side, it has more assets than liabilities. This indicates that the Société Générale (to a limited degree) performs

Table 4.11
Degree of Maturity Transformation, 1979

	Ratio of short-term assets to short-term liabilities	Ratio of long-term assets to long-term liabilities
NIM	15.0	0.74
Société Générale	0.68	1.17

Source: Computed from Table 4.10.

a banking function in that it borrows short and lends long. The reverse picture is obtained in the case of the NIM. On the short side, the assets are fifteen times higher than the liabilities and, on the long side, the assets are about 25 per cent below the liabilities. This leads to the conclusion that the NIM tends to borrow long and to lend short. Put differently, the NIM is an institution attracting mostly long-term funds which it partly transforms into assets with a shorter maturity.

One can conclude from the preceding sections that in terms of employment gain there does not seem to be a justification for continuing investment in the NIM. The continuing loss of society's real capital does not enable it to gain additional employment. A similar conclusion holds for the second objective: there is no evidence that the NIM enlarges the stock of equity capital for society.

The question now is what other social benefits the NIM achieves to justify the average real rate of return of −5 per cent of its portfolio since its existence and the destruction of equity capital? Unfortunately it is practically impossible to evaluate these other social benefits. Unless these can be made more explicit by policy makers, the conclusion must be that there is no evidence that these other social benefits outweigh the substantial costs resulting from the loss of equity capital for society.

FINANCIAL ANALYSIS OF NIM COMPANIES

In the previous section the evolution of the rate of return on NIM investment was analysed. In this section a more detailed financial analysis is performed, focussing on the results of companies in which the NIM has an equity participation.[17] This allows more detailed conclusions about the nature of NIM investment policies to be drawn. In addition, this section takes all NIM investments into account, that is, those that are performed with the NIM's own resources and those that are made possible by direct state contributions. This is done in order to evaluate state investment policies in their entirety.

In order to do this, the balance sheets of all companies in which the NIM is a shareholder were analysed.[18] Different ratios of financial performance were computed. In addition, these ratios, whenever possible, were compared with financial ratios of a representative sample of Belgian companies.[19]

Financial Performance of NIM Firms

Table 4.12 contains a series of financial ratios of NIM firms and compares these with a representative sample of Belgian private firms. This sample was obtained from the Kredietbank. The results reported in Table 4.12 illustrate how poorly NIM firms performed in terms of traditional financial ratios. In fact, these ratios probably overstate the quality of NIM management control. For they were obtained by giving each NIM firm the same weight. If, however, each firm is weighted by the percentage share the NIM has in the firm, the ratios given in Table 4.13 appear.

It can be seen that the financial ratios deteriorate substantially. This means that on average the financial performance of firms deteriorates with an increasing equity participation of the NIM.

This result is also brought out by classifying in three groups firms in which the state has an equity share: firms with a minority share owned by the state (less than 20 per cent); firms with a blocking minority share owned by the state (20–50 per cent); and firms in which the state has a majority share (more than 50 per cent).[20] The result is shown in Table 4.14.

Table 4.14 confirms that the more important the share of the state is, the weaker the financial performance of the firm. The differences here are quite dramatic. Firms in which the state has only a minority share, and thus relatively little influence on management decisions, exhibit a financial performance which is

Table 4.12
Financial Ratios of NIM Firms and of Kredietbank Sample of Belgian Firms

	1977	1978	1979
Net rate of return on equity (in %)[a]			
NIM firms (total)[e]	−12.4	−15.5	−12.3
NIM firms (industrial)[d]	−20.7	−45.7	−56.3
Average Belgian firms (total)[f]	2.7	5.5	8.1
Average Belgian firms (industrial)[f]	− 2.6	− 1.1	4.8
Net profit margin (in %)[b]			
NIM firms (industrial)[d]	− 0.8	− 3.8	− 2.1
Average Belgian firms (industrial)[f]	1.6	21.1	—
Gross profit margin (in %)[c]			
NIM firms (industrial)[d]	4.1	2.4	4.3
Average Belgian firms (industrial)[f]	6.3	6.8	—

Sources: Computed from balance-sheet data of the National Bank, Kredietbank; and G. Clémer and K. Rogiers, *Roodboek over de Staatsinterventie* (Antwerp: Vlaams Economisch Verbond, 1980) pp. 28–31.
[a] Nominal rate minus the inflation rate.
[b] Net profit divided by sales.
[c] Gross profit divided by sales. Gross profits are equal to net profits plus amortisation.
[d] Industrial NIM firms are industrial firms in which the NIM has an equity participation.
[e] NIM firms (total) refers to all firms in which the NIM has an equity participation. Only firms with sales over BF 25 million are included.
[f] The average Belgian firms relate to a sample of Belgian firms as used by the Kredietbank.

Table 4.13
Financial Ratios of NIM Firms Weighted by Degree of NIM Participation

	1977	1978	1979
Rate of return on equity of NIM firms	−45.8	−75.8	−153.2
Net profit margin	− 4.3	− 6.0	− 4.9
Gross profit margin	1.7	− 0.3	1.7

Source: See Table 4.12.

comparable to other Belgian firms. On the other hand, the financial performance of firms in which the state has either a blocking minority or a majority share can only be labelled catastrophic.

Table 4.14
Financial Ratios of Firms, Classified According to Size of State Participation

	1977	1978	1979
Net rate of return on equity			
minority share	4.1	− 18.0	3.1
blocking minority	− 25.7	− 29.0	− 41.5
majority	−125.5	−129.7	−349.2
Gross profit margin			
minority share	6.7	4.8	9.3
blocking minority	2.3	1.7	1.3
majority	− 8.8	− 8.4	− 3.5

Source: See Table 4.12.

This negative correlation between size of participation by the NIM (state) and financial performance of the firms can be explained by two alternative hypotheses.

(a) The negative correlation can be due to the fact that increasing control by the NIM (state) leads to increasing politicisation of the management of the firm and, as a result, to increasing financial mismanagement. The evidence to corroborate this hypothesis is the fact that important executive positions tend to be distributed through party politics.

(b) The negative correlation can also be due to the fact that the NIM tends to invest in 'lame-duck' firms or industries. The weaker the financial position of these firms, the more the NIM (state) is forced to invest in these firms in order to save them from bankruptcy.

The evidence of this section, when compared with the evidence of the previous section, allows one to conclude that hypothesis (b) must have played a significant role. In the previous section the net rate of return on the NIM's own resources (equity) was found to be −1.4 in 1977–78 and +1.1 in 1978–89. On the other hand, the net rate of return realised on all participation, including that financed by direct state contribution, was found to be substantially lower (−15.5 per cent in 1978 and −12.3 per cent in 1979). This suggests that NIM investments forced by the state are much less financially sound than NIM investments financed by its own resources.

Wage Bill and Public Investment Policies

To gain additional insight into the nature of public investment policies the ratio of total labour cost to value added in NIM firms was computed. These ratios are shown in Table 4.15.

Table 4.15
Average Ratio of Labour Cost to Value Added in NIM Firms (per cent)

	1977	1978	1979
Unweighted average			
NIM firms	71.7	67.5	61.7
NIM firms (industrial sector)	84.2	90.2	85.1
Weighted average			
NIM firms	90.9	98.1	91.6
NIM firms (industrial sector)	103.9	110.5	90.5
Average whole industry	82.0	83.0	—

Sources: *Service de Conjoncture* (Louvain-la-Neuve: Institut de Recherches Economiques et Sociales, various issues); see, also, Table 4.12.

Typically the wage share in value added of NIM firms operating in the industrial sector is larger than the wage share of private firms in the industrial sector. More significantly, when the wage share of NIM firms is averaged by weighting these firms according to the size of NIM participation (instead of giving all NIM firms the same weight), the average wage share increases substantially. This indicates that the larger the equity share of the NIM in a firm, the larger also is the ratio of labour costs to total value added.

Similar evidence can be obtained by classifying firms into three groups depending on the proportional importance of the state participation (see Table 4.16).[21] A striking result is that in those firms in which the state has a majority share, the wage bill tended to be 7–20 per cent above total value added in these firms. Here, again, there is a negative correlation: the lower the share of the state in the firm, the smaller the wage bill in total value added. The question again arises how this result should be interpreted.

Table 4.16
Total Labour Cost to Value Added in State Firms (per cent)

	1977	1978	1979
Firms with state minority share	77	83	70
Firms with state blocking minority	89	92	96
Firms with state majority share	119	120	107
All state firms	84	90	85

Source: Computed from balance-sheet data of the National Bank, Kredietbank.
Note: The sample of state firms (140) in 1979 is larger than the sample of NIM firms. It includes all firms in which the state has a participation. Total labour cost refers to the total outlays for personnel. See, also, Chapter 4, Notes and References no. 20.

Obviously, it is related to the previously analysed phenomenon. It also suggests, however, that public investment policy is geared towards protecting the wage bill of employees.

By systematically investing in firms with excessive wage bills the NIM (state) allows these firms to stay alive and allows wage earners to gain an income which exceeds their contribution to the national product. In addition, the evidence provided here is in accord with the hypothesis that state participation in a firm allows its employees to increase their wage claims.

This policy of systematically protecting firms with excessive wage bills is an endogenous reaction of the political authorities to the wage explosion which the Belgian economy has experienced since the mid-1970s. This wage expansion is illustrated in Figure 4.2. It can be seen that the Belgian wage bill in industrial value added increased faster than in most other countries of the European Community. Whereas in the early 1970s the Belgian wage bill in industrial value added was among the lowest in the Community, it had increased to the highest by 1978. One result of this wage shock was to reduce industrial employment in Belgium at a much faster rate than in the other Community countries.[22] (See Figure 4.3.)

Given the character of political pressure in a democracy, it became inevitable that the NIM would rescue failing firms which, given the nature of the economic shock, generally were firms whose wage bill had increased to such a level as to make continuing activity unprofitable. Thus the NIM, together with the increasing state subsidies to failing firms, became an institution which, by allowing high wage firms a lease on life, helped to sustain a high wage level in the economy. The NIM may not have

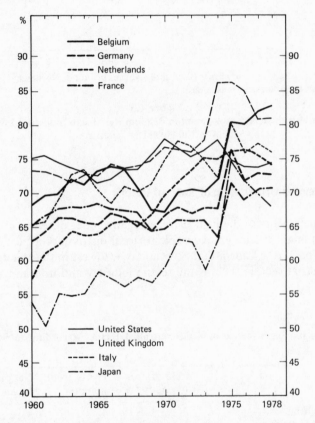

Source: *Service de Conjoncture* (Louvain-la-Neuve: Institut de Recherches Economiques et Sociales, various issues).

Figure 4.2
Wage Share in Value Added (Manufacturing Sector)

wanted this but the economic shock of the mid-1970s and the political pressure subsequently exerted on it forced the NIM to follow this wage-protection policy.

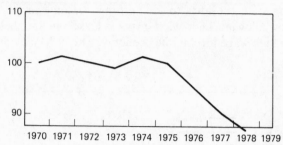

Source: *Service de Conjoncture* (Louvain-la-Neuve: Institut de Recherches Economiques et Sociales, various issues).

Figure 4.3
Index of Industrial Employment in Belgium Relative to Industrial Employment in Industrialised Countries

Sectoral Distribution of Rates of Return

One reason for the high average negative rates of return of NIM firms might be the unfavourable sectoral distribution of the NIM portfolio. It is known that profitability is lowest in the traditional industrial sectors such as the textile industry and iron and steel.

Table 4.17
Financial Performance of State-controlled Firms[a] According to Sector, 1978

	Rate of return of equity (%)	Gross profit margin (%)	Net profit margin (%)
State firms[b]			
Textile industry	−80.3	−3.1	−8.5
Metallic construction	−11.4	4.4	
Machinery	−66.2	−3.6	
Average of Belgian firms[c]			
Textile industry	− 5.1	6.6	1.8
Metallic construction	− 5.0	6.9	
Machinery	2.0	8.5	

[a] Including NIM firms.
[b] Firms in which the state has an equity share. The sample is larger than the sample of NIM firms. See Chapter 4, Notes and References no. 20.
[c] The sample is from the National Bank of Belgium, Kredietbank.

Given the relatively high share of the NIM investment portfolio in these sectors, it might at least partially explain the low average rates of return.

The evidence presented in Table 4.17, however, allows us to refute this interpretation. There, it is seen that the rate of return on the equity of firms in which the state has an equity share, as well as their gross profit margins, are uniformly lower — and substantially so — than the same indicators of performance of other firms in the same sector.

CONCLUDING REMARKS

The analysis of the preceding sections allows one to derive the following conclusion. The NIM has failed to achieve its major objectives. The real rate of return on investments financed by its own resources (equity) has been negative (-5 per cent per year) since it came into existence. In addition, the rate of return on equity investment financed by its own resources and by direct state contributions has been much lower. A typical firm in which the NIM has an equity share has realised an annual nominal rate of return of *minus* 13 per cent during 1977–79.

This poor financial performance has not allowed the NIM to achieve its employment objectives. In fact, the decline of employment in firms controlled by the NIM has been faster than total dependent employment in Belgium. Whether the NIM has been able to achieve other objectives (modernisation of industry, a more dynamic management) is difficult to evaluate. It is doubtful, however, that the NIM has achieved much as far as these other objectives are concerned. NIM investment policy during recent years has consisted of protecting high-wage firms from failing. In addition, this wage protection policy has effectively led the NIM to transform equity capital into consumption. Through the NIM, capital provided by society is transformed into consumption by employees in lame-duck industries. The question arising, therefore, is why the NIM has failed so dismally to achieve its objectives?

The answer is that most of the objectives entrusted to the NIM are impossible to realise, given the fact that the NIM has become an instrument of the executive branch of Government. In a political democracy, politicians will be guided by vote-maximising behaviour. When given the ultimate power to decide where to allocate investment funds, these funds will tend to be allocated where the political benefits are the highest. Thus the political decision mechanism channels resources to the best-organised pressure groups.

This process, which is common to most industrialised countries, has been exacerbated in Belgium as a result of the wage explosion of the mid-1970s and the resulting increasing unprofitability of the industrial sector. This has led to the mushrooming of pressure groups aimed at obtaining state subsidies. The political pressure exerted on the NIM has led to a situation in which the NIM has become an instrument of protection of failing firms and of preserving the incomes of their employees at an otherwise unsustainable level.

Recently, the Belgian Government decided to enlarge substantially the role of the state investment companies, especially the regional investment companies ·and the Fund for Industrial Renewal. The finances which will be made available to these institutions in the coming years are large enough to enable them to control a substantial part of the Belgian industrial sector. At the same time, however, nothing has been done to reduce the political leverage on these institutions — on the contrary, it has been increased. There is reason to fear, therefore, that future state investment policies will be the same as those of the past. The only difference will be that state investment policies will become much more important, dwarfing the past inefficiencies and poor performance of the state investment company.

NOTES AND REFERENCES

1. In French it is Société Nationale d'Investissement.
2. The law of 2 April 1962, Article 2(1). All laws are published in *Belgisch Staatsblad* (Brussels: Belgian Government Printing Office).
3. Note that at about the same time J. Drèze developed his now well known argument that small open economies have a comparative advantage in the production of relatively homogeneous goods, for example, steel, basic chemicals *et cetera*.

The reason is that, because of large information costs, the development of more heterogeneous goods requires a large home market. See Drèze, 'Quelques reflexions sereines sur l'adaptation de l'industrie belge au Marché Commun', in *Comptes Rendues des Travaux de la Société Royale d'Economie Politique* (Brussels: Société Royale d'Economie Politique, 1960) No. 275.

4. The law of 30 December 1970; the law of 30 March 1976; and the law of 4 August 1978.

5. *Annual Report* (Brussels: NIM, 1978) pp. 5–6.

6. *Belgisch Staatsblad* (Brussels: Belgian Government Printing Office, 17 August 1978).

7. The 'industrial policy' of the government is a rather vague term. It has been given more precise content in an official document of the Ministry of Economic Affairs.

8. In Appendix 4.1, more statistical information about the regional and sectoral composition of the NIM portfolio is provided.

9. In French it is Société Nationale de Credit à l'Industrie.

10. The only exception is that the NMKN is allowed to invest in shares of the NIM.

11. Technically, the King appoints.

12. This procedure is only a rough approximation. It does not take into account the changes in the market value of the firms in which the NIM invests. It is unclear, however, whether our procedure biases the results upwards or downwards. We take comfort in the fact that other researchers have found broadly similar results.

13. See S. Beckers, P. Sercu and J. Fabry, 'Een Evaluatie van die NIM als Autonome Investeringsmaatschappij', in *Vijftiende Vlaams Wetenschappelijk Economisch Congres* (Louvain: Louvain University Press, 1981) pp. 161–78.

14. *Ibid.*

15. Note that, since the NIM has a large part of its equity investment in the tertiary sector (approximately 30 per cent in 1979, see Appendix 4.1), the relevant comparison of the NIM employment index is with total employment in Belgium.

16. In response to the present study, the NIM has calculated an employment index in NIM firms using a constant sample of firms during 1972–79. In 1979 the index stood at 100.2. It is clear that this index tends to over-estimate the employment trend in

NIM firms, since it eliminates all firms that failed during this period.

17.   The calculations reported in this section were performed in collaboration with Kris Rogiers of the Flemish Association of Employers (VEV).

18.   As of 1979, there were ninety firms in which the NIM had a participation. Since its origin the NIM has invested (through equity or bonds) in 387 firms. An unknown number of firms has failed. For more information see G. Clémer and Kris Rogiers, *Roodboek over de Staatsinterventie* (Antwerp: Vlaams Economisch Verbond, 1980) pp. 28–31.

19.   We used the balance-sheet data of the National Bank of Belgium ('Balanscentrale'). Unfortunately, these exist only for the years 1977, 1978 and 1979, so that the analysis of this section is limited to these three years.

20.   The sample of 'state-firms' includes the firms in which the NIM has a participation. It also includes those firms in which the state has taken a participation either directly or through one of the other state investment companies described above. It does not include here the traditional nationalised sectors, such as the National Railway Company, SABENA, public savings and loan associations.

21.   We were unable to do this classification for NIM firms separately.

22.   For an analysis of the effects of this shock, see Paul de Grauwe, *Symptoms of an Overvalued Currency: the Case of the Belgian Franc*, International Economics Research Paper No. 26 (Louvain: University of Louvain, 1980). There, it is also argued that the simultaneous policy of effective currency appreciation speeded up this 'de-industrialisation'.

Appendix 4.1
Composition of the NIM Portfolio

	1971–72	1978–79	
	%	BF million	%
Food industry	6.18	108.9	1.71
Textile	3.82	462.7	7.27
Glass, fibre	1.34	90.6	1.42
Timber and plastics	2.03	266.4	4.19
Paper, printing and publishing	10.09	452.2	7.11
Chemical industry	14.90	826.2	12.99
Basic metals	11.89	637.4	10.02
Machinery	14.46	726.8	11.43
Energy	7.66	390.5	6.14
Construction and construction materials	2.82	173.7	2.73
Electricity	—	284.0	4.47
Transport	8.37	816.3	12.83
Financial	10.45	817.8	12.86
Other	5.85	307.3	4.83
Total	100.00	6 360.8	100.00

Source: *Annual Report* (Brussels: NIM, various issues).

Regional Composition of NIM Investment, 1976–77

	BF '000 million	%
National investments	1 680	27.3
Investment in Flanders	1 869	30.2
Investment in Wallonia	2 066	33.4
Investment in Brussels	540	8.7
Foreign investment	27	0.4
Total	6 193	100

Source: *Trends Magazine*, Brussels, 15 January 1977.

Appendix 4.1 cont'd

Composition of NIM Investment in Firms According to Size

Yearly sales (BF million)	Percent of total number of firms			
	1974–75	1976–77	1977–78	1978–79
< 50	22.1	25.8	24.8	19.8
50 < 100	11.6	9.0	8.9	7.5
100 < 200	20.9	15.7	13.9	20.7
200 < 300	14.0	10.1	8.9	14.3
300 < 400	5.8	9.0	9.9	8.5
400 < 500	5.8	2.3	5.9	5.7
> 500	19.8	28.1	27.7	23.6
Total	100	100	100	100

Source: *Annual Report* (Brussels: NIM, various issues).

CHAPTER FIVE

United Kingdom: An Experiment in Picking Winners—the Industrial Reorganisation Corporation

Brian Hindley and Ray Richardson

The Industrial Reorganisation Corporation (IRC), which was in operation between 1966 and 1971, was a public corporation whose major task was to promote changes in the structure and management of industry in the United Kingdom. It was set up by a government whose expressed view was that much of British industry was unduly and inefficiently fragmented and that greater concentration or 'rationalisation' was needed. In the words of the first IRC Annual Report, the role of the corporation was 'to seek out those sectors of industry where structural change should be happening but is not'.[1] Mr Michael Stewart, the minister responsible for the passage of the enabling legislation through Parliament, expressed things more soberly when he said that the job of the IRC was to help secure 'the optimum size of firm — the firm which is neither unwieldy nor menaces the consumer though the danger of monopoly but which is able to obtain all the advantages of scale which modern conditions of industry make possible'.[2]

The IRC should be viewed in the wider context of the economic policy of the time. There had been for some time a widespread recognition that Britain's rate of economic growth was disappointingly low, at least when compared with growth rates abroad. The Labour Party's return to office in 1964, after an extended period in opposition, was widely believed to be due in considerable part to the expected effectiveness of its economic policies.

While in opposition, the Labour Party had, naturally, attacked the detail of the macro-economic policies of successive Conservative Governments. Its more fundamental criticism was, however, that Keynesian macro-economics, of whatever specification, was not enough. Keynesian principles, the Labour Party claimed, needed to be supplemented by certain kinds of planning, with widespread institutional reforms and with very substantial structural changes. A picture was painted of a private industrial sector that had invested too little, had innovated too slowly, was obsolete in structure and was dominated by old-fashioned managerial attitudes. The Labour Party claimed that what was needed was, in a word, modernisation.

In an effort to produce this industrial renewal, the new Government introduced a range of policies, including the National Plan, new schemes of investment incentives, a much enlarged regional policy and encouragements to scientific research and development. Within this portfolio of policy experiments the IRC had the explicit role of helping to change the structure of private industry.

That structure, as the Government recognised, was already changing. As the White Paper that introduced the IRC noted, 'many industries have already substantially altered their structure and organisation through mergers, acquisitions and regroupings'. The White Paper even admitted that this 'process has been accelerating in recent years and may be expected to continue'. It asserted, however, that 'the pace and scale of change do not yet match the needs of the national economy'.[3]

The basis on which such an assertion was made, or could reasonably be made, is not clear. Even with the benefit of hindsight, present day scholars would have great difficulty in reliably estimating the optimum size of firms in British industry in the mid-1960s. Still less could they pronounce with any confidence on the then optimal pace and scale of structural change. Scholars have one duty, however, and those who draft White Papers have another. An examination of the public discussion of the time, and later, suggests that two factors lay behind the White Paper's rather bold and sweeping assertion.

The first factor was the view taken by certain prominent individuals active in the worlds of finance and industry. A number of these evidently knew of, or believed that they knew of, situations where mergers failed to occur even though their consummation would have been beneficial. The benefits might have accrued privately or have been 'in the national interest' but there was clearly a fairly widespread view among experienced and practical men that potentially useful rationalisations were frequently not taking place. As Sir Frederick Catherwood, then Director of the National Economic Development Council (NEDC), observed, after the IRC had been wound up: 'At the time that the IRC was set up there were a number of groups which I think everyone felt required to be merged for various reasons.'[4] The IRC itself noted, in its first Annual Report, that it 'soon became apparent that many businessmen recognised the need for structural change in their industries, and welcomed the assistance of an independent agency'.[5]

The second factor was of a very different kind and stemmed from the belief that Britain had persistent balance-of-payments difficulties that were partly the result of the inability of small British firms to compete successfully with large foreign firms. In seeking to understand economic policy between 1964–67 it is hardly possible to overstate the role and significance of real and imagined balance-of-payments problems. Certainly the IRC White Paper was heavily influenced, even analytically deformed, by them. For example, it asserted that the 'need for more concentration and rationalisation to promote the greater ... international competitiveness of British industry ... is now widely recognised'.[6] The necessity of large firm size for international success was taken to be almost beyond question, as was the proposition that British firms were generally somewhat smaller than their foreign competitors. Neither the necessity nor the proposition was, or is, obviously true. They were taken to be so, however, and were factors which were widely deployed in justifying the IRC.

Having concluded that there is 'no evidence that we can rely on market forces alone to produce the necessary structural changes at the pace required',[7] the Government thought it necessary to create a new body — one that would supplement, not supplant, existing institutions. The IRC was therefore seen as an organisation 'whose special function is to search for opportunities to promote rationalisation schemes which could yield substantial benefits to the national economy'.[8] The key words here are 'special' and 'search'.

The Government's view was that the IRC would have a distinct advantage over existing institutions, such as merchant banks, part of whose business was to organise mergers. This view was based on the proposition that the IRC would be single-minded and a merger specialist.[9] It is, however, not easy to see why single-mindedness and a specialist status would, automatically, be valuable qualities, especially as there was nothing to stop private firms from having or acquiring them.

The other key word, 'search', related to the view that existing merger brokers were essentially reactive, that in general they acted only at their client's instigation. In contrast, it was implied that the IRC would succeed by actively, and even aggressively, seeking out 'desirable regroupings' which would otherwise 'fail to take place through lack of initiative and sponsorship, or because, when opportunities arise, there is no one ready to grasp them'.[10] In short, the IRC would succeed because it was designed to lead rather than follow.

The Government's case for the IRC was, therefore, rooted in two distinct forms of private market failure. The first was in the industrial sphere, where optimum firm size was held to be only belatedly, if at all, attained in certain industries. The second was in the financial world, where merchant banks and others were held to be too passive in the presence of potentially desirable mergers. The source of this second failure, it could be argued, might be the existence of high private risks affecting the broker if the proposed merger failed to come to fruition. In the presence of such risks, it might be argued, it would not be privately worthwhile to invest resources to decide which potential mergers might pay off.

All this might seem to many to be a slender and rather too speculative basis on which to establish an important government initiative. Clearly, an economy's industrial structure is most unlikely to be 'perfect', in the sense of meeting textbook conditions. Equally clearly, a public agency might be able to improve the structure. The key question, however, is not the one framed in possibilities but the one which seeks to establish the presumption that such an agency is likely to deliver the goods. In this respect the Government thought it an important point in favour of the IRC that it could take a longer view than would normally be done by a purely private organisation. This was not to say that the IRC was to act uncommercially, for it was under an obligation to earn a 'commercial' rate of return. It was claimed, however, that the IRC 'would not be obliged (as would a private merger broker) to look so much to the immediate profitability of a transaction'.[11]

It must be said that the ability to wait for one's return does not automatically improve the soundness of one's decisions. Transactions whose expected profits accrue in the relatively distant future are likely to be particularly hard to evaluate in the present; this is perhaps even more likely if the profits depend on organisational change rather than, say, on the exploitation of some natural resource. This difficulty in evaluation does not, of course, mean that private calculations are appropriately discounted; it merely implies that accurate valuations and appropriate discount factors are hard for anyone — including those with the best will in the world — to establish with any confidence.

In one sense, the above discussion is academic. The more closely that the record of the period is examined, the clearer it becomes that the attraction to the Government of the IRC did not lie in the formal rigour of the arguments deployed by its parliamentary proponents. Rather, it lay in an intuition that the British economy had been slow to change and that, *if the right people could be recruited*, a catalytic agency could have a very useful role. It was the quality of the men in charge and the calibre of its staff and advisers that made the IRC seem potentially worthwhile to the Government. In certain hands such an organisation would doubtless have no useful role; in the hands of gifted individuals, however, it could be effective. This may not be a secure basis on which to set up a new organisation, certainly not one with a permanent role. It was, however, a basis that was fully consistent with the style of (the then) Mr George Brown, the first head of the Department of Economic Affairs, the Government's new economic ministry.

Our interpretation, therefore, is that the creation of the IRC was rather sudden and depended on the receptiveness of a politician with singular qualities to the proposition that talented men, given a fairly free hand, could achieve good results. This view gains support from a consideration of the IRC in the context of the Labour Party's traditions in industrial policy.

Unusually for Labour Government initiatives in the field of industrial policy, the IRC had no party pedigree. The virtues of rationalisation or increased concentration had not figured prominently in party discussions in the preceeding fifteen years, particularly if the firms concerned were to remain in the private sector. Indeed, the reverse was the case. There was a long history of Labour Party antagonism to private amalgamations which was still alive in the early 1960s. Far from the IRC being, in the words of *The Economist*, 'the first distinctively Labour imprint on Britain's industrial and financial structure since the heady days of 1945–51',[12] its purpose and justification ran counter to the party's traditions and current inclinations.

This departure was underlined by the Government's position on whether the IRC should retain any assets acquired from the private sector. The clear expectation was that any such assets would fairly shortly be sold, at a profit. Indeed, the Government stressed that such a turnover would increase the impact of the organisation by allowing it to put its resources to work in more situations. The IRC was explicitly not to be a state holding company and its activities were not to be seen as 'back door' nationalisation or creeping socialism — as one junior minister expressed it, 'the purposes of the Corporation are rather not to encourage Socialism to creep but to encourage private enterprise to gallop'.[13]

It is notable that, in the House of Commons debates on the IRC, left wing, or even centrist, members rarely spoke and when they did their tendency was to seek to diminish the IRC's importance. The push behind the measure came very much from those in the Labour Party who wished to see the private part of the mixed economy function more effectively. As *The Economist* expressed it, looking somewhat wider than the Labour Party, its instigators were 'for the most part "apolitical men"' – where they were not, they tended to be 'grammar school conservatives'.[14]

FUNCTIONS, CRITERIA AND PROCEDURES OF THE IRC

The principal functions of the IRC were set out in Section 2(1) of the House of Commons IRC Bill. This stated that the 'Corporation may, for the purpose of promoting industrial efficiency and assisting the economy of the United Kingdom or any part of the United Kingdom:

    a) promote or assist the reorganisation or development of any industry or section of an industry; or

    b) if requested so to do by the Secretary of State, establish or develop, or promote or assist the establishment or development of, any industrial enterprise'.[15]

Section 2(1)(a) sets out the IRC's most important and distinctive role, the restructuring function. Section 2(1)(b) was clearly intended to be subsidiary and its application normally implied financial assistance from the IRC. In addition to these statutory responsibilities, the Corporation also acquired the role of giving advice on a variety of industrial situations. The advice was usually sought by the Government but the Corporation's Annual Reports indicate that private concerns also received guidance.

The White Paper which introduced the IRC suggested or implied three criteria which the Corporation should use in discharging its statutory responsibilities. First, it was not to support ventures which had no prospect of achieving eventual viability. Interpreted strictly, this could not have been a very restrictive condition because there must be few ventures which have *no* prospect of *eventually* achieving viability. The IRC itself interpreted its responsibility here more narrowly, referring, for example, to a target of earning an overall commercial return on any of its money disbursed. There was also a significant difference between the IRC Bill, which referred to 'promoting industrial efficiency', and the eventual IRC Act, which referred to 'promoting industrial efficiency and profitability'. The White Paper's wording, therefore, might reasonably be interpreted to mean that no ventures should be supported (financially or otherwise) unless they were thought likely to achieve long-run commercial profitability.

In addition to some profitability condition, the White Paper indicated that the Corporation should have regard to ventures that promised to secure improvements in the nation's balance of payments and/or offered a good prospect of increased employment in areas of high unemployment.

The existence of three not always compatible objectives raises the problem of how they were to be weighted. For example, confronted with a choice between two projects, one with a greater probability of commercial success, the other with a greater probability of substituting domestic production for imports, how should and how would the IRC have chosen? And, if, in fact, it chose the project with less chance of commercial viability, to what extent should an eventual failure of that enterprise be taken into account when assessing the IRC's performance?

In practice, however, this problem is less severe with the IRC than with most public bodies. The authors of the IRC White Paper do not seem to have been in any doubt that the British economy offered many cases of commercially viable reorganisations which were not going forward, either for lack of private sector finance or because of an excess of private sector caution. Thus, finding profitable projects was not seen to be a problem for the IRC; the balance of payments and regional employment objectives merely limited and directed the choices it was to make from within the set of commercially viable projects that was available. In short, the defects of the private sector were thought to be so large that profitable operation of the IRC was possible, even though it might be able to make a better financial return if released from its balance-of-payments and regional employment objectives.

During the course of its operations the IRC itself developed additional criteria by which it judged situations. In its first Annual Report it stated that: 'In assessing any reorganisation proposal the IRC has regard to the importance of the industry in the national economy, [and] the extent to which the industry suffers from structural weaknesses [particularly in relation to its overseas competitors]... '[16] In addition, the Corporation declared that it 'paid particular attention to those industries which can make a major contribution to the development of technology'.[17] These additional criteria do not all have a straightforward and clearcut meaning. Their existence and use, however, serves to reinforce the proposition that the Corporation felt that it had a large field of projects and reorganisations from which to choose. Sometimes it might stress the trade implications, on other occasions it might stress regional benefits or technological advance. On all occasions, except perhaps when requested by the Secretary of State under Section 2(1)(b), it evidently felt bound to put weight on the prospects of commercial profitability.

Most of the reorganisations sponsored by the IRC did not involve the Corporation in extending any financial assistance. The companies involved evidently saw, or were persuaded to see, potential private benefits in the venture. This, in a real sense, was the pure milk of the IRC, what Sir Ronald Grierson, the first Deputy Chairman and Managing Director of the IRC, termed its 'catalytic role'. He described this as involving the Corporation in 'chatting up firms, putting them on a kind of psychoanalyst's couch, talking to them, enthusing them, energising them, putting ideas into their minds'.[18] When successfully executed, the catalytic role did not require the provision of finance so much as the effective transmission of what was hoped to be the IRC's superior vision.

In some of its activities, however, the IRC did provide finance. It was endowed with £150 million (worth about £750 million in terms of 1982 money values) largely on the argument that 'you might run into situations in which, after all the persuasion has been applied, there would finally be some possibly small financial element that could hold up the desirable development and it would be very useful to have something to prime the pump'.[19] That pump priming was sometimes required was confirmed by Lord Stokes, then Chairman of British Leyland, who, when asked whether the Leyland/BMC (British Motor Corporation) merger would have taken place without a loan from the IRC of £25 million, replied: 'No, I do not think we would have done it. We would never have undertaken it.'[20]

In its first Annual Report, the Corporation noted that 'IRC finance comes into the reckoning when a *commercially sound* project would be impossible or unduly delayed without IRC funds'[21] (emphasis added). The second *Annual Report* observed that the IRC '... only commits funds where this is essential in pursuit of its statutory objectives: it is determined to operate on a commercial basis and it seeks the best return on its funds consistent with its objectives'.[22]

There was clearly some tension between those who saw promise in the IRC's catalytic role and those who wished to arm the Corporation with money to 'prime the pump'. There was even more tension, however, over a third element in the Corporation's procedures and activities. This involved the selection of certain combinations of firms as superior to other possible combinations. Given that reorganisation in a certain sector had been judged in principle to be desirable, the IRC on occasion backed one restructuring at the expense of others; the backing was sometimes very aggressive and 'obviously carried the influence that one would expect an organisation like the IRC to have'.[23] This influence or power was widely held to be unreasonable or unfair because the IRC was acting 'almost like a tribunal without any of the normal judicial safeguards'.[24]

ACTIVITIES OF THE IRC

The four Annual Reports of the IRC list seventy-four projects in which the Corporation was involved in one way or another. Of these, thirteen can be quickly dismissed for our purposes. Five were surveys of particular industries or situations which were requested by government; one was a recommended merger that failed to go through; four derive from the period of Conservative government when the IRC was somewhat in the doldrums and was pressured by the Government to consider favourably applications for finance for re-equipment by companies in the cotton and allied textile industry; finally, three, dating from the same period, did not involve IRC finance and resulted in expression of its support for arrangements made by British firms with foreign companies.

Of the remaining sixty-one projects, seven came under Section 2(1)(b), that is, were the result of requests from the Secretary of State that assistance be given. One possible inference is that these were projects, not directly involving rationalisation, where the Corporation was obliged to act and could not realistically deploy to the full its usual criteria. If this were the case, it would clearly be appropriate to use any commercial failure among the Section 1)(b) cases to criticise the IRC's ability to discover neglected commercial opportunities. On the other hand, a consideration of their outcome is relevant to a fuller assessment of the IRC. It can be argued that the existence of the Corporation made it much easier for the Government to intervene, perhaps in response to immediate pressures, in areas which, on reflection, might have been better ignored. We will, therefore, consider the outcomes of the seven cases.

The remaining fifty-four projects may be taken to reflect unambiguously the judgement of the IRC's management. They may be categorised in a number of ways, for example, by size or to the extent that they were emergency rescue operations. We have chosen to divide them into the following three classes of transactions, details of which are given in Appendix 5.1).

(a) IRC sponsored mergers or acquisitions without IRC finance; this was much the largest class, covering thirty-one projects.

(b) Sponsored mergers with IRC finance, either in the

form of loans or purchases of shares; there were eighteen of these.

(c) Five other cases, all involving IRC loans, but not in connection with mergers or acquisitions.

The basic division here is between projects with and without IRC finance. Such a division allows us to make potentially interesting comparisons, that is, those between an unusual feature of the IRC — the fact that its operations did not normally involve finance — and the more common activities of state investment corporations, whether of the IRC or not, which do involve finance. It should be noted, however, that some of the projects are difficult to categorise on this basis. For example, the original project with Davy-Ashmore did not involve finance but finance was subsequently provided. In some cases, therefore, we have had to use our judgement to determine in which class a project should be placed.

Sponsored Mergers without IRC Finance

This is possibly the most interesting of the three classes, directly raising the question of how the IRC managed to achieve reorganisations without offering direct financial inducements. One possibility is that the IRC's catalytic potential was both real and realised, in that what seemed to be neglected opportunities were made apparent and induced management action. There is, however, another possibility. Horizontal mergers may increase the monopoly power of the combined firms, a development for which the Monopolies Commission existed, in part, to restrain. What the IRC might have represented to the owners and managers of the firms involved was assistance in clearing the Monopolies Commission hurdle.

Some evidence to support this proposition exists in a statement made by (the then) Sir Arnold Weinstock, Chairman of GEC, with respect to the GEC/AEI merger. Having noted that 'the IRC took the initiative in the case of the acquisition by GEC of AEI', Sir Arnold observed that 'it is also true that we were looking for a very long time at AEI'. He then continued: 'I suppose its [the IRC's] principal contribution was it eased the passage of the acquisition, of the mergers, through the Government and removed obstacles that the Government might have put in the way such as reference to the Monopolies Commission and this sort of thing.'[25]

The assistance that might be offered to merging firms in this respect can also be seen in the following detailed and sympathetic analysis of the IRC.

'The most regular contact of all with a department was that over monopolies with the Board of Trade (and after its dismemberment in October 1968 with the Department of Employment and Productivity). The IRC obviously did not want to be seen to be in conflict with the Board of Trade Mergers Panel, whose function it was to process all proposed mergers to help determine whether or not the President [of the Board of Trade] should refer them to the Monopolies Commission. The result was that an extremely close working relationship was established. The Mergers Panel probably informally advised IRC executives that if certain conditions existed in a proposed link-up, or in the industry in which the new firm was involved, then the proposed merger would be unlikely to be referred to the Monopolies Commission, even it if technically came within the provisions of the 1965 Monopolies and Mergers Act.'[26]

In fact, no IRC sponsored merger was ever referred to the Monopolies Commission; in one case (the merging of the trawler fleets of Ross Group and Associated Fisheries) an IRC project which ran counter to an earlier negative recommendation of the Monopolies Commission was permitted to pass without challenge.

These facts suggest that for at least some firms the IRC was *primarily* a means to short-circuit the monopolies and merger legislation. More precisely, the IRC might have been seen as a way of reducing the probability of a Monopolies Commission reference, if only because it was a powerful 'friend in court'. This is not to say the initial IRC sponsorship or interest guaranteed a result, for we do not know how many potential mergers were quietly vetoed by the Board of Trade. If firms did view the IRC in this way, however, it would not have been short of applications from monopolistically-inclined firms eager to merge in the name of rationalisation.

Sponsored Mergers with IRC Finance

The major new issue raised by the presence of IRC finance is whether such finance was 'hard' or 'soft', that is, whether the terms of the loan were worse or better from the point of view of the borrowing firm than could be obtained elsewhere.

In terms of objective market conditions, this is difficult to judge. IRC loans were typically medium-term, unsecured and subordinated. In so far as such loans are available in the market, the rate of interest charged will vary with the circumstances of the particular company. Moreover, the IRC often imposed other conditions on its loans. W. McClelland, a founding member of the Board of the IRC, has commented that the IRC '... never... had a long queue of would-be borrowers because it was known to be an exacting lender, not in the financial terms of the loan, but in the conditions with respect to commercial plans and performance'.[27]

In the present context, however, it is the financial terms of the loan that are relevant and, on *a priori* grounds, it seems highly probable that IRC loans were soft. Some direct evidence to support this judgement is given in the following exchange between Lord Stokes and Mr William Rodgers, then MP, in connection with the merger between Leyland and BMC:

> Lord Stokes — 'We wanted some sign of good faith on the part of the Government of the time and they [really, the IRC] lent us £25m, but you must remember, we paid normal commercial rates on that loan. It was not aid in that sense. It was a commercial loan at what was then roughly the going rate, which was, I think, if I remember, 7½%.'
> Mr Rodgers — 'Which was not a rate you would have got from the City at that time?'
> Lord Stokes — 'I think it would have been difficult.'[28]

Apart from underlining the fact that it is not always easy to define a commercial loan, Lord Stokes does suggest that IRC loans were sometimes soft. Further, if IRC sponsorship was available with or without acceptance of a loan, the fact that some firms accepted loans suggests that the financial conditions attached were better than they could hope to obtain elsewhere. Another possibility that leads to the same conclusion is that the IRC might on occasion have used the offer of finance as an inducement to companies to accept its plans.

On the other hand, the fact that many sponsored mergers did not involve finance suggests either that the IRC conditions were not very much softer than could be obtained elsewhere or that the IRC rationed its loans, limiting them to those firms that could demonstrate a 'need' for them or where they were essential to obtain compliance with IRC plans.

The Five Other Cases

These involved IRC loans for purposes other than the financing of a specific merger or acquisition, though they did not preclude, and possibly encouraged, future mergers or acquisitions by the recipients.

ASSESSING THE PERFORMANCE OF THE IRC

As is discussed above, the IRC used a number of criteria when evaluating the possible ventures known to them. One way of assessing the Corporation, therefore, is to consider the appropriateness of these criteria. Is it socially useful, for example, for public money to be risked in an attempt to make a major contribution to the development of technology? Again, are state-sponsored mergers and rationalisations a promising way, largely free of adverse side effects, of achieving an improvement in the nation's balance of trade? An alternative assessment procedure, and the one that is broadly followed here, is to take the criteria as given and seek to discover how far the targets implied by the criteria were achieved.

In the case of the IRC, it is not possible to use this latter procedure with complete success. Firstly, the IRC's own criteria were complex, potentially involving delicate trade-offs and not easily made commensurable with one another. Secondly, the available data do not permit a worthwhile assessment to be made in respect of some of the criteria. The impact of the Corporation's activities on regional employment patterns was probably negligible but we cannot be sure. Similarly, the Corporation's impact on

technical developments, and the value of any impact, are extremely hard to gauge. More importantly, in the light of the emphasis
placed on it at the time, the consequences of the IRC on the
balance of payments are profoundly difficult to judge. Many other
policy instruments were used, and have since been used, to effect
trade flows. To take a specific example, British imports of ball
bearings have been restricted by a voluntary export restraint since
at least the early 1970s. With the available information it is not
possible to separate the effect on the trade in ball bearings of the
activities of the IRC — through its support for the formation of
Ransome, Hoffman and Pollard Ltd — from the effects of the
voluntary export restraint.

These difficulties having been recognised, it is still possible to
say something about a major criterion by which the IRC should be
judged, that is, the extent to which it contributed to the profitability of British industry. This may be only a partial yardstick of
performance but it is one that the IRC itself decided was a
necessary part of success. In its second Annual Report the
Corporation indicated that its 'client is the national interest where
this is identifiable'. More practically, it went on to declare that the
'real test of the IRC's judgment is the capacity of the companies
which it assists to prosper in world markets and satisfy their public
shareholders'.[29] This statement alone makes it appropriate to
investigate the profitability consequences of the IRC and to use
them as a basis by which the idea of state-sponsored rationalisations can be evaluated.

When estimating profitability it is, in practice, necessary to
confine the investigation to those firms who participated in the
relevant rationalisations. This may not be a complete accounting.
First, assistance, of whatever kind, to one set of firms may have
imposed losses on other British firms; in the last few years, for
example, public subsidies to British Leyland and Chrysler UK
have surely had adverse consequences for Ford UK and Vauxhall
Ltd. IRC ventures may well have had similar consequences for
the rival firms who were not parties to the mergers. It was, after
all, explicit policy to take markets away from foreign rivals; to the
extent that the policy was successful it must usually have done the
same to domestic rivals.

A second reason why our profitability measures may be incom-
plete goes in the other direction: the measures may understate the

impact of the IRC ón the profitability of British industry. The Corporation observed that 'wherever possible the IRC tries to identify and push forward the strategic move which will have the widest repercussions throughout the industry'. Again, 'even a small merger, in an industry which has resisted structural changes, can influence the attitudes of the other companies in the field and thus break the log-jam which has held back rationalisation'.[30]

The possibility exists, then, that IRC-sponsored mergers generated consequential mergers elsewhere, thereby possibly raising profits elsewhere. It is even possible that the consequential effects were so profound that the feedback effects on the sponsored firms were substantial and negative. That is, the galvanising effect of IRC intervention could, in principle, have damaged the long-run relative profitability of the sponsored firms. No doubt this is no more than a theoretical *curiosum* but it does underline the possibility that any measure of profitability that focusses on the sponsored firms may omit important benefits.

Our index of performance is therefore partial and may not fully capture even the profitability effects of the IRC's activities. Nevertheless, it bears directly upon a central issue raised by the IRC: that of whether the Corporation was able, as it persistently asserted, to discover commercially profitable ventures which had been neglected by the private sector.

Even with this narrower focus, the criterion of profitability raises problems of interpretation. These appear most sharply in the sponsored mergers that did not receive IRC finance. As we have already noted, the IRC may have been able to arrange such mergers simply by being able to persuade managements of the existence of hitherto unperceived opportunities for profitable rationalisation. In such cases, it would be appropriate to take the additional profits as a first approximation of social gain and to regard them as an indication of IRC success. But it is also possible, at the other extreme, that the IRC served as a means by which previously willing but previously frustrated monopolists evaded the Monopolies Commission. At this extreme, the IRC might have achieved no rationalisation whatsoever but all of its ventures might have been highly profitable because of the increased monopoly power of the sponsored firms. Hence, the use of private profitability as an indicator of achievement would bias the results in favour of the IRC, perhaps substantially so.

When IRC finance is involved, a second source of bias appears, stemming from the possible softness of IRC funds. If one group of firms gets cheap finance, it would not be surprising if they also enjoyed relatively high profits. The importance of this bias will depend upon the softness of the terms and the size of the loan relative to the assets of the borrower, and in the case of the IRC it may not be large. Nevertheless, it pulls in the direction of making our criterion of performance most unlikely to disfavour the IRC.

Measuring Profitability

Information about profitability can be obtained either directly through accounting data, the economic interpretation of which is often dubious, or indirectly by observing stock market performance. Here, we present an analysis based on stock market performance.

This approach has the great advantage that it eliminates the need for direct assessment of changes in performance following an IRC intervention. The stock market at any time will value shares so that the expected return to holding one share is the same as that from holding any other share. Thus, the shares of companies that are in the future given some currently unanticipated advantage (as supporters of the IRC would regard its interventions) should on average show returns superior to those of companies not receiving that advantage. The approach also raises problems however. Three are of primary importance.

First, there is the problem of knowing what the market has already discounted at the start of the period of observation. For example, if it is known that the IRC is about to sponsor XYZ Ltd, and if the market expects XYZ profits to increase as a result, the anticipation will cause XYZ shares to rise before the event. Even if the IRC is in fact succcessful, there is no ground to expect that the future performance of XYZ shares will reflect that success: indeed, if the market were over-optimistic about the effect of the IRC action on XYZ profits, the performance of the shares might record a failure even though there had in fact been a success.

In an attempt to avoid this problem, we started our observation of share prices at 30 December 1966, roughly concurrent with the passing of the IRC Act but before the first IRC initiative, announced on 22 June 1967. This seems to be a safe procedure because it is not plausible to suppose that before this date market participants could have forecast where the IRC would choose to intervene.

The position with respect to Section 2(1)(b) actions (that is, those requested by the government) is less clear. Although it would have been difficult on 30 December 1966 to anticipate those firms that the IRC would choose to sponsor, it would have been less difficult to guess which companies the Government would instruct it to help. Thus, we cannot exclude the possibility that the 'lame-duck' shares reflected the appearance of the IRC at the start of our period of observation. In this respect, it may be important that the first Section 2(1)(b) case occurred on 17th Janury 1967, some five months before the first voluntary decision of the IRC; it concerned Rootes Motors, which later became Chrysler UK and, then, Talbot UK.

The second problem in using stock market performance occurs because the expected return to a share-holding takes at least two forms, anticipated future dividends and capital gains. To discover whether a share has performed better or worse than it was expected to, it is therefore necessary to take account of both forms of return.

One method of doing so is to reinvest conceptually dividends in the shares of the company paying them which gives rise to a single figure measure of performance. This is, however, a computationally expensive method: here we have chosen to present two figures for each company examined; first, the capital gain on its shares between 30 December 1966 and 28 December 1979 and, second, the algebraic sum of its dividends over the same period. To express performance in two figures rather than one will give rise to problems if, for example, one company has larger capital gains but smaller dividends than another. This problem, with reference to the present sample, is slight. Moreover, the relation between capital gains and dividends is stable for alternative cut-off dates, so that it is unlikely that discounting dividends will substantially affect the relative positions of companies in the different groups examined.

The third problem is the purely technical one of dealing with stock splits, rights issues and the like. Details of the procedures adopted are given in Appendix 5.2.

Finally, there is a problem of comparison, which is not specific to the measures adopted here but is inherent in any study of this type. What we really want to know is whether IRC-sponsored companies increased their profit streams as a result of the sponsorship and as compared with what would otherwise have happened. But obviously this cannot be known, even in principle. The best that can be done is to compare the performance of the sample group of companies with the performance of some similar group which has not received IRC sponsorship.

In the case of stock market performance, an obvious standard of comparison is the *Financial Times* Ordinary Share Index (FTOI). For each of the companies entering that index, calculations were made on dividends and capital gains in the same manner as for the IRC-sponsored companies. From these, two figures were produced. The first gives an index of the capital gains that would have accrued to a £1 investment made on 30 December 1966 in each of the companies entering the Ordinary Share Index; the second gives an index of the sum of the dividends that such an investment would have realised on 28 December 1979.

To the extent that the FTOI is representative, we would expect that the performance of a sample of randomly chosen companies would on average match its performance. If the IRC did succeed in increasing the profitability of its selected companies, or even in merely identifying companies whose merits had not yet been fully appreciated by the market, this should be reflected in a performance of IRC-sponsored companies that is superior to that of the FTOI companies.

SOME RESULTS

The fifty-four projects listed in Appendix 5.1 do not translate into a sample of fifty-four separate companies to be investigated. First, a single company was sometimes the focus of more than one merger or project. Second, some sponsored companies were wholly owned subsidiaries of much larger companies and separate performance figures for the sponsored unit are not readily available. Third, sponsored firms were sometimes private and occasionally foreign, so that usable data are unavailable. What remains after losses for these reasons is a list of thirty-two companies sponsored by the IRC at its own volition, plus five Section 2(1)(b) cases pressed on it by the Government.

Table 5.1 gives some results. They are unweighted average outcomes for the four categories of IRC activity. They suggest that the IRC had a varied success. The sponsored mergers without finance seem on average to have turned out well, on the basis of either capital gains or dividends. When finance was made available, however, the merger activity seems to have produced poor results, again with respect both to capital gains and dividends. The small group of other cases was more successful but the Section 2(1)(b) group evidently performed badly.

Table 5.1
Average Performance of Different Classes of IRC Project

	Capital appreciation	Dividends
19 Sponsored mergers without finance	4.53	1.37
	(6.58)	(0.418)
11 Sponsored mergers with finance	1.30	1.06
	(1.174)	(0.979)
2 Other cases	2.39	1.15
5 Section 2(1)(b) projects	0.98	0.72
	(1.049)	(0.754)
FTOI	2.16	1.13

Note: Figures in parenthesis are sample standard errors.

From a statistical point of view, the average capital gain accruing to shares of sponsored companies to whom no IRC finance was given are significantly different at the 5 per cent level both to the capital gains accruing to companies involved in sponsored mergers with finance and to the Section 2(1)(b) cases. No other differences in either column are statistically significant.

When the company by company results are examined, these average results are confirmed. That is the success or failure of a group is not attributable to extreme results for isolated projects. Table 5.2 shows that among the mergers where no finance was made available nine companies were unambiguously successful, in the sense of outperforming the FTOI on both counts: only five companies were unambiguously inferior. Of the nine successes, some were outstanding by any profit yardstick. Thus, for part of its activities the IRC was clearly associated with financial success.

Where the mergers involved IRC finance, however, the results are very different. Only one of the eleven companies is unambiguously successful, while no fewer than nine are unambiguous failures. The probability of a similar or more extreme result occurring by chance, if success or failure each have a probability of 0.5, is quite low: 0.0654 in a sample of eleven and taking account of the opposite extremes (that is, to have observed nine or more successes).

Further, if an attempt is made to relate performance to the amount of financial assistance from the Corporation, the results are, if anything, worse. For example, the British Leyland merger involved the largest amount of assistance and was, by our criteria, the worst failure. It is not easy to compare the different packages of financial assistance because the IRC sometimes made loans and sometimes provided equity but a reasonable rough judgement is that the greater the assistance the less likely would be eventual profitability.

It is worth noting, however, that the financial judgements of the IRC may not always have been wrong. Implicitly the Corporation may have judged the Section 2(1)(b) cases adversely and the outcomes certainly support such a judgement.

Before conclusions are drawn from the results in Tables 5.1 and 5.2, it is appropriate to consider three criticisms that might be made of our procedure. First, it might be argued that the FTOI is too broad an index against which to compare the outcome of the IRC projects. It is certainly true that the latter tended to be in a relatively narrow range of industries. Might it, therefore, not be more appropriate to compare them with an index that captures just that narrow range?

It is by no means obvious that this is an appropriate procedure. The IRC was not instructed, explicitly or implicitly, to concentrate on certain industries. Its choices must therefore have reflected its judgements as to where it could make the best impact. If it had concentrated on relatively unsuccessful industries, but within those industries had done relatively well, its activities could still have been consistent with failure. Thus, if, as a result of the IRC, more money was invested in generally unprofitable sectors it would not necessarily have been socially beneficial, even if the

Table 5.2
Performance of Individual IRC-sponsored Companies

Company	Capital appreciation	Dividends
Sponsored mergers without finance	£	£
Amalgamated Power Engineering[a]	2.22	1.71
BICC	1.76	0.86
BOC	1.84	1.81
British Rollmakers	1.20	1.79
BTR	5.57	1.12
Coats Patons	1.14	1.14
Davy-Ashmore	4.91	2.07
Dobson Park Ind.[b]	2.85	1.80
Dowty Group	5.37	1.16
Dunford and Elliott[d]	2.46	1.06
GEC	8.04	1.23
GKN	1.54	1.20
Hawker Siddeley	3.88	1.34
International Compressed Air	1.71	1.11
Peglers Hattersley	1.78	1.59
Portals Holdings	1.84	0.86
Racal Electronics	30.38	2.09
Reyrolles Parsons	1.26	0.65
Rowntree Mackintosh	6.35	1.36
Sponsored mergers with finance		
Allied Textiles	1.27	1.20
British Leyland	0.03	0.27
Clarke Chapman[d]	4.57	3.87
Geo. Kent[d]	0.64	0.44
Klinger	0.83	0.46
Lucas	1.08	1.07
Plessey	1.44	0.95
Ransome and Marles (RHP)[c]	1.26	1.00
Steel Group[d]	1.66	0.78
The Weir Group	0.79	1.06
Whessoe	0.70	0.61

additional money earned a higher return than that prevailing in the sector.

In general, if one sector is earning 10 per cent and another is earning 5 per cent it is not obviously right to channel extra

Table 5.2 cont'd

Company	Capital appreciation	Dividends
	£	£
Other cases		
Laird Group	2.43	0.97
Spirella	2.35	1.34
Companies assisted under Section 2(1)(b) of the IRC Act		
Peter Dixon[d]	2.81	1.90
Reed Paper	0.86	0.91
Rolls-Royce	0.24	0.15
Rootes Motors[d]	0.43	0
Samuel Osborn[d]	0.55	0.65

[a] Amalgamated Power Engineering was formed from W. H. Allen and Bellis and Morcom. This is no clear indication as to which of these is the dominant partner. If W. H. Allen is treated as dominant, the relevant figures are (capital gain first) £2.39 and £1.82; while, if Bellis and Morcom is so treated, they are £2.05 and £1.60. The figures in the table are arithmetic averages of these.

[b] Dobson Park Industries was formed from Dobson-Hardwick and Wm Park but there is no clear indication of which is the dominant partner. If Dobson-Hardwick is taken to be dominant, the relevant figures are £3.37 and £2.14; while, if Wm Park is taken to be dominant, they are £2.23 and £1.45. The figures in the table are arithmetic averages of these.

[c] The IRC action with respect to Ransome & Marles was to use the company as a basis for the formation of RHP by acquisition of Pollard Ball and Roller Bearing and Hoffman Manufacturing. Ransome & Marles has therefore been entered in the Table. Similar calculations for Hoffman Manufacturing give £2.44 as the final value of £1 invested and dividends of £1.11. However, Pollard gives £3.89 for final value and £2.09 for dividends. According to the IRC's *Statement on the U.K. Ball and Roller Bearing Industry*, Pollard announced on 8 April 1969 that it had agreed with Skefco that Skefco should acquire a 15.6 per cent interest in Pollard by subscribing for new shares at a price (to quote the IRC) 'considerably above the then market price'. The IRC then supported Ransome & Marles in an offer for Pollard later in the month. The need to compete with the Skefco offer may explain the vastly superior performance of an investment in Pollard in 1966.

[d] Company was itself acquired during the period of observation. Details are given in Appendix 5.1. The figures to the final date in all such cases are obtained by investing in the successor company the market value at the time of the merger of the original £1 invested.

resources to the latter. By the same token, if the IRC had concentrated on the highly profitable industries, but had done less well there than was typical, it would not be good evidence that its activities constituted failure. Our preferred indicator, therefore, is a broad one. In recognition of the fact that some might not agree, however, we did look at the performance of some of the disaggregated *Financial Times* share indices over the period 1966 to 1979.

The performance of the capital goods' index was roughly the same as that of the all-industry index; there were temporary divergences but there was nothing sufficiently large to affect the conclusions drawn from the comparisons using the FTOI. We also plotted the performance of the *Financial Times* index of the mechanical engineering sector (and its previous incarnations). It tended to do somewhat less well than the other indices but the use of it rather than the FTOI would not have significantly affected our earlier conclusions. In particular, the mergers not receiving finance would have remained generally profitable and the others would still have done badly. We therefore conclude that plausible alternative indices, whose use we would not advocate anyway, do not in practice affect our broad conclusions.

A second objection to the above conclusions drawn from Tables 5.1 and 5.2 is that they treat each of the mergers as having a similar importance to the companies concerned, which was clearly not the case. Thus, the merger involving Hawker Siddeley and Brook Motors was relatively unimportant and is unlikely to have made a big impact on the whole group's subsequent performance. It follows that it might be misleading to use the group's performance as an indicator of the success of the merger. In contrast, some of the other mergers involved amalgamations of firms of roughly equal size, so that the fortunes of the combined group do reflect the merger. This is a fair objection in our view and it implies that the above conclusions do not necessarily indicate the extent to which the IRC was able to identify and associate itself with relatively successful management teams.

A third criticism of our procedures would reflect the assertion that privately arranged mergers of the late 1960s and early 1970s were generally financial failures. Within this perspective, it has been suggested that a fairer test of the IRC would be to compare the results of its sponsored mergers with those of privately arranged ones. This suggestion does not appear to us to have merit. If mergers indeed are generally a mistake, there seems little point in the state encouraging even more of them. This is so even if the state's (bad) decisions are less bad than those made in the private sector.

Finally, a fourth objection is that our procedure of starting all of our observations on 30 December 1966 is unfair to the IRC. This date was adopted, it will be recalled, in order to avoid a possible source of bias *against* the IRC: if the initial share price observed contains an anticipation of an IRC intervention expected to be good for the returns to the shares of the company concerned, our test procedure will fail to pick up that beneficial effect. It was suggested to us, however, that many of the cases involving IRC finance had displayed a marked deterioration between 30 December 1966 and the date of the IRC intervention, so that if our results had been calculated from that low point, the IRC's performance would have appeared in a much better light.

In order to check this possibility, we obtained share prices for each of these cases at three monthly intervals up to the date of the IRC intervention. Inspection of these and comparisons with the movements of the FTOI did not support the suggestion that our results would have been substantially different, had we used an alternative starting date or a different date for each company a given number of months prior to the announcement of IRC involvement.

Returning to the results of Tables 5.1 and 5.2, it seems clear that there was a marked difference between the IRC-sponsored mergers that involved finance and those that did not. In some respects this result might be taken to vindicate those who, while supporting the principle of an IRC, were sceptical of the desirability of providing it with money. Sir Ronald Grierson was perhaps expressing this view when he said: 'When I was asked to take on the IRC the Government had already decided to equip it with £150m. I did not at the time see clearly what the use of this money was, nor indeed that a catalytic organisation like the IRC necessarily required any money.'[31]

The general lack of success of these projects involving finance seems well established. The evaluation of the other mergers, however, must remain more ambiguous. One interpretation is that the IRC ably discharged its catalytic function, identifying and achieving useful reorganisations. A second interpretation is that the profitable possibilities had already been identified by the participants but had not been acted on because of the fear of a referral to the Monopolies Commission. This second interpretation has two variants. The first possibility is that the resulting mergers would have produced only monopoly profits and no social gain (indeed, a social loss). In this case the existence of the Monopolies Commission had produced a socially desirable situation until the IRC persuaded the Board of Trade otherwise. The second possibility is that the resulting mergers would on balance have produced some social gain (with or without additional monopoly profits) but that the prospect of a monopoly investigation had inhibited reorganisation. In this case the value of the IRC was to reduce the deleterious effects of the monopoly legislation. As an example, we know from Sir Arnold Weinstock's testimony that GEC had previously considered taking over AEI and that they regarded the IRC's main assistance as being one of eliminating a monopoly reference. We also know that the merged group has been highly profitable. The material presented here, however, does not indicate whether that performance was the result of greater efficiency or greater monopoly power. As a consequence we cannot know whether the IRC's role in this case was socially beneficial or socially harmful.

The overall conclusion must be that, judged by our criteria, one type of IRC activity, that of encouraging mergers without providing finance, produced results that are consistent with success. The 'success', however, is by no means well established, in that it could be the result of diminished competition and greater consumer exploitation. The other main type of IRC activity involved the provision of finance, and in this respect the Corporation was a more typical industrial intervention agency. Our results indicate that in this capacity the IRC was unsuccessful.

Acknowledgements

We are grateful to Steve Ambler for his intelligent research assistance at the start of the project, of which this paper is a result, and also to Dick Baldwin for gathering data and calculating the results for sponsored mergers without finance.

NOTES AND REFERENCES

1. 'Industrial Reorganisation Corporation; First Report and Accounts', *Parliamentary Papers, 1967/8 Session* (London: H.M.

Stationery Office, 1968) Vol. 24, p. 6, hereafter cited as IRC First Report.

2. *Parliamentary Debates (Hansard)*, House of Commons, 16 October 1966 (hereafter cited as *Hansard*); *House of Commons Official Report, 1966–7 Session* (London: H.M. Stationery Office, 1967) Vol. 743, col. 218.

3. *The Industrial Reorganisation Corporation* (London: H.M. Stationery Office, 1966) Cmnd 2889, p. 2.

4. 'Public Money in the Private Sector', 6th Report from the Expenditure Committee, *Parliamentary Papers, 1971/2 Session* (London: H.M. Stationery Office, 1972) Vol. 27, p. 234.

5. IRC First Report, p. 5.

6. *The Industrial Reorganisation Corporation, op. cit.*, p. 2.

7. *Ibid.*

8. *Ibid.*

9. Michael Stewart in the House of Commons debate, *Hansard*, 16 October 1966, col. 222.

10. *The Industrial Reorganisation Corporation, op. cit.*, p. 3.

11. Michael Stewart in *Hansard, op. cit.*

12. *The Economist*, London, 29 January 1966, p. 425.

13. Harold Lever in *Hansard*, 1 February 1967; *House of Commons Official Report, op. cit.*, Vol. 740, col. 659.

14. *The Economist, op. cit.*, p. 426.

15. 'The Industrial Reorganisation Corporation Bill', in *Parliamentary Papers, 1966/7 Session* (London: H.M. Stationery Office, 1967) Vol. 4.

16. IRC First Report, p. 6.

17. *Ibid.*

18. 'Public Money in the Private Sector', *loc. cit.*, vol. II, p. 261.

19. Sir Eric Roll in *ibid.*, p. 262.

20. *Ibid.*, p. 199.

21. IRC First Report, p. 7.

22. 'Industrial Reorganisation Corporation; Second Report and Accounts', in *Parliamentary Papers, 1968/9 Session* (London: H.M. Stationery Office, 1969) Vol. 33, p. 9, hereafter cited as IRC Second Report.

23. Sir Ronald Grierson in 'Public Money in the Private Sector', *loc. cit.*, Vol. II, p. 262.

24. *Ibid.*

25.   *Ibid.*, p. 273.

26.   S. Young and A. V. Lowe, *Intervention in the Mixed Economy* (London: room Helm, 1974) p. 99.

27.   W. McClelland, 'The IRC 1966–71: an Experimental Prod', *Three Banks Review*, Edinburgh, June 1972, pp. 32–42.

28.   'Public Money in the Private Sector', *loc. cit.*, vol. II, p. 195.

29.   IRC Second Report, p. 8.

30.   IRC First Report, p. 7.

31.   'Public Money in the Private Sector', *loc. cit.*, vol. II, p. 261.

Appendix 5.1

The Fifty-four Relevant IRC Projects and the Section 2(1)b Cases

Where a merger occurs, an arrow points from the company that ceased to survive and towards the surviving company. Where this is unclear, the companies are separated by a stroke '/'. The date by each transaction is the 'publication date', listed in the IRC *Annual Reports*. More detailed information is available from that source. Where finance was involved, the amount is indicated (in millions of £) after the transaction.

Companies selected as 'IRC sponsored' are indicated by '*'. Where a company has been sponsored twice, the second occasion is indicated by '**' and so on. Private or unlisted sponsored companies are indicated by 'P' or 'U'.

Sponsored Mergers without Finance

28/9/67	AEI → GEC*
24/10/67	Hadfields → Dunford & Elliott (Sheffield)*
10/1/68	West Riding Worsted & Woollen Mills → Coats Paton*
13/1/68	Edwards High Vacuum International/the British Oxygen Co.* (Finance to BOC 5/68 2.5M)
18/1/68	W. H. Allen Sons & Co. (and) Belliss & Morcom → Amalgamated Power Engineering*
6/2/68	Davy-Ashmore* Acquisitions
4/68	Broom and Wade (and) Holman → the International Compressed Air Corp.*
8/68	Armstrong Whitworth (Metal Ind) → Davy Ashmore**
9/68	English Electric Co. → the General Electric Co.**
11/68	Harland Engineering → the Weir Group*
11/68	Sigmund Pulsometer Pumps*/Plenoy & Son Ltd*
12/68	Johnsons Rolls → British Rollmakers Corp.*
1/69	Weir Group**/Studebaker → Worthington Inc. (Worthington-Simpson)

1/69	Controls & Communications → Racal Electronics*
2/69	Newman Hender → Pegler Hattersley*
3/69	R. H. Windsor → Guest Keen & Nettlefolds*
3/69	Bruce Peebles → Reyrolle Parsons* (Finance later stand-by 4M 4/69)
3/69	Dobson Hardwick ⎫ → Dobson Park Industries* William Park & Co. ⎭
4/69	Ross Group ⎫ → British United Trawlers* (U) Associated Fisheries ⎭
4/69	Rowntree & Co. ⎫ → Rowntree Mackintosh* John Mackintosh & Sons ⎭
5/69	Fletcher & Stewart ⎫ Richard Sutcliffe ⎬ → Richard Sutcliffe* A.G. Wild & Co. ⎭
6/69	Bonser Engineering → Dowty Group*
7/69	BICC* Acquisitions
7/69	Supertension Cable Divisions of Pirelli/Enfield Standard → BICC
9/69	BTR ⎫ → BTR* Leyland and Birmingham ⎭
10/69	Airmec-AEI → Plessey*
11/69	Super Oil Seals → Aeroquip* (U)
12/69	Reavell & Co. → International Compressed Air Corp.**
1/70	Brook Motors → Hawker Siddeley*
4/70	Permutit Co. Ltd → Portals Holdings Ltd*
5/70	Gateshead Division Booker McConnell → Ingersoll Rand*

Sponsored Mergers with Finance

22/6/67	Elliott Automation → English Electric (→ GEC) 15M
6/12/67	Acquisition by Nuclear Enterprises* (U) of Nucleonic Instrument Activities from EMI, Hayes and Wells, Elliott Automation and Baldwin Instrument Co. 0.6M
17/1/68	Leyland and BMC → Brit. Leyland Motor Corp.* 25M
22/3/68	Whessoe Acquisition* 3.5M
6/68	Cambridge Instrument → Geo. Kent* 6.5M
7/68	Nuclear Reorganisation 0.41M
1/69	IRC offer for Brown Bayley Ltd 5.8M
4 & 5/69	Formation of RHP* 9.4M
1/69	Donside Paper Mill → ⎧Reed Paper Corp. ⎨Bowater Paper Corp.
2/69	Clarke Chapman* Acquisitions 2m
4/69	H. F. Hartley → Allied Textiles* 1M
7/69	Osborn-Hadfields Steel Founders Ltd → the Weir Group*** 1.25M
9/69	Priestman Bros → Steel Group* 1.5M
11/69	Lucas* Acquisition 3M

12/69	Ferranti Numerical Control Activities → Plessey** 3M
1/70	Klinger → Qualitex* 2M
5/70	Miles Roman* Acquisition (P) 0.211M
6/70	John Thompson → Clarke Chapman** 5M

Other Cases

7/69	Loan to Davy Ashmore*** — 'Serious overrun on major contract' — Total 5M, IRC share of which 1.2M
3/70	Loan to Marwin (Holdings) for expansion in production of numerically controlled machine tools 1.5M
6/70	Loan to British Leyland** to purchase machine tools 10M
6/70	Cammell Laird Reorganisation → Laird Group* 6M
6/70	Spirella* Restructuring of household textile ind. 1.3M

Section 2(1)b

17/1/67	Rootes Motors/Chrysler		
1/2/68	Reed Paper Group	1.5M	Paper
7/68	Peter Dixon	0.35M	Paper
2/70	Samuel-Osborn & Co.	1.75M	Steel
5/70	Rolls-Royce	10M	Aero Engines
5/70	Herbert-Ingersoll Loan	2.5M	Machine Tools
12/70	Kearney and Trecker	0.3M	Machine Tools

Appendix 5.2
Calculating Stock Market Performance

The basic calculation is to discover the number of shares in the company that could have been purchased with £1 on 30 December 1966. The dividends accruing to that number of shares until 31 December 1979 is then summed to give the dividend figure recorded in the tables and the price at which that number of shares could have been sold at the later date gives the final value of £1 invested.

However, the original number of shares may change due to issues of scrip or of rights. Such issues are always taken up for purposes of the calculation and, if a monetary payment is required of the shareholder, this is obtained by (conceptually) selling just sufficient of the existing holding to realise the necessary cash.

For example, suppose that a rights issue offers R shares per ordinary share already held and at a price P_r. The base shareholding at this point consists of X shares with a market price of P_m. Then to buy the XR shares offered, it is necessary to sell Y of the base holding where $XRP_r = YP_m$.

Then the net additional number of shares is given by the difference between the number purchased under the rights issue and the number sold to finance their acquisition:

$$\Delta X = XR - XR.\frac{P_r}{P_m} = XR(1 - \frac{P_r}{P_m}).$$

Thus, after the offer has been taken up, the number of shares in the holding is:

$$X + \Delta X = X + XR(1 - \frac{P_r}{P_m}).$$

This is the base number for which dividends are not calculated and the number that will be conceptually sold on 31 December 1979.

An issue of shares requiring no payment by the shareholder directly increases the number of shares in the holding and requires no further calculation. If S shares are issued for each of the X already held, then the new base number is $X + XS$.

When a sample company is acquired, the basic procedure is to continue the calculation to 31 December 1979 on the basis of the acquiring company's dividends and share price. Thus, if the acquiring company offers Z of its own shares for each share in the sample company, the new base is ZX shares of the acquiring company and dividends and capital gains to this holding are calculated from the date of acquisition. Where the acquisition is with cash, the cash is converted into shares of the acquiring company at the price of its shares prevailing on the last business day of the month in which the acquisition becomes effective. If shares of a third company are involved, or loan stock or some other financial instrument, this is sold on the last day of business of the month in which the acquisition becomes effective and shares of the acquiring company purchased with the proceeds.

Data on dividends was obtained from the *Stock Exchange Year Book*, London, for years to 1968. From 1968 on, the Extel *Yearly Dividend Record* was used.

CHAPTER SIX

Sweden: Problems of Maintaining Efficiency Under Political Pressure

Gunnar Eliasson and Bengt-Christer Ysander

Industrial policy can work in two different directions. It can be oriented towards improving the market process by stimulating competition and making price signalling more reliable, thereby leaving decisions regarding investments and production in the hands of the firms. The other approach consists of direct interference in the micro-decision machinery of industry through legislation, controls or direct ownership.

Swedish policy towards manufacturing used to be almost entirely of the first, anti-monopoly, kind. But, since the end of the 1960s, Swedish industrial policy has moved in the second direction and the creation of Statsföretag (SF) can be viewed as part of this change.

Swedish industry entered the post-World War II period in an extremely favourable position. Modern and intact industrial production machinery driven by cheap hydro-electric power could supply much needed investment goods to the war-damaged countries of Europe. At the same time Swedish basic raw materials — iron and wood — enjoyed rising prices. These advantages were reflected in a fast generation of resources, a high proportion of which was reinvested, producing an exceptionally fast growth of gross national product (GNP). The Swedish policy orientation until the end of the 1960s was in fact rather to check strongly expanding industrial investments to make room for activities considered socially more desirable, like public sector growth or residential construction.

From the peak of the Korean boom, however, the competitive situation of Swedish industry began to deteriorate. New competi-

156

tion emerged in Europe, America and the Pacific which resulted in falling price trends for Swedish staple goods. The downward trend was temporarily halted by an investment boom in the late 1950s and the early 1960s. Trade liberalisation, economic integration in Western Europe, the lifting of internal war-time restrictions on and impediments to industrial investment and construction were driving forces behind a revival of growth through the middle 1960s.

During this period of industrial expansion and fast productivity increase the Government did little to influence the direction of industrial development. The industrial policy strategy was to facilitate structural change by smoothing its social effects. Government and unions aimed at subjecting the manufacturing sector to further competitive pressure while concentrating on redistributing the rapidly growing output through increasingly ambitious public budgets.[1] Profits and losses remained with industrial owners and business tax rules were generous as long as profits were reinvested in industry. A tight fiscal policy that diverted resources to public sector growth, combined with a union policy of equalising wage levels from below across firms, regions and industries (the so-called 'solidaric' wage policy), served to pressure manufacturing firms into increasing productivity — or going out of business. An *active labour market policy*, directed towards regional pockets of unemployment created by this squeeze, at the same time helped to speed up geographical and professional mobility. These policies included retraining as well as financial stimuli for workers to move geographically. Emphasis, furthermore, was on internally financed expansion within big firms favoured by generous fiscal write-off rules, while a tougher tax treatment was accorded the small businessman who tried to keep his business within the family.

Around the mid-1960s the growth effects of the investment boom had petered out. New international competition was on the increase and the ongoing deterioration of the competitive position of Swedish basic raw-material industries again became visible. With hindsight the mid-1960s can be said to mark a change for the worse in trends for Swedish industry.

Other producing sectors had shown a quite different development. The normal growth in demand for education, health care and old-age security that comes with an increased standard of living had been further stimulated by increased subsidy programmes. Since the production of these sectors was almost 100 per cent in the public domain this meant strong growth in the public sector. In this way, a dual economy was created with a decentralised and privately organised manufacturing sector producing internationally traded goods contrasting with a centralised social service sector.

There were also other sectors that were, to a great extent, in the public domain. The construction sector was strongly influenced from the demand side by government housing subsidies and by a growing share of local government and cooperative ownership of residential buildings. After World War II, the credit system was used more strongly to divert household savings to other uses than manufacturing investment. Formally under private ownership, the banking system, through regulations and controls, came to be more or less in the public domain. Public control of the credit system was further enhanced in 1960 by the creation of a supplementary pension scheme (the ATP system) with a huge funding arrangement (the AP funds). The three initial funds were later supplemented with a fourth, designed to operate as part of a new industrial policy strategy by direct acquisition of shares in companies. This huge financial institution (the four funds) was imposed upon a highly regulated capital market. As a consequence the AP funds, to a large extent, became the main source of cheap (below the market interest rate) finance for the housing sector.

With the continued integration of the Swedish economy with the other economies of the Organisation for Economic Cooperation and Development (OECD) in terms of trade, production and investment, however, a parallel financial integration followed that began to make itself felt towards the middle of the 1960s. Fiscal and monetary policy making in Sweden was no longer solely a domestic issue.

From the late 1960s, the still growing social and redistributional ambitions were thus straining the resources of an industrial engine whose conditions were deteriorating both internally and externally. Politicians and professional economists alike, however, both seem to have been largely unaware of this at the time.

Two alternative ways of responding to changing economic conditions were available to the government in principle — if indeed it wished to react. The old policy of *market support* could be both modified and strengthened to create a more favourable climate for new and aggressive industrial ventures. The alternative was a *selective industrial policy*, that is, more central government involvement in the production machinery and less reliance on the self-regulatory mechanisms of the markets.

The market support policy would probably have required a major restructuring of the capital market and an improvement in the relative benefits allowed for private share owners. The combined effect of accelerating income taxes and tax laws that favoured profit flow-back of capital gains and reinvestment at the expense of dividend distribution worked well during the favourable conditions of the 1950s. Relative — as well as absolute — price development was then quite stable and predictable and investment went, as it should, to those industries where profits had been generated. In the new, changing, competitive situation, however, the same system began to pull the growth machinery into reverse. Cash flows — later reinforced by subsidies — were channelled into long-term losers like the iron mines and the steel and shipbuilding industries.[2]

To provide resources for the needed industrial restructuring, the expansion rate of the public services would probably have had to be moderated. The growth of public consumption — for example, of 'medicare', education, public transport, city clearance — accelerated in the first two decades after World War II, adjusting upward to the fast GNP growth rate. This expansion kept going and even further accelerated during the slow-down of industrial and GNP growth during the 1970s. In the early 1970s, income redistributional ambitions by way of the income tax system were moreover drastically raised which in later inflationary years led to severe distortions in the capital market.

The Swedish Government, however, opted for the alternative of abandoning piecemeal its general policies *vis-à-vis* the manufacturing sector. To begin with, this consisted of new policy approach measures, explicitly designed to overcome deficiencies in the capital market and perceived restrictions on the supply of industrial finance. These measures could not be said to be part of a consistent policy programme but were, rather, the result of *ad hoc* responses to the current and unfamiliar economic situation. To some extent, official documents of the time do reflect worries about the increasingly competitive international environment. This, however, was by no means the only, or dominant, political concern behind the new policy approach.

Of at least equal importance was the increasing anxiety about the social costs of expansion. Environmental damage, regional imbalances and social distress associated with rapid structural change are emphasised in the documents of the time as the most important reasons behind the policy revision. The new regional policies of the mid-1960s constituted the first deviation from the old Swedish policy model.

The concentration of industrial power and also, possibly, of private industrial wealth resulting from increasing scale and specialisation were also in the forefront of political discussion at the time. Demands for a more direct representation of labour and of the public interest in the boardrooms of private business were frequently voiced from the beginning of the 1970s and eventually materialised in the form of changed legislation.

As part of the new industrial policy orientation, a set of new institutions for more active government intervention and participation has been organised in the following areas: (i) planning procedures; (ii) financial resources; (iii) company laws; and (iv) state companies.

An organisational structure for a central coordination of industrial development, somewhat similar to the French plan, emerged in the late 1960s. In 1969 a new Ministry for Industry was formed out of a separate department already set up two years earlier within the Ministry of Finance (Treasury). Attached to this new Ministry was an advisory industrial council and associated with this were several branch committees making reconstruction plans for the branches of industry most acutely affected by the new international competition. In 1973 this work on detailed studies and sector programmes was incorporated into a new industrial agency (Industriverket). Meanwhile, responsibility for technological and industrial research had been delegated to another new agency, STU, set up in 1968. The development of the organisational structure for industrial policy soon was followed up by a similar structure for regional development, being integrated at the agency level with the labour market policy and supposedly working in close collaboration with its industrial counterpart.

The creation of new bureaucratic institutions, designed to ease the financing of risk ventures into new industrial fields and to support latent innovations until commercial fruition, had already begun in 1967 with the establishment of the State Investment Bank (SIB). Although assumed to operate according to the normal profitability criteria of commercial banks, the SIB was supposed to enjoy a much greater freedom than the banks when it came to evaluation of long-term risks and demands for bonded security. Through a subsidiary, the SIB could also give financial and moral support to socially desirable industrial mergers.

A Special Development Fund (Utvecklingsfonden) was later added to the group to complement STU (a Department of Industry research and development organisation) and the SIB by offering financial support in the early stages of innovative ventures, that is, between research and production. This development fund was formally a part of the industrial agency (Industriverket). Various financial companies were also set up to accommodate the special needs of small business, like 'Industrikredit', 'Företagskredit' and 'Företagskapital'. 'Regioninvest' was later added (in 1976) to support industrial activities in regionally distressed areas and in particular to ameliorate the side effects associated with the aborted 'steel work 80' project. The Government also attempted initiatives on its own. Through SU — a development company set up in 1968 — unexploited industrial innovations were to get a chance of being presented in the market. Another new state company — Svetab — was set up in 1969 to help in establishing new, state-supported, production companies to turn ideas into jobs.

Two general comments may be added here. It should first be understood that access to long-term capital-market bond and debenture finance has been selectively regulated in Sweden throughout the post-World War II period. The capital market has been dominated since 1960 by the huge supplementary pension fund; but high risk investments were offered at the same regulated market terms through the special institutions mentioned above. These institutions could thus be interpreted as an attempt to compensate for a possible tendency towards exaggerated risk-aversion or short-sightedness on the part of the Government's own regulations. It did, however, usually go further, implying a form of selective government subsidisation of the costs of credits.

The second comment has to do with the corporate income tax system in Sweden, characterised by generous fiscal write-off rules.[3] Firms have access to interest-free government (tax) credit, the amount of which can be increased through increases in their level of investment. It is an open question whether firms feel a responsibility to earn a market return on the part of their 'implicit net worth' which is made up of this credit or if they simply restrict their ambitions to earning a return on this book-value of assets. The second case implies that firms lower their internal rate of return standards to adjust on the margin to the interest free credit.[4] Capital market dominance and regulation and the corporate income tax system (with special mention of the investment funds) together represent the major vehicles for government intervention in the resource allocation process in Swedish industry, in terms of the resource flows involved.[5]

One of the first tasks of the new Ministry of Industry was to prepare new legislation requiring public representation on the board of directors of all large companies. Two other pieces of legislation and collective agreements arising out of the experience of the 1960s were to have an important impact on the business sector. One was concerned with the security of jobs, making it considerably harder and more costly for a company to lay off labour. The other dealt with internal decision making in a company, requiring consultation with employees and union representatives before taking any action affecting work conditions and job security.

The Government also chose to enter the business sector directly by forming new companies or taking over responsibility from existing firms. There were some bold ventures into so-called 'future industries'. The most typical were computers and nuclear technology — in particular the state half-interest in Data-Saab, Udd-Comb and Asea-Atom. The Swedish Government shared this hope of picking future 'winners' with other European governments like the United Kingdom, West Germany and France. In retrospect, however, the Swedish ventures, like the majority of similar experiences abroad, cannot be judged as successful. The successful government interventions took, rather, the form of the joint development of complex high technology products, either in the form of a development-purchasing contract or by an institutional arrangement like Ellemtel between LM Ericsson and the Swedish Telecommunication agency.

Having encouraged industrial mergers and concentration, the Government sometimes considered it part of its anti-trust responsibilities to have the public interest represented as shareholders in the dominant firm. This was, for example, the case with the new, private cement monopoly, Cementa, formed in 1969. Similar arguments acccompanied a series of government purchases in manufacturing sectors, considered vital to public health or security. The Government thus has bought a majority interest in the dominant Swedish brewery (Pripps, in 1975), purchased a drug company (Kabi, in 1969), established a state monopoly in drug distribution (Apoteksbolaget, in 1971), and has formed a series of new companies for technical testing purposes — Semico and Statens Anläggningsprovning, for example.

The 1970s also witnessed a sometimes heated political discussion on the nationalisation of the pharmaceutical industries — being, by some, considered the natural sequel to government control of the pharmaceutical distribution system — and, on similar grounds, on the nationalisation of commercial banks. Nothing came of this, however.

The rapid proliferation of state businesses soon made administrative control through ministries appear unwieldy. Potential political embarrassment, furthermore, easily emanated from routine business decisions. Considerations of this kind led, in 1968, to the formation of a government business delegation (Affärsverksdelegationen). In some political quarters the aim was that this delegation should develop into a coordinating agency for all government business activities, irrespective of judicial form and activity. Instead, in 1970, a more narrowly defined entity was formed: Statsföretag AB (SF), a state-owned conglomerate under the direct control of the Department of Industry. The board of SF was almost identical to the earlier delegation. The major part of the government-controlled business companies — twenty-two firms in all — were thus bundled together under one corporate hat. Only the main financial institutions and the fiscal monopolies were excluded.

It was hoped, at the time, that with so much of industrial power under government control it would prove possible to push industrial development into socially desirable areas and regions and to increase the influence of works and unions without having to sacrifice profitability. This hope was built on the hypothesis that private industrial power sometimes creates unnecessary social problems by default or neglect even when socially more acceptable and equally profitable solutions exist. The SF, however, never had a fair chance to test the merits of this argument. Structural problems, barely camouflaged during the 1960s and early 1970s, came into the open during the recession of the late 1970s. SF was forced to accept the role of midwife to governmental reconstructions of bankrupt companies, designed to solve short-run employment problems. A series of new 'national' companies emerged in shipbuilding, steel and textiles (Svenska Varv, SSAB and Eiser) with the government as the controlling party.

Only recently, with Svenska Varv forming a wholly separate group and with SSAB as a portfolio interest only, has SF been stripped of non-business commitments to the extent that it may be able to begin acting as a normally operating industrial group. SF top management has also been trying to obtain special government contract offers for activities in what they call 'special programmes', that is, problem industries.[6]

The new industrial policy did not stop either the Government or private business from making bad investments — ploughing back profits or tax-money into long-term losers such as the steel industry — but the experiences of the 1970s taught everyone a costly lesson and have created an opening for new approaches in the 1980s. What the lesson consisted of and how it was learned is very much the story of SF.

CONGLOMERATE OF PROBLEMS: DEVELOPMENT OF STATSFÖRETAG

When SF was formed in 1970, it ranked immediately as number three among Swedish companies in terms of employment, with 34,000 employees. At the end of the decade it was still the third largest company in the country, although now with almost 47,000 employees. Its importance as an employer was matched by its importance as an exporter. More than half of its sales are abroad, making up some 5–6 per cent of Sweden's total exports. SF was initiated as a normal commercial enterprise although it was expected to show special concern for the social effects of its managerial actions — and the ambition of the ruling social democratic party was to develop it into one of the main instruments of industrial policy. In the public mind SF became closely associated with the financial reconstruction and nationalisation of some major branches of Swedish industry. (Table 6.1.)

Table 6.1
Government Share of Total Employment and Investment (per cent)

	Employment (persons)		Investment (gross)	
	1970	1979	1970	1979
Statsföretag AB[a]	0.9	1.1	1.3	2.0
Other state-controlled stock companies (incl. credit institutions[a,b])	0.6	1.8	0.5	2.4
State business agencies	3.7	5.7	6.9	6.5
State services	6.3	7.5	5.2	5.2
Central government total	11.5	14.1	13.9	16.1
Local government joint stock companies	n.a.	0.9[d]	10.6	7.8
Local government business agencies	1.0	1.2	6.4	4.4
Local government services	14.3	22.3	16.6	11.7
Local government total	15.3[c]	24.4	33.6	23.9
Total Government	26.8[c]	38.5	47.5	40.0

[a] The partition of the state-owned companies has been made possible by the use of data from the publication *Statliga företag* (Stockholm: Liber, 1980). As this source diverges somewhat from the national accounts otherwise used, especially in 1970, the figures should be interpreted with caution.
[b] The figures for 1979 include the newly acquired Södra Skogsägarna, previously a production company belonging to the farmers' cooperative movement in forestry. The figures also cover AB Samhällsföretag, a company created for the employment of handicapped people.
[c] These total figures exclude local government joint stock companies for which data concerning 1970 are not available.
[d] The estimate of employment in local government joint stock companies has been derived from data available at the Association of Swedish Local Governments, while the other employment figures have been calculated using official employment statistics from the National Central Bureau of Statistics.

Backdrop of the Problems: the Swedish Economy During the 1970s

Swedish economic policy of the 1970s will probably be best remembered for badly timed demand management which added to the already existing adjustment problems on the supply side. The decade started as it ended, that is, with stagflation and a rising trade deficit. In 1971, the Social Democratic Government, to correct a growing external deficit, braked so resolutely that, combined with a sudden decrease in housing investment and an equally sudden and unexpected increase in household savings, the economy went into deep recession for two years. The economy emerged in late 1972, however, in very good shape to meet the steep recovery in raw materials demand and prices of 1974.

The impact of the international upswing in 1973–74 was reinforced by the raw materials' boom affecting Sweden's basic industrial resources and was further supported by a very expansionist fiscal policy. Swedish export industries experienced a great profits' boom in 1973–75, present in no other OECD country but Finland. Tight fiscal and monetary policies were applied much too late and huge wage increases were let through in 1975–76, coinciding with a sudden collapse of exports and export prices. To prevent a sudden increase in unemployment at home, the government boosted domestic demand *inter alia* by accelerated public expenditures and by paying the business sector to increase inventories and keep employment at normal figures.

This traditional contra-cyclical policy programme was followed through by the new, non-socialist, government that came into office in 1976. But investments boomed in the wrong sectors. Both the business sector and the Government went on a spending spree, partly misreading the market signals. By further expanding capacity in steel, shipbuilding and the petro-chemical industries, new structural problems were added to old ones. As a consequence, the competitive situation for Swedish industry changed dramatically between 1974 and 1976.

From 1970–74 Swedish manufacturing unit labour costs equalled the OECD average and were some 15 per cent under those of West Germany. Two years later the Swedish figure was 15 per cent above that of West Germany and 30 per cent above the OECD average. To maintain profit margins, Swedish firms priced themselves out of many traditional export markets and over the next few years registered a dramatic downturn in market shares, profits and industrial investments.

The economic situation worsened in late 1976, and 1977 saw a series of devaluations. By this means, the new Government managed to rectify most of the overvaluation of Swedish currency. Before that, however, the Government had felt forced to pull several firms out of bankruptcy by various kinds of subsidies. In fact, during the years 1977–78, Swedish industry 'earned' more by state subsidies than it generated as gross profits. Part of this 'profit crisis' can be attributed to the overvalued currency but a large part of the profitability crisis was more permanent or structural. The major recipients of government cash support were the iron and steel, shipbuilding and, later, some forestry industries. In some cases outright nationalisation was the final outcome. For some of these firms the situation was not only disastrous in the short run but, according to many observers, hopeless in the long term too.

Some firms had by then been caught up by their investment spending mistakes in the mid-1970s. In this way, for example, the Government in 1979 acquired a controlling interest in two wood-processing firms earlier owned by farmers' cooperatives. In the same year, workshops especially adjusted for physically or socially handicapped workers, part of which had earlier been financed by relief work grants, merged into one big company (Samhälls-företag), employing around 25,000 people.

Even without the bad timing of demand management, the Swedish economy would have had trouble adjusting on its own with sufficient speed on the supply side. Decentralised market adjustment had become harder to achieve: labour laws made it very difficult for firms to lay off labour, short of bankruptcy, and tax laws made it hard for expanding firms to attract labour through wage offers. Progressive income tax locked labour into the wrong sectors and corporate income laws locked venture capital into the wrong sectors. The result was that the Swedish economy entered the 1980s with an undersized and wrongly proportioned industrial sector.

Statsföretag Charter

Little or none of this was foreseen when SF was initiated in 1970. Official documents emphasised the managerial efficiency advantages and the political gains of being able to delegate specific commercial decisions to the new holding company. Visions of a new industrial policy, however, reappear in the public objectives set out for the new company which were to attain the fastest expansion consistent with a profitability requirement. Another recurring theme in the documents is the hope that the new company, by the power of its sheer size and capital resources, would be able to fulfil particular social and industrial obligations without having to sacrifice profitability unduly.

The new company was to show particular concern for regional employment and the development of new employee relations and working arrangements and it was to support and spread commercial and technical innovations in the industrial field.[7] Execution and financial reconstruction of whole industrial sectors was a task added later. SF in the 1970s thus had five different roles, as: (i) manager of a business conglomerate; (ii) entrepreneur and industrial innovator; (iii) pioneer in employee relations; (iv) trustee of regional development and employment; and (v) official 'receiver' of businesses in need of overhaul and reorganisation. Its performance in each of these roles will be considered in turn.

SF as Conglomerate

SF was faced with several difficult initial tasks as a conglomerate. Its corporate basket contained a very wide assortment of eggs, some oddly shaped. The spread between sectors is illustrated in Table 6.2 which gives the composition of SF in 1970 and 1979. In terms of employment in 1970, the iron and steel subsidiaries made up almost a third and food and tobacco a quarter. In terms of sales, the importance of iron and steel halved over the period while that of wood processing and building materials doubled. Food and tobacco, engineering and shipbuilding commitments also diminished in relative size while the chemical industry and services expanded. A new block of textile firms was added to the group after 1976. Table 6.2 also shows that the financial importance of the so-called industrial development companies has been negligible and thus not at all in proportion with the hopes and headaches associated with them.

The administrative set-up of SF reflects both its commercial ambitions and special social obligations. Of the fourteen board members, one is the chief executive and one represents the Ministry of Industry. The remaining twelve seats are divided equally between the business community and the unions, four of the latter being chosen by the employees of the SF group. The

Table 6.2
Composition of Statsföretag, 1970 and 1979[a]

	Average number employed ('000)		Sales (SKr. million)	
	1970	1979	1970	1979
The SF group[b]	34.1	46.5	3592	12177
Iron and steel	10.6 (31%)	7.7 (17%)	1485 (41%)	2230 (18%)
LKAB	7.1	7.7	1131	2174
NJA	3.4	−339	56	−
Engineering and			171 (5%)	
electronics	2.3 (7%)	5.1 (11%)	8.1	1167 (10%)
Kalmar Verkstad	1.1	1.0	−	339
Kockums Industri	−	2.2		440
Ship building	4.4 (13%)	−	310 (9%)	−
Uddevallavarvet	2.8	−	257	−
Karlskronavarvet	1.6	−	53	−
Wood-processing building materials	4.3 (13%)	12.4 (29%)	585 (16%)	3028 (31%)
ASSI	4.3	9.4	570	2897
Rockwool	−	2.6	−	743
Chemicals	1.2 (4%)	3.6 (8%)	140 (4%)	1528 (12%)
Kabi	1.0	2.5	118	701
Food and tobacco	9.0 (26%)	7.8 (17%)	762 (21%)	1963 (16%)
SARA	6.9	4.6	357	726
Svenska Tobak	2.1	3.2	405	1237
Services	1.1 (3%)	3.5 (8%)	120 (3%)	697 (6%)
ABAB	0.5	2.1	23	192
Liber Crafiska	−	1.2	−	461
Textiles	−	5.7 (9%)	−	719 (6%)
Eiser	−	5.7	−	719
Industrial development companies and others	1.2 (3%)	0.6 (1%)	48 (1%)	156 (1%)

[a] In parenthesis is the percentage of the whole of companies in which SF holds a half interest without having them as subsidiaries.
[b] After internal group adjustment.

members of the executive staff of the holding company are represented on the boards of the main subsidiaries.

The main task assigned to SF was to disburden the Government of ownership responsibility directly related to the operations of individual firms. After the establishment of a holding company, furthermore, it was thought that it would be possible to distinguish between decisions of a more general kind made by the political decision makers in relation to the holding company and decisions of a more operational character made by the holding company in fulfilling its ownership obligation relative to its subsidiaries.[8] A possible interpretation of these rather vague formulations is that the politicians wanted to be protected from blame for unpopular commercial decisions and wanted to avoid the role of hostage to local employment problems.

To judge from the outside how well SF has been able to fulfil this function is extremely difficult. The politicians' wishes to stay away from down-to-earth operational problems may be more than cancelled by their desire to cash in politically on employment-creating investments. Experience in the 1970s seems to indicate that the problem of balancing immediate concerns about unemployment against ambitions to establish a sound economic footing for long-term economic growth is, indeed, a difficult and politically hazardous one.[9]

Alternatively, however, the instructions quoted above might be seen as a way of protecting managers of the state companies from political meddling. At that time, though, the major state companies concerned voiced no need to be 'protected from' their political owners. They were sceptical both of the need for coordination and of the potential efficiency gains to be had by reshuffling profits within an extremely heterogeneous conglomerate. The non-socialist opposition in Parliament expressed the concern that the proposed holding company might become a means of hiding inefficiency.

Whether SF and its staff (of some sixty persons) have been able to protect its subsidiaries from political and/or competitive pressures in any significant way is impossible to tell. SF management has certainly made use of the possibilities of short-circuiting parliamentary intentions by the internal reshuffling of profits. By transferring profits within the conglomerate, SF — like any similarly structured private group — can avoid paying local taxes and tax and dividends to the state.

By this kind of internal manoeuvring, which is a normal practice within large corporate entities, SF has 'disbursed' at least half a billion Swedish crowns of potential local government taxes and more than a billion of potential state taxes, without reference to either Government or taxpayers. Profit flows may be further aggregated by integrating permanent loss operations with subsidiaries generating handsome profits (as in the integration of Sinject into the Swedish Tobacco Company). Whether, and to what extent, this has gone beyond normal and accepted behaviour for a private commercial firm is hard to know: no comparable private conglomerate exists.

One way of insuring SF from political, non-commercial, influence would be to sell it, as a whole or in part, on the equity market — for example, by accepting private shareholders in the state companies and making exchanges of shares in private and state companies a normal procedure. This would ensure adherence to market rate-of-return requirements. The idea was, indeed, explicitly mentioned as an alternative to the setting up of SF by the Conservatives in 1970, echoed in 1978 by the Royal 'One Man' Commission[10] set up to survey the future of SF and again in a publication from the Federation of Swedish Industries in 1980.[11] There has so far, however, been no official attempt to follow up these suggestions.

Another kind of exchange between private and state business sectors, also aiming at the application of tougher internal rate-of-return standards, might be engineered through the buying and selling of individual firms within SF. So far, SF has acquired many firms but sold few. There is, however, no reason to believe that SF does not want to rationalise its rather varied assortment of production lines. Many of the firms purchased have been taken over by SF unwillingly — and only after political prodding — because they were in bad financial shape and there was a lack of presumptive buyers. Moreover, political and trade union considerations do undoubtedly place considerable obstacles in the way of selling off any part of the state business empire on grounds of bad profit performance.

When operating units are as varied as those of SF, some order must be brought into the organisational maze by discovering what firms can gain by being more closely associated. SF has chosen to build sub-groups, or subsidiary units, designed to exploit technical and commercial potential, while the holding company concentrates on (i) finance, (ii) some organisational matters and (iii) more general policy questions. In this way the wood processing group (ASSI) grew rapidly during the 1970s to become a conglomerate in its own right. Many of the management problems of SF have been delegated to this group.

The same kind of managerial technique has been used in attempts by the Ministry of Industry to reorganise entire sectors of industry, such as steel and shipbuilding. In these cases, it has been a major aim to construct a group with a satisfactory balance sheet — or at least one that appears satisfactory — and, then, as in the case of Svenska Varv (shipbuilding) and SSAB (standard steel), to leave it on its own or, rather, to leave it to the mercy of the Ministry of Industry. As will be seen later, the separation of shipbuilding and standard steel production from SF is the major reason for the movement to better profit performance in 1978. (See Figure 6.2 below.)

Undistinguished Innovator

SF's record of industrial innovation and entrepreneurship is less than impressive. This is true whether one looks at the overall production growth of the group or at the specific accomplishments of the industrial development corporations, that were established by SF to generate and transmit innovative impulses to the rest of industry. Sure enough, new ideas have been launched and new products marketed, some of them with startling success — one example is the new truck developed by Kalmar Verkstad. Another — and financially much more important — commercial success is the pipe tobacco Borkum Riff. With this brand the tobacco company has managed to capture 9 per cent of the American pipe tobacco market which is no small accomplishment. As a result, the Swedish Tobacco Company has been able to pay almost three quarters of a billion towards losses elsewhere within the group. This was especially true after the collapse of the iron ore market: before that, LKAB was the main supplier of golden eggs. These examples, however, are exceptions to the general picture which is characterised by a relatively low level of research and development (R and D) expenditure, by few product developments and by remedial action to patch up the results of loss making.

Official statistics on industrial research and development are notoriously unreliable. The proportion of these costs in the budget of the SF group has been somewhat below the level of private firms in the corresponding branches, however. Moreover, the group's R and D efforts seem to have been directed more towards basic research and process improvements than to market-oriented product developments. Compared with the rest of the business community, SF group companies on average seem to pay more for outside patents and to earn less on patents of their own.

The industrial development corporations Svetab and SU have been involved in regional employment problems from the very start. In this way they became heavily engaged in, and responsible for, a number of small and middle-sized firms, most of which were to become financial burdens rather than development resources. By the time SF took over final responsibility for them, around the early and mid-1970s respectively, each employed between one and two thousand people and they both faced major financial problems. SF managed to untangle their affairs by selling off some of the small firms and by distributing others to the care of more solvent subsidiaries. SU was reconstructed as a small central advisory group focussing on industrial techniques for energy conservation. The investment function within Svetab was decentralised to four regional venture capital companies charged with the task of engaging on a minority basis in innovative ventures within the regions.

It soon became clear, however, that SF could not function as a leader of industrial advance. Too much of its time was used in fighting rearguard actions for industries falling behind. There is a general lesson to be drawn from this. Instruments designed for very long-term purposes should perhaps be kept out of reach from decision makers whose concerns and preoccupations naturally tend to be more focussed on the problems of the immediate future. This was also one of the original ideas behind the forming of SF.

The Model Employer

SF was also charged with special obligations of coordinating and representing the state employers in the business sectors and of being a pioneer in the new methods and arrangements in employee relations. The state, as employer, was expected to give both authoritative interpretations and an exemplary execution of the new laws dealing with labour security and labour participation. Particularly during the last few years SF, by all accounts, has put much effort into educational and experimental activities within the field of personnel relations. Due to the circumstances in which SF has found itself, much of this work has been concerned with finding ways and means of compensating, training and re-employing laid-off workers. Unfortunately, there are as yet no studies of how this activity of SF compares with that of private firms.

Trustee of Regional Development and Employment

From its birth, SF, was charged with special obligations for regional development and employment, in particular in Northern Sweden where most activities in basic industries, like mining, steel and wood processing, were centred. The official goal — or illusion — was that regional interests could be taken into account in decisions on sites and sizes for investment, without any effect on profits.

Reviewing the past decade, there is no doubt that considerations of regional employment have weighed heavily in many of the investment decisions made by SF. It is equally clear that some of these have proved very costly in terms of profitability. Examples have already been cited. By far the most important, however, is the capital sunk into steel and shipbuilding. A combination of employment considerations and over-optimistic forecasts of foreign and domestic demand were the main reasons behind an expansion and modernisation of steel capacity at NJA in Luleå.

In the middle of the 1970s the Government was even on the brink of adding a huge plant to the one already existing — very much against the advice and desires of SF management. This so-called 'steel work 80' project produced great political turmoil in Sweden. Although these plans were finally scrapped, the money put into the northern steel works up to 1978 corresponds to a capital consumption of some 75,000 Swedish crowns per man per year, if the figures carried on the balance sheets are accepted. Swedish shipyards are currently subsidised to the tune of 2,500 crowns per taxpaying household per year. The government-operated shipyards are, however, no longer part of the SF group.

Here again, there are more questions than satisfactory answers.

In some instances SF undoubtedly managed to stave off immediate local unemployment. What SF did to the long-term regional employment situation is, however, far less certain. Nor is it possible to compare the results of the money invested in selective industrial measures with the gains that would have accrued from more general policies, such as regional differentiation of business taxation or of the collective labour fees born by employers.

Structural Surgeon

SF is, no doubt, by now best identified with its role as official receiver and surgeon-general of industrial sectors in need of financial reconstruction. The major examples of this are the reconstructions of shipbuilding, standard steel and textile industries from which emerged the new state-controlled business groups Svenska Varv, SSAB and Eiser. In all three cases the final 'nationalisation' was carried through after a series of earlier supporting measures had failed to put the industries back on their feet. The magnitude of the task and of the money involved was such that responsibility for the major decisions automatically fell back on the Government which used the SF partly as a technical and financial intermediary and partly as a means of unloading a responsibility it did not want. The distinction between being a structural surgeon and a dump for impossible political problems in industry is, therefore, extremely thin. The unloading in 1978 of two of the worse cases — the northern steel plant and the shipyards, to SSAB and Svenska Varv respectively — may, however, indicate the strength of SF top management ambitions to be a commercially viable company.

From the very beginning the new selective industrial policy contained both defensive and offensive ambitions. The offensive ambitions were concerned with finding new avenues for industrial expansion by, for example, funding and transmitting innovative ideas and providing the risk capital necessary for the new ventures and industrial combinations. The defensive purpose was to deal with the social costs of structural adjustment by better tailoring industrial investments to the needs of regions and the wishes of employees as expressed in active participation. The offensive aims were soon thwarted by the turn of events, partly brought about by the Government's own bad timing of demand policy. As the problems created by currency over-valuation, domestic inflation and a profitability crisis grew, so did the clamour for more selective measures and subsidies. SF was a major instrument of these selective measures and had to foot part of the bill.

In spite of the difficulties of evaluating the overall (social and private) performance of SF in terms of stated objectives, the Royal Commission of 1978 expressed its conclusion in the following terms: 'Even though stated objectives and ambitions [about] maximum expansion subject to a profitability criterion', about the 'contribution to industrial expansion' and to 'activities where size, risk and long-term commitments are central' and about employment *et cetera* were not fulfilled, the current economic situation would have been even 'more difficult to control with the earlier organisation of government business activities. It was therefore appropriate to form SF'.[12]

COMMERCIAL AND/OR SOCIAL PROFITABILITY: RESULTS OF STATSFÖRETAG

The SF group provides an excellent example of the intricacies involved in profitability analysis. But what does profitability mean in a group that initially earned large profits from rents on capital that traditionally is not fully (or at all) activated in the books; a group that turned into a heavy and seemingly permanent loser? The best examples are the 'stock of forests' and 'the mine deposit' in the north. How should capital be valued in such a group?

Profit Performance of SF

Due to generous fiscal write-off rules, assets in an average Swedish manufacturing operation as recorded in the books are normally considered to be under-valued compared with the real market value. But this is not so for SF — at least after 1975. Assets in shipbuilding and standard steel operations, net of formal debt, have no market value. SF would in fact have to pay to get rid of some of its assets, at least as long as an employment responsibility was attached.

The standard procedure is to calculate real rate of return figures, as in Figure 6.1, based on replacement values for plant and equipment. One common procedure is to cumulate investments from the past, corrected for inflation and net of depreciation. In Figure 6.1, the rate of return has been calculated in a way comparable to similar calculations for all industry. One curve (SF)

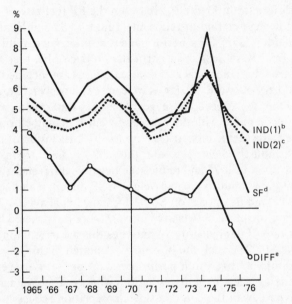

[a] Assets are valued at replacement costs from cumulated, price-corrected investment. Same depreciation rate in denominator and numerator.
[b] Real rate of return of all manufacturing, excluding mining.
[c] Real rate of return, when IND(1) has been reweighted to reflect SF sector composition. Note, however, that mining is not included.
[d] Real rate of return of SF.
[e] SF minus IND(2).

Figure 6.1
Real Rate of Return to Total Assets in Statsföretag and in Total Manufacturing[a]

shows the real rate of return, before tax, on total capital in Statsföretag. This can be compared to the same measure [IND (1)] calculated for all manufacturing. The third curve [IND (2)] gives the same real rate of return for total manufacturing reweighted to obtain the same branch composition as SF. The data on 'SF before

1970' have been calculated from the accounts of all the large firms that were bunched together as SF in 1970.

The official target set for the SF group in 1969 in fact was to expand within a 'satisfactory' profitability constraint. What satisfactory profitability meant was not very clearly stated but the two measures defined above could be used as a reference.

The difference in Figure 6.1 between the SF real rate of return and the reweighted rate-of-return measure for all manufacturing is positive until 1975: SF's performance is quite good until 1975. After 1975 LKAB losses, in particular, reduce SF's real rate of return strongly. Due to lack of data, mining is not included in the total industry measure. As far as we can see, however, there is no evidence in the Figure to suggest that SF was not a well-run company compared with the average Swedish manufacturing firm with the same sector mix, at least up to 1976. Inclusion of mining in total industry figures would probably reduce the positive difference before 1975 and reduce the negative difference thereafter. Mining has a much greater weight in SF than in manufacturing as a whole and its impact on SF performance is heavy.

The rate-of-return curves in Figure 6.1 were constructed by way of a flat rate of depreciation. What does this mean to a long-term loser like SF? The real rate of return calculated in this way tells a sad story of very bad profit performance. Suppose, however, that this is due to a few large investment mistakes. The company will then have to await the end of a slow depreciation process to show good profitability figures, even though current operations are quite profitable. Why not cut the permanent losses immediately through writing off all dead capital? In a company with SF's background of relying on the commercial capital market this would have happened long ago through bankruptcy or financial reconstruction.

This can be reformulated as follows. Suppose all investments in SF have been a complete waste of resources: they have no capital value and should be written off the books.[13] Does SF have an earnings potential after this financial surgery? With no depreciable assets on the books a relevant profit concept is the gross operating profit margin. Does it show a positive contribution and what are the future prospects? Gross operating margins of SF are shown in Figure 6.2. The same pattern appears here. Until 1975 the SF index developed well ahead of the manufacturing average. Then it nose-dives together with the other crisis industries. It does not recover until SF has managed to divest itself of standard steel and the shipyards in 1977 and 1978.

When we know how much the Government paid, the next question to ask is what the Government had hoped to get in return

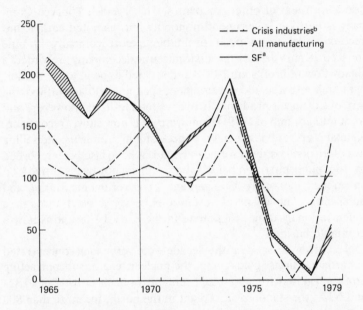

[a] SF profit margins have been measured both in terms of sales and valued added. The difference is, however, negligible.

[b] Crisis industries are defined as mining, steel, forest industries and shipping. There is an interesting accounting device in the shipping profit series. Despite large losses, adding shipping to the crisis industries increases profit performance in the years 1976–79. The reason is probably that ships being built or ships completed but not sold are entered at cost plus a reasonable mark up in the profit and loss accounts; when sold at a staggering loss, they appear as a write-off.

Figure 6.2
Profit Margins in Statsföretag, Crisis Industries and All Manufacturing
(100 = 1970–79 average)

for the money. How much of the money was considered a normal commercial investment and how much was paid to get other policies executed or to get SF to perform special duties?

Winners and Losers

The winners in the post-oil crisis situation are easily counted. When ASSI and LKAB became seemingly permanent-loss operations after 1975, the task of propping up financially was taken over by the tax payers, by the Swedish Tobacco Company and by an odd assortment of other companies. The Swedish Tobacco Company is partly a government monopoly but, as noted earlier, has succeeded in becoming a profitable export company in pipe tobacco. KabiVitrium, the pharmaceutical company, recorded a steady flow of profits until 1978 and seemed to be a future winner, with high research and development spending and a good-looking mix of advanced products. It over-extended itself, however, and went into a slump in 1979[14] from which it is now slowly recovering. Kalmar Verkstad has been very successful in producing and selling heavy trucks. Positive profit contributions have also been recorded by the publishing company Liber. Liber, however, thrives on an implicit monopoly arrangement for government printing and publishing. The chain of restaurants, SARA, went through a tough rationalisation programme in the early 1970s and is now a profitable business.

Net current losses over the decade were very much concentrated in particular firms. Udd-Comb, the nuclear reactor subcontracting firm, accounted for about 200 million Swedish crowns in losses and NJA, the standard steel plant in the north, for more than 800 million. These figures would be much larger if losses from the early part of the 1970s were upgraded to take account of inflation; however, they are peanuts in comparison with the big losers. SSAB (the new standard steel group, including NJA) and Svenska Varv (the new shipyard group), both publicly owned but now separated from SF, generated losses of 670 and 1,650 million Swedish crowns respectively in 1978 alone.[15] For SSAB this amounted to 15 per cent of turnover and for Svenska Varv almost 35 per cent.

Financing Investments

Throughout the 1970s both the value of sales and the book value of capital in the SF group trebled. To expand, SF needed a great deal of new financing. Taken together, for 1971–79 more than 17.5 billion Swedish crowns of external finance was used. 1.25 billion of this went into covering losses within the group, so that 16.25 was available for capital accumulation, of which around 11.5 were investments in buildings and machinery and 3 billion for inventory increases. About 1.25 of the remainder was invested in shares *et cetera*, much of it in connection with the financial reconstruction of the steel and shipbuilding industry. The remaining half billion is accounted for by increases in financial assets and net purchases of new firms.

The amount of real investment sunk into SF is undoubtedly high, even taking into account the capital intensity of its major firms. Again, the investments are very much concentrated in a small number of firms. The main part of investment expenditure was in LKAB, ASSI, NJA, Berol Chemicals and the shipbuilding firm, Uddevallavarvet. The rather unfortunate allocation of part of this investment money has already been noted: throughout the 1970s, and especially during the investment boom in the mid-1970s, more than a billion crowns was sunk into a shipbuilding yard and into a new plant for basic chemicals both of which are still showing a very unsatisfactory return, while more than 2 billion crowns was invested in the steel works at NJA in Luleå. If we accept the book value of 700 million at which NJA was sold off in 1977 to the newly established SSAB, the capital consumption at the steel works in Luleå was of the order of 2.3 billion crowns between 1971 and 1977. The investment boom of the mid-1970s was common to all industry. The major share of the investment boom, however, occurred among the crisis-stricken industries (mining, steel, forestry and shipbuilding), accounting for about 40 per cent of manufacturing investments and in the relatively profitable engineering sector. SF, itself heavily burdened by crisis industries, followed the investment path of the crisis industries but did not cut investment spending enough in 1977, in spite of a much earlier drop in earnings.

Of the financing needed in the period 1971–79, 7 of more than 16 billion crowns were contributed by the state, either in issues of shares or in other forms, while 5½ billion were taken up as loans. Some 800 million crowns were obtained by selling off assets. The wide divergence in the profit performance of the subsidiaries is again evident, with the Swedish Tobacco Company as the leading profit maker, LKAB second and ASSI third. NJA is the great loser. There was a substantial shifting around of profits in the form of intra-group subsidies, together amounting to some 1½ billion crowns over the decade. The dramatic change that has taken place between the first and the second half of the 1970s, however, is the transformation of the principal cash provider of the early 1970s (mining operations) into a long-run problem for the SF group.

Equally interesting is the development of investment spending within the group. There is a perverse relationship between investment and profit contributions. Not only did low-performance subsidiaries receive a relatively higher contribution of total finance for investment in the good years 1973–75 but, during the bad years that followed, the low-performance companies and the big losers have been the relatively heavy recipients of investment capital within the SF group. The internal allocation of investment funds within SF thus exhibits an extreme version of the misallocation of resources within Swedish manufacturing during the 1970s. It should of course again be remembered that most of these 'misallocations' are of the 'special programme' type, the enactment of which, for all practical purposes, has been imposed on SF by the Government and, to our knowledge, often against the will of SF management.

To evaluate the degree of government subsidisation, apart from the 7 billion crowns of direct contributions, it is necessary to know how much of the 5½ billion of loans were 'soft' or specially tailored for the needs of the SF group. It appears that most loans were obtained with the usual commercial conditions in the capital market. It is more difficult to judge to what extent the special standing of SF as a big government-owned group made for more easy access to long-term borrowing than is normal for a private firm. What can easily be calculated is that the outside supply of financing has allowed the SF group to retain a slightly higher formal net worth/debt ratio than has generally been possible for the rest of industry.

Government Contract Offers: a New Line of Business

It is particularly difficult for a publicly operated business to adhere strictly to the profit motive. A firm of SF's size cannot close down an unprofitable plant in a regional unemployment area to protect its profits without generating political turmoil. Nor can the Swedish railroad monopoly (SJ) terminate transport services simply on grounds of an insufficient number of customers to cover costs. Thus, a system of government contracts has been used for many years by the railroad monopoly to finance unprofitable transport services. This idea can be — and has been — extended to cover the employment of a certain number of people in a region or the restructuring of a particular loss company.

The problem for the Government is then (i) to determine what the companies would have done were there no such subsidies and (ii) to determine the need for — say — extra transport or employment services. This is no easy thing. The efficient solution is for the Government to put the unprofitable service on the market as soon as SF asks for subsidies and invite competitive offers from both private and public firms. Competitive bidding between several independent companies is essential for this to work, both in the sense of determining the magnitude of the task and in minimising costs.

It still remains, however, to determine how desirable the activity is from a welfare point of view. How much is the public willing to pay for it? If a market for subsidy payments of this kind is to be more than an accounting device, its social net benefits have to be clearly specified and evaluated.

Actual Swedish practice displays a wide spectrum of such subsidy arrangements. Some examples, like the opening of the new mine of Stekenjokk, seem to fulfil the competitive conditions mentioned. On the other side of the spectrum, however, are many cases where the subsidy was tied to a financial reconstruction or was a straight hand-out to cover current losses. As long as there are no strict rules about the use of the offer system, the appearance of the word in various accounts of subsidies does not really help to delineate what part of total subsidies should be considered as payment for special tasks.

For SF, the contract offer system was formally recognised in the bill to the Parliament in January 1980 (prop. 1979 180:79). At the same time the profitability objectives originally formulated in 1969 were repeated and emphasised. Contract offers had also been emphasised in the 1978 annual report as the best method to compensate SF for non-commercial business ventures urged upon it by the Government.

The money disbursed to SF to take care of defunct companies

suggests that this is very profitable business. SF, however, argues that this is not a fair assessment.[16] For one thing, the assets of defunct companies usually have no value. SF does not want to write them off against its own profits. Second, the salvaging of defunct companies takes an unduly high proportion of management resources and attention away from more profitable activities elsewhere. Furthermore, SF management does not learn very much from such activities.[17] Third, and perhaps even worse, the very fact that SF engages in these activities means that it becomes even more difficult to apply tough, internal profitability standards elswhere within SF.[18] Fourth, many of these activities have no real business future, even after being rescued and reorganised. To engage in such activities SF wants to be well paid.

It is very difficult to assess the merits of such arguments. Any firm with a profit motive will of course charge as much as the market can absorb. So the problem is rather whether the Government is paying an undue amount of taxpayers' money to a select group of workers in defunct companies.

Kockums Industries (making equipment for forestry work), with 1,250 employees and 385 million Swedish crowns in annual sales, received an equity contribution of 235 million crowns and a 150 million crowns loan with conditional repayment obligations to cover losses in 1980–81.[19] The equity contribution amounts to 190,000 crowns per employee for three years, or almost 75 per cent of wage costs for the three years. To pay out that much, a huge amount of accumulated losses must have been hidden away in the Kockum accounts. There was an immediate outcry from the three competing firms in the market. They argued that the Government, by supporting Kockums, was driving them out of business. If any firm should go out of business, they said, it should be Kockums.[20]

The Eiser (textiles) rescue operation is more explicit on the subsidy purpose. The government bill (prop. 1979–80, 79 p. 25 f) stated that 29 million Swedish crowns would be handed out to keep production alive at 'the Norsjö and Sollefteå' plants from 1 January 1979 to 30 June 1980. These plants employed less than 180 people during that period. The subsidy thus amounted to 160,000 Swedish crowns per employee for a period of one and a half years. This is just about the entire wage sum including all additional charges (retirement fees, payroll taxes *et cetera*). The explicit intention was to maintain production.

CUSTOMER VERSUS TAXPAYER: EVALUATION OF STATSFÖRETAG

After this guided tour of the SF accounts, let us return to the crux of the matter: the customer versus taxpayer confrontation. The taxpayers undoubtedly have had to pay quite a lot. What the customer has gained seems quite unclear.

The non-profitable part of the government-invested capital mostly seems to have gone into (i) ill-timed capacity increases, (ii) the covering of losses on current operations and (iii) the payment of various other tasks of regional and industrial policy. In this way, the taxpayer may have had to subsidise inefficiency within government firms, even though there are, as yet, no signs that such policies have undermined the competitive positions of other firms at home or abroad. It is also far from clear to what extent the objectives of the policy, say more secure employment, have been reached. In several of the sectors in which SF is engaged, there have been complaints by domestic competitors about the unfair advantage of the easy financing enjoyed by the state combine. There are, however, no data to sustain or refute this contention.

Achievements

The original aims of SF were (i) to 'achieve maximum expansion under a minimum profitability restriction' and (ii) at the same time to fulfil a series of social objectives, like improving industrial structure, making the regional distribution of job opportunities more acceptable, softening the unemployment consequences of structural change *et cetera*.

The Royal Commission that was set up to view SF's performance concluded that the first objective (i) was not attained[21] and we concur on the basis of our analysis. As for the second ambition (ii) the discussion here will be restricted to the efforts to keep up employment in especially afflicted locations.[22] Our conclusion may be summarised in the following way. The efforts can be evaluated by asking two successive questions: (i) could SF achieve these results by less costly means and (ii) is there a different and socially less costly alternative?

With respect to the first question, SF management has been systematically pushing the commercial profit motive, often against the desires of its owners. This is illustrated by the fact that the really 'terminal cases' (the shipyards and standard steel plant) have been forced out of the SF organisation and the responsibility 'handed back' to the Swedish Government. With standard steel and the shipyards out, SF exhibits a profit performance that is close to other industries with the same sector mix. The data even seem to suggest that SF has been very skilled in obtaining profitable government contracts to reconstruct ailing firms and to solve short-run unemployment problems. If this has been costly for the Government, the problem is one of government competence that should be solved by a more competitive bidding for government contract offers. Given the charter of SF, its internal allocation of resources has probably been considerably more efficient than would have been the case if the same activity had been organised directly under ministerial control. As to whether there is a different and socially less costly alternative, one could consider the following three alternative suggestions to arrangements of the SF type: (i) a selective subsidy programme with no direct management involvement, or (ii) a general cost-reducing, fiscal policy package, simply allowing the non-viable firms to close down, or (iii) stimulating more private competition against SF for government contract offers.

We cannot here present a thorough evaluation of these alternatives against each other and against SF. Our earlier discussion suggests, however, that a selective subsidy programme must be inferior to the SF arrangement. It would in fact mean returning to the situation before SF was organised, that is, having no profit-oriented financial intermediary between the politicians and the production units. In so far as private firms in distress are to be 'socially managed' during the adjustment period, a politically managed subsidy programme is likely to be more costly than a professional management solution. It may slow down or even worsen the adjustment process and, with or without intention, subsidise lenders to, and share owners in, distressed companies as well.

The second suggestion is exemplified by proposals, often put forward during the 1970s in Swedish policy discussion, to combine currency depreciation with regionally differentiated cuts in the payroll tax and to pay out financial inducements to firms for marginal increases in capital investments and employment. With no subsidies and several closedowns of firms, a temporary increase in frictional unemployment would most likely follow before the growth effects begin to dominate. We think that, with hindsight, most political decision makers would now tend to prefer such a solution. It is extremely difficult to evaluate such policies empirically. We have so far neither a satisfactory dynamic theory nor fully tested empirical tools for such an analysis.[23]

In the third suggestion the Government purchases management competence not only from SF but also from private firms. If the SF administrative solution is a viable alternative to the *ad hoc* handing out of subsidies, then it would do no harm to make a more efficient use of management competence in other firms as well by engaging them on a larger scale in bidding for a minimum cost solution to the social adjustment problems. Furthermore, future SF management teams may not be as good as the current one and may prefer to fall back into more comfortable and politically more yielding behaviour. With no competitors to provide a comparison for its performance, SF may, in the longer run, become less efficient. A further check on SF management of course is to put part of SF equity out for competitive bidding in the stock market. This has been discussed[24] and would be a natural continuation of the current SF management philosophy with its emphasis on market solutions for achieving social objectives.

A LESSON TO BE LEARNT

The story of SF and of Swedish industrial policy in the 1970s, as reviewed above, does not sound very edifying to an economist — not, at least, if economic efficiency is the overriding goal. In the Swedish economy, where factor markets are closely regulated and in which almost two-thirds of all disposable money is channelled through public budgets for reasons other than efficiency, a more complex judgement is needed. Applying efficiency criteria to SF in isolation would be unfair and also wrong. It would be equally misleading to polarise our view so that social motives are the only ones that cause government intervention in the business sector. This is why we decided to introduce and analyse SF in the context of direct state intervention in business management activities.

From official records accompanying the new kind of direct government involvement in business management in the 1970s, we learn that it was originally propelled by high ambitions to improve and innovate. From the records of the 1970s, we can read that such involvement became mostly defensive, supporting declining industries in the hope of getting them back on their own feet. Records of success are restricted to a few activities, notably within SF, where efficiency and profitability stubbornly have been pushed as the overriding objective, often against the wishes of the political governing bodies.

The lessons from the SF story in the 1970s are mostly concerned with proper and less proper ways of handling losers. Any industry contains a tail of losers. Any firm of a certain size has a string of both profit and loss operations. Normally luck shifts around over time but, even so, a careful inquiry would probably show that medium-sized and large firms continue with loss-making operations for years, wasting resources that could have been employed more profitably elsewhere.

One reason for this is, of course, uncertainty about the future: by closing down something a future winner may be lost. The special situation of SF is that the company is paid to continue operating plants whose future is deemed completely hopeless by SF management. The tax payer pays for the extra costs to fulfil a social objective. Such government contract offers are not unique to SF or other public bodies. When a private firm enters the subsidy market the intent, however, is to make a profit *above* the subsidy, at least in the long run. The Swedish engineering combine Electrolux has done that several times by moving its own products into the factories of defunct firms. ('Facit' is a case in point.) Conceivably, this could be a prosperous business part of SF as well. Viewed from this point of view, the optimal policy of the Swedish Government should be to put rescue operations on the market, with as many bidders as possible, in order to secure a minimisation of its subsidy costs. Whether intended or not, a major part of industrial policy so far has consisted of disbursing subsidies to impossible operations to preserve employment in the short run.

One should note that this is just the opposite to a profit-oriented firm or merchant bank that absorbs losses for years on the chance to cash in handsomely some time in the long-run future. Private conglomerates are based on the idea of a tightly reined-in merchant bank and investment institute in combination: they are the extreme form of remote management control and guidance. The efficient operation of such a firm requires delegation through simple measures of performance such as profit controls based on good standardised profit measurement systems.

One is tempted to say that this should be the last organisational form to choose for a politically dependent body like SF. Multiple conflicting objectives like profits and employment responsibilities would jam the decision process. Strictly enforced profit targets on defunct operations do not tally with the presence of elected politicians in the neighbourhood of the decision process. Considering this, it is surprising that SF has performed so well in comparison with other firms and especially during the last few years of crisis. Furthermore, the alternative, where all decisions are passed one by one in a disorganised fashion within the ministries, must surely be an inferior one.

Given the circumstances, the SF arrangement may be a second-best solution — with a first-best fiscal policy, not a politically feasible option — provided a highly qualified and politically independent management team can be rounded up. Since this cannot be guaranteed in advance with the current charter of SF, suggested improvements are (i) to engage private firms actively in the bidding for the 'social offer' contracts performed by SF and (ii) to put SF itself in the equity market to ensure that enough interests are locked up in the profit motive. Praise, however, undoubtedly must go to top SF management that has, so far, performed beyond expectations. A further test of it will come, however, when the northern iron mine and its associated city, Kiruna, may have to be reduced to a fraction of their present size.

NOTES AND REFERENCES

1. The philosophy behind this policy was outlined in several documents from the Central Union Organisation (LO). See, for instance, *Utredningen angående economisk efterkrigsplanering*, SOU, Stockholm, 1944, Nos 7, 12, 13, 25, and 57, and 1945, Nos 11, 30, 31, 36, 42 and 54. See also, *Fackföreningsörelsen och den fulla sysselsättningen* (Stockholm: LO, 1953).

2. See G. Eliasson and J. Sodersten (eds), *Business Taxation and Firm Behavior*, IUI Conference Report (Stockholm: Industries Utredningsinstitut [IUI], 1981) No. 1; and B. Carlsson, F. Bergholm and T. Lindberg, *Industristödspolitiken och dess inverkan på samhallsekonomin*, IUI Working Paper No. 39 (Stockholm: IUI, 1981).

3. Or even ahead of the actual acquisition of a capital good through the renowned Swedish Investment Fund system. See Eliasson, *Investment Funds in Operation* (Stockholm: Konjunkturinstitutet, 1965).

4. See the paper by Eliasson and Lindberg in Eliasson and Sodersten, *op. cit.*

5. At least until the extensive subsidising of failing industries began in the late 1970s. See Carlsson, Bergholm and Lindberg, *op. cit.*

6. These special programmes currently include Berox, Eiser, Kockums, LKAB, Svetab, Udd-Comb and Ceaverken, employing some 35 per cent of SF's Swedish employment in 1979, most of it in distressed regions.

7. For a documentation of these ambitions, see 'Angående ett statligt förvaltningsbolag m m', *Royal Parliamentary Bill No. 121*, (Stockholm: Government Printing Office, 1969), and *Statligt företagande i samhällets tjänst* (Stockholm: SOU, 1978:85).

8. *Royal Parliamentary Bill No. 121*, *op. cit.*

9. That these problems occur on a larger scale in planned economies is demonstrated in J. Kornai, *The Economics of Shortage* (Amsterdam: North-Holland, 1980).

10. See *Statligt företagande*, *op cit.*

11. See N. Lundgren and I. Stahl, *Industripolitikens spelregler* (Stockholm: Industriförbundets Förlag, 1980) pp. 141 *et seq.*

12. See *Statligt företagande*, *op. cit.*, pp. 11–15.

13. Thomas Lindberg at IUI has been very helpful in providing data for this analysis from his research project at the Institute.

14. See *Affärsvärlden*, Stockholm, No. 46, November 1979.

15. See *Affärsvärlden*, No. 20/21, May 1980.

16. See 'Utfragning om Statsföretag', *Ekonomisk Debatt*, Stockholm, No. 4, 1980, pp. 306 *et seq.*

17. See interview with the Managing Director of SF, Per Sköld, in *Affärsvärlden*, No. 40, 1980. See also Eliasson, *Business Economic Planning* (New York: Wiley, 1976).

18. See again interview with Sköld, *loc. cit.*, and the interview with the Finance Director of SF in *Dagens Industri*, Stockholm, 4 March 1980, p. 12.

19. 'Om Kapitaltillskott till Statsföretagsgruppen m m', *Royal Parliamentary Bill No. 79* (Stockholm: Government Printing Office, 1979/80).

20. Complaints were immediately filed with the Minister of Industry by one competing firm (AB Börjes Mek. Verkstad, 28 January 1980), by all competing firms (2 February 1980) and jointly by the unions for workers, salaried workers and supervisors at another competing company (Östbergs Fabriks AB, 12 February 1980).

21. See, for example, *Statligt företagande*, *op. cit.*, ch. 1.

22. *Ibid.*, p. 15.

23. A recent study on the long-term allocation effects of the Swedish subsidy programme using a complete micro(firm)-to-macro-economic model sets a general subsidy programme against a general decrease in the payroll tax costing the same amount in the first year. The subsidy programme tends to stimulate demand in the short-term, increasing the utilisation of inefficient capacity that would otherwise have been closed down. The wages share in total output is higher than would otherwise have been the case. The demand effect on total output dominates for more than five years. After that time, the effects from improved allocation in the no subsidy alternative begins to generate substantially higher total output. The employment differences, however, are quite small and of short duration especially if firms expect the subsidy to be only temporary. With general lowering of the payroll tax, labour released from closed down firms is rapidly rehired in growing firms. The experiments suggest that subsidies tend to hold back this growth in other firms. (These results are preliminary and should be regarded as merely suggestive of the time dimension involved.) See further, Carlsson, Bergholm and Lindberg, *op. cit.*

24. See 'Statsföretag privatiseras: Per Sköld vill sälja ut dotterbolag över börsen', *Veckans Affärer*, No. 7, 19 February 1981, p.3.

CHAPTER SEVEN

France: Enlisting the Aid of the Private Sector

Diana M. Green

The Institut pour le Développement Industriel (IDI) was set up in July 1970 to assist French industrial development by strengthening the financial structure of private-sector companies. It was launched at the time of, and was seen as an integral part of, the 'New Society' approach to economic and social policy sponsored by the then Prime Minister, the Gaullist radical Jacques Chaban-Delmas. Its creation was preceded by a protracted debate about its role, the desirable size of state investment (and extent of government control) and the funds it should have at its disposal. Typically, these issues were not settled once and for all at the launching. On the contrary, the debate has continued during the decade since it was created.

ORIGINS AND AIMS OF THE IDI

The Institute's role should be viewed in the wider context of French economic and industrial development. Industrialisation has taken place in France, very belatedly and very rapidly, largely since the end of World War II. As late as 1936, about 35 per cent of employment was in agriculture while the industrial sector was still composed of small, predominantly family-owned firms. The share of French manufactures in world trade at that time was half that of West Germany or the United Kingdom. The balance of payments was secured by income from overseas investment and imports were restricted by high tariff barriers.

During the post-World War II period, governments have continuously intervened in and monitored the pace and direction of industrial change. An important feature of the French approach, because of these structural weaknesses, has been intervention to prompt, and underwrite, industrial restructuring. The aim was two-fold: first, to promote a long overdue specialisation and, second, to rationalise the industrial structure by creating 'national champions' capable of competing in international markets in designated 'key' sectors.[1] In spite of the modernisation and rationalisation which took place in the 1950s and 1960s, the industrial structure was still characterised, in the early 1970s, by a proliferation of small and inefficient firms. Moreover, the tendency of these firms to rely on short-term bank credit to finance their expansion plans had resulted in a progressive deterioration of the corporate sector's financial structure, [2] in spite of previous policy measures, such as the establishment of regional development agencies, to be discussed later in this chapter.

The creation of the IDI can therefore be seen as a response to two different types of perceived market failure. First, in the industrial sphere, it was called on to promote mergers in a bid to reach optimum firm size in 'key' sectors. Second, by taking holdings in the share capital of small firms, the Institute strengthened their financial structure, allowing them to finance internal growth from their own resources and/or gain access to external financing (medium- or long-term loans) through conventional financial channels.

Initially, the IDI's issued capital was set at 333 million francs though provision was made for this to rise to 1,000 million francs. According to its initial charter, its funds were to be used mainly to assist small and medium-sized firms in the manufacturing sector by taking share holdings. No official limit was set on the size of the holdings,[3] but its interventions were expected to be temporary. Thus, it was expected to dispose of its holdings, as soon as commercially and industrially feasible, in order to redeploy its funds for further projects.[4]

After a protracted debate, the state's holding in the Institute was eventually fixed at 39.1 per cent. Other shareholders included the Crédit National[5] (15 per cent), the three nationalised banking groups (6.9 per cent), the Crédit Agricole (7.5 per cent), the Regional Development Agencies and a number of private banks.

Once it became operational, the IDI met with opposition because of its hybrid nature and also because of the continuing uncertainty surrounding its role. On the one hand it was regarded with suspicion as yet another mechanism by which the state could tighten its grip on industry. At the other extreme, it was seen as a hospital for lame industrial ducks. Crédit National and the Regional Development Agencies resented its intrusion into what they considered their own territory and the private banks resented the fact that a competitor, headed by an ex-banker, was being handed potentially large profits in the shape of (potentially) lucrative holdings.

The opposition was fuelled by two of its early ventures. In 1971, it took shares in the Compagnie Internationale pour l'Informatique (CII), under instructions from the Government.[6] This seemed to confirm its role as a tool of government policy. Suspicion was however to some extent alleviated by its refusal to bail out the Lip company in 1973,[7] a move which seemed to demonstrate a measure of independence. Unfortunately, however, its involvement in the Lip affair served to reinforce the impression that its main function was bailing out inefficient firms.

CHANGING ROLE OF THE IDI

Over time, both the role of the IDI and the nature of its participations have changed. As a result of a financial crisis and a change of management in 1973,[8] the banking sector was eventually persuaded that the Institute was not a competitor but a partner.[9]

Technically, the IDI is a private sector investment company and, as such, is expected to operate according to commercial criteria. In practice, however, state control has increased in a number of ways. First, the state has increased its holding (to 49.9 per cent) as a result of which more than two-thirds of its equity is in the hands of the state or the financial institutions it controls.[10] Second, a new Letter of Intent was issued in 1976 which stated quite explicitly that the Institute is an instrument of the Government's industrial and, more broadly, economic policies:

'The Institute should act in the National Interest, thus justifying the public funds invested in it. Its role is to make its decisions in the light of the Government's priorities, not only in respect of those sectors in which it intervenes but also in that its actions should be governed by the Government's more general objectives, notably those relating to balance of payments considerations, regional policy and maintaining the level of employment.'[11]

This greater control was underwritten by a commitment to increase the IDI's capital by 120 million francs per annum until 1980, when it would total 1,200 million francs. After that date, no further state assistance would be forthcoming: the Institute was expected to be self-financing.

The severity of the 1973 recession prompted the Government to re-think its industrial policy and helped the IDI to find its real role. Companies were instructed to postpone redundancies for as long as possible and a plethora of support 'plans', covering almost all industrial sectors, was launched. This defensive reaction was presented as an integral part of the new 'Industrial Redeployment Strategy'. In principle, this differed from earlier responses to industrial problems in being more coherent and systematic ('planned'). In practice, it was neither new nor strategic.[12] It did, however, provide an intellectual framework within which the Government could carry out its restructuring operations and some sort of rationale for its pragmatic interventions. Thus, in the Letter of Intent which redefined the IDI's role in 1976, the Institute's actions (particularly the promotion of mergers) were presented as an integral part of the process of redeployment 'either by strengthening the resources of those firms best able to exploit openings offered by the market, notably those which appear equipped for assuming the role of industrial 'poles' [*poles de regroupement*], or by participating in merger operations for this purpose'.[13]

At the same time, a clutch of new government committees was set up to coordinate and/or implement government action in this policy area. The first of these was the Comité Interministériel pour l'Aménagement des Structures Industrielles (CIASI), set up in 1974 to bail out lame ducks.[14] This introduced a kind of division of labour, as a result of which the IDI was able to revert to its original role, restricting its interventions to *efficient* firms and leaving 'difficult' cases to the state. In other words, an explicit distinction emerged between the activities of the IDI, which acted like a private sector investment company and was expected to show a profit on its investments, and mechanisms which were more directly state-controlled, like the CIASI, where losses were countenanced — at least in the short term. This distinction should not, however, be exaggerated. Indeed, as is shown later, a tightening-up of the terms of reference of the CIASI reflecting the more market-oriented principles of the Government of Raymond Barre, resulted in a considerable overlap in the functions of the IDI and this committee.

An analysis of the Institute's actual interventions during the 1970s reveals a mixture of changes in policy and continuity in policy decisions. Although a large proportion of IDI's resources continued to go to firms wishing to expand by internal growth, merger operations gained increasing prominence after 1974, in line with the Government's emphasis on redeployment. A sectoral analysis on the other hand, reveals continuity rather than change. From the beginning, the mechanical and metallurgical industries have accounted for the bulk of IDI's interventions. In the first five years of its existence, the number of *dossiers* considered relating to firms in this branch was three times higher than in the next highest group (textiles and clothing), accounting for 27 per cent of the total number of investments considered by the Institute in this period. In terms of actual investment, too, IDI's effort has been focussed on this industrial branch, in respect of both the number of investments and total funding (over 30 per cent of the total in both cases).

There has, however, been a shift, over time, in respect of the size of the companies in which IDI has invested. In the first five years of its operation, the majority of its actual participations was in firms with a turnover of less than 150 million francs.[15] It has tended, since then, to invest in larger firms. Indeed, in 1978 it formalised this shift by hiving off its small business activities into a joint enterprise with the Banque Populaire group, (Sopromec-IDI, see later in this chapter).

The third change which has occurred during the first decade of the Institute's existence can be detected from an analysis of its participations by region — (Table 7.1). Firms in the Paris region not only constitute the largest group seeking assistance, they have also benefited from the largest share of participations by the IDI, a trend which has increased over time. The Institute's investment in the depressed regions, on the other hand, remains modest (two firms in Lorraine, for example, in 1978, in spite of the increasingly

Table 7.1
Regional Analysis of the IDI's Operations, 1970–78

Region	Number of firms seeking funds	Actual interventions 1975	1978
Paris	466	18	31
Alsace	27	4	3
Aquitaine	88	3	3
Auvergne, Centre, Poitou-Charente	129	3[a]	4
Brittany	64	6	3
Champagne-Ardennes	47	4	1
Franche Comté/Bourgogne	46	5	2
Languedoc	20	3[b]	0
Lorraine	89	3	2
Midi-Pyrénées	37	6	5
Nord	60	3	2
Normandy	51	3	4
Loire	76	4	6
Picardy	40	2	1
Provence-Côte d'Azur	52	4	5
Rhône-Alpes	240	11	12
Total	1 532	82	84

[a] Auvergne, Limousin, Poitou/Charente.
[b] Languedoc-Centre.

severe problems of this region in the late 1970s). This suggests that its participations are not motivated by regional policy considerations, in spite of the fact that it is expected to act in concert with the Regional Development Agencies to promote development in the regions. Nor do job creation or employment maintenance criteria appear to be critical in determining its investment policy, (although they are important when firms seek assistance through schemes directly controlled by the state), underlining the extent to which the Institute attempts to concentrate on profitable investments.

Given the vast range of private sector and para-public agencies providing investment finance in France, and the multitude of mechanisms through which the state provides financial assistance at concessionary rates,[16] why do firms go to the IDI? The key seems to be the very narrow range of firms at which it is aimed, that is, small, mainly family-owned firms which cannot obtain funds through the banking sector and are wary of the merchant banks and the state, fearing that the intervention of either would inevitably mean loss of control. For these firms, the IDI is a *neutral* agency, neither banker nor government agency. Moreover, it provides a range of other forms of assistance such as management advice. In this respect, the Institute's small size and flexible organisation is an asset: it sees its own role as 'between the family and the Bourse'.

Organisation and Control

The IDI is small and organised in a flexible way. Investment decisions and general policy are determined by a management council consisting of twelve members, drawn mainly from private industry,[17] and two government officials.[18] The day-to-day work of the IDI is carried out by twenty-five *chargés de mission*, organised sectorally. Administration is coordinated by a director-general who is appointed by, and reports to, the council.

The extent of the state's control is difficult to determine. The IDI insists that it is a private sector organisation, carrying out 'commercial' operations (so that it is under an obligation to earn a commercial rate of return on its investments) and subject to minimal control. It is certainly true that it is not accountable to Parliament, nor are its activities monitored by the Court of Accounts. Control is, however, exercised to the extent that it relies, for part of its resources, on government funding. Moreover, its activities are clearly *influenced* by the mixture of gentle pressure and moral suasion which characterises government-industry rela- tions in France.[19] According to the IDI, its contacts with the Government are close and frequent. Pressure on it to intervene in specific firms is exerted through informal contacts with the council members rather than in the formal council meetings. Conflicts are rare, but do occasionally take place, generally when government pressure runs counter to the IDI's financial and/or industrial judgment, underlining the tension which continues to be gener- ated by the Institute's hybrid nature.

Although the guidelines for the IDI's interventions are spelt out in its charter, an examination of its strategy over time suggests a progressive divergence from its remit, in line with its evolving role. Over the last three or four years, there has been a clear attempt to rid its portfolio of those acquisitions which have turned out to be 'losers'. This appears to be a bid to divest itself not only of unprofitable ventures but also of the rescue agency image. In some cases (the paper and agricultural machinery sectors, for example) this has meant disposing of its holdings to other stockholders (para-public or private), while in other cases it has meant liquidation, (for example, Ratier-Forest, in the machine-tools sector). At the same time, there has been a move to take a more strategic and longer-term approach to its acquisitions. The IDI has always pursued an *active* policy, searching out potential acquisitions and/or merger operations. Its interventions are normally preceded by detailed analyses of the strengths and weaknesses of the relevant firms and their medium-term prospects.[20] Indeed, it has built up an extensive bank of sectoral information through these studies and is frequently used by the Government in a consultative capacity, especially in difficult rescue cases.

Recently, however, this approach has been refined. Adopting the methods of the Boston Consulting Group, it has focussed on efficient firms (*vedettes*), regardless of the sector. Consequently, despite the nominal time-limit on its holdings, it has decided to enter into a limited number of longer-term investment projects, extending and reinforcing its investment in firms which have turned out to be 'winners'. To take one example from the electronics sector, a 35.7 per cent holding in Benson in 1977 was followed by a further capital injection (to the tune of 5.4 million francs) in 1978, underwriting Benson's expansion in the domestic market and in the United States.[21] The aim is quite clear: to forge a more regular and permanent relationship with efficient firms which are well placed to extend their share of world markets. In this respect, its actions are in line with, and complement, the state's actions in the industrial policy area.[22]

Financial difficulties have continuously threatened the IDI's viability. This is, of course, partly a function of its *modus operandi*. Although its holdings are, in principle, temporary, in practice it has not always been possible to turn companies round or sell them off as profitable concerns within the nominal five-year limit.[23] Moreover, the policy decision to make longer-term investments has added to the funding problem. At the same time, an increasing proportion of IDI's funds has been required for *supplementary* interventions. Indeed, in 1978 the cost of supplementary interventions exceeded that of new operations (Table 7.2). Additionally, although the Institute expects to receive a return on its investments, the nature of the firms in which it participates means that in many cases this does not materialise. This is arguably not so much a function of the riskiness of the ventures or the inefficiency of the firms in which it invests as of their *size*. In the case of the smaller firms in its portfolio, especially the family-owned firms, the payment of dividends is not generally a first priority.

As indicated above, the 1976 Letter of Intent provided for injections of state funds until 1980, after which date the Institute was expected to be self-financing. It has therefore been forced to

Table 7.2
IDI – Pattern of Interventions, 1970–79 (Fr.F million)

Type of intervention	1970/71[a]	1972	1973	1974	1975	1976	1977	1978	1979
New investments	219.9	168.9	50.4	48.1	93.2	124.9	181.4	112.4	227.2
Supplementary operations	—	8.1	52.2	42.6	105.8	46.0	89.7	157.4	—
Special operations	—	—	—	—	19.2[b]	44.0[c]	—	—	—
Other assistance	—	0.8	0.1	6.1	5.6	3.7	4.0	4.6	47.6
Total	219.9	177.8	102.7	96.8	223.8	218.6	275.1	274.4	274.8
Nature of intervention									
Convertible bonds	126.2	89.9	53.5	44.2	62.6	47.2	81.2	73.0	—
Shares	93.7	87.9	49.2	52.6	161.2	171.4	193.9	201.4	—
Total	219.9	177.8	102.7	96.8	223.8	218.6	275.1	274.4	—

[a] Eighteen-month period.
[b] Shares bought back from the SED (subsidiary of CN).
[c] Gaz et Eaux.

prepare itself for the end of state assistance and look for ways of obtaining additional finance. It has sought to mobilise funds in four main ways. First, although IDI's *modus operandi* remains holdings in share capital, it has shown an increasing preference for convertible bonds. These provide it with a means of deferring its decision on acquisition for two to three years until such time as it gets a better idea of the likely success of the venture. This seems to suggest that the IDI has become increasingly cautious, not to say risk averse, over time. To what extent this is dictated by the number of 'losers' in its portfolio (particularly those which require constant injections of capital simply to stay alive), is an open question.

Second, the Institute has had recourse to external funding. Thus, in 1979 it raised 110.8 million francs (60 million francs by the sale of equity and 50.8 million francs by the issue of bonds, underwritten by the insurance companies).

Third, funds have been mobilised by rationalising and/or extending its activities into new areas. Thus, certain activities have been hived off in new joint ventures with other institutions to bring in additional funds. For example, intervention in small firms is now carried out by Sopromec-IDI, a joint subsidiary of IDI's small firms division and the Crédit Populaire group, set up in 1978. Participations are limited in respect of both the cost of the intervention (below 2.5 million francs) and the size of the firm (a turnover of less than 100 million francs) and may take the form of holdings, convertible bonds or loans.[24] Similarly, regional operations have been partly hived off to the extent that IDI has participated in the setting up of a number of private sector investment agencies (*instituts de participation*, see below) at the regional level, for example, Siparex (at Lyons) and Participex (at Lille).[25] More recently, it has collaborated with a number of insurance companies in setting up the Compagnie de Développement Industriel et Financier (CODIF) to provide share capital for industrial and financial firms. This move not only allows the Institute to augment its own capital, it also enables it to undertake investment projects which are technically outside the terms of reference laid down in its charter.[26]

Fourth, in 1976, IDI acquired a 25 per cent interest in the successful financial and industrial group, La Financière et Industrielle Gaz et Eaux, a portfolio company which is quoted on the

Stock Exchange. The investment cost IDI 80 million francs, but gave it effective control of the group.[27] Gaz et Eaux is well placed to buy some of the Institute's holdings, thus helping to speed up the rotation of its capital. Indeed, in 1979 the IDI sold to Gaz et Eaux the printing company Leonard-Danel, a deal in which it made a handsome profit. The acquisition of Gaz et Eaux has proved to be useful to the extent that it has provided the IDI with a back-door means to the financial markets. It can also use Gaz et Eaux for ventures which its statute prevents it from undertaking. For example, during 1980 Gaz et Eaux took control of Harpener AG, a West German conglomerate with a quoted value of 930 million francs and interests ranging from power stations to chemicals.[28]

The IDI, then, has two main aims today: to assist the expansion of efficient, medium-sized firms (either by internal growth or mergers) and to promote wider sectoral restructuring. In carrying out these objectives, its activities are distinct from, although complementary to, those of agencies more directly under state control, a distinction underlined by the fact that it is expected to obtain a return on its investments. To what extent this distinction is meaningful and to what extent the IDI operates as a successful private enterprise will be discussed in later sections of this chapter. In the next section, some of the other agencies which have aims and functions broadly similar to those of the Institute are examined.

Regional Development Agencies

In 1955, Sociétés de Développement Regional, Regional Development Agencies (SDRs), were set up to provide a source of finance at the regional level for small and medium-sized companies wishing to undertake investment by taking holdings in share capital. They were subsequently given the right to arrange bond issues on behalf of groups of companies within their region and underwrite those issues. There are now fifteen SDRs covering all the provincial regions of France. Situated in the principal towns, they may either restrict their activities to a single region or a wider area (for example, the Sodeco covers Poitou, the Auvergne, Limousin and four of the six *départements* of the Centre).

The SDRs are technically private sector investment companies and are generally quoted on the (regional) stock exchange. They enjoy considerable fiscal benefits (for example, they are exempt from taxes on net profits or capital gains from portfolio operations) and are subject to state control.[29] Like the IDI, the SDRs are primarily interested in projects which are commercially sound and potentially profitable.[30] Nevertheless, the special relationship with the state, (which now effectively subsidises a substantial part of their operations) casts some doubt on their actual independence in respect of investment decisions.

Prima facie, there is a considerable overlap between the functions of the IDI and the SDRs. Indeed, the Institute was set up largely because the SDRs had manifestly failed to carry out the task set for them — the strengthening of the financial structure of the small business sector. There are, however, a number of differences. First, the SDRs offer a much wider range of types of funding, including loans, whereas the IDI was essentially designed to provide share capital.[31] Second, there is a limitation on the size of the holdings the SDRs may take (35 per cent on the capital of the firm and 25 per cent of their own capital) while the IDI is free to take majority holdings. Third, their activities are restricted geographically (that is, they may operate only within their region) while the IDI operates at the national level. Fourth, unlike the IDI, they do not, in principle, engage in 'industrial engineering', (that is, take holdings to promote mergers). This is partly because of the regional nature of their operations. In practice, however, this restriction has been overcome by creating a national organisation, the Association Nationale des Sociétés de Développement Regional (ANSDER), which 'coordinates' inter-regional action, including mergers. Finally, there is a difference in the kind of firms in which they invest. As a general rule, the SDRs tend to take holdings in smaller firms than the IDI (generally those with an annual turnover of less than 100 million francs). Unlike the IDI, their interventions are not limited to manufacturing industry.[32] Broadly speaking, then, the SDRs appear to complement the IDI's role at the regional level.

Direct State Action: Two New Committees

As the rate of economic growth in France slowed down after 1974, and as international competition became increasingly intense, the number of firms experiencing severe financial difficulties increased sharply.[33] In spite of its 'liberal' (that is, non-interventionist) posture, the French Government responded to the worsening crisis by creating a number of new industrial policy instruments, primarily, although not exclusively, providing selective financial assistance. A number of interministerial committees were set up to coordinate or implement these actions. The first of these was the CIASI. Since then, three new committees have been created: the Fond Special d'Adaptation Industrielle, Special Fund for Industrial Adaptation (FSAI), set up in September 1978 to assist the conversion of those regions particularly affected by the crisis;[34] the Comité Interministériel pour le Développement des Investissements et le Soutien d'Emploi, Interministerial Committee for Industrial Development and the Support of Employment (CIDISE), set up in March 1979 to assist the expansion of small and medium-sized firms; and the Comité d'Orientation pour le Développement des Industries Stratégiques, Interministerial Committee for the Development of Strategic Industries (CODIS), set up in October 1979 to promote 'strategic' industries.[35] Only the CIASI and the CIDISE will be examined here.

All these committees are authorised to grant 'participatory loans' (*prêts participatifs*), long-term loans which become part of a company's equity for their duration.[36] Although nominally providing the state with temporary holdings in private sector funds, their very long-term nature (up to seventeen years) means they provide the French authorities with a further means of controlling the pace and direction of industrial development.

CIASI: Entrepreneur or Rescuer?

Towards the end of 1974, the problem of firms getting into financial difficulties had become sufficiently acute that it was felt necessary to set up some mechanism to deal specifically with this problem. This had, of course, been the main reason for setting up the IDI. Whether, in the wake of the oil crisis and a policy of strict credit controls, which resulted in the drying up of credit (and which particularly affected smaller companies), the problem was simply too big for the Institute to handle is a moot point. In any event, as the number of firms forced into liquidation increased, it became clear that more radical measures were needed. Nationalisation was out of the question for political as well as economic reasons and the formula eventually adopted was based on the IDI model: joint interventions combining public and private capital. Moreover, in any intervention, the state would make a *minority* contribution, generally of the order of 10–15 per cent of the cost of the operation.

The CIASI is a committee which brings together the most senior officials in the main economic ministries and the Governor of the Bank of France.[37] Officially, it was set up to recommend intervention in firms 'which are basically sound and whose management is satisfactory but which are experiencing severe financial difficulties',[38] whose disappearance would be detrimental either with respect to the unemployment which would result or the damage to the industrial fabric.[39] In practice, during the first four years of its existence, it dealt primarily with lame ducks. Indeed, the composition of the committee was to some extent dictated by the need to ensure rapid action: the seniority of the civil servants involved meant that they could short-circuit cumbrous administrative procedures.

The CIASI was initially seen as both a social and an economic instrument, providing loans to small and medium-sized companies facing short-term cash-flow problems. Only in very exceptional circumstances did it consider intervening in high-risk ventures. This can be seen from an internal report on its performance in the first four years of its operation (1974–77) which used performance indicators such as the number of jobs 'saved'.[40]

Under the Barre Government after 1978, there was a change in both the scale and the nature of its interventions. Thus, in 1980 alone, 649 firms received financial aid through this scheme, compared with 434 over the preceding four years. In spite of the increase in the scale of interventions, however, and perhaps because of the alarming increase in the number of firms in difficulty,[41] there was a general tightening up of the criteria for intervention. Rescues only took place after an extensive and detailed scrutiny of the longer-term industrial and financial viability of the firm, together with an appraisal of managerial competence. As the collapse of Manufrance showed, saving jobs was an important factor in considering rescue operations but was not the sole determinant.[42]

There appear to have been two main reasons for this change.

First, the chief obstacle to the success of the scheme was the reluctance of private capital to join rescue operations. Given that the cornerstone of the scheme was a partnership arrangement between public and private capital with the burden of financial support being assumed by the latter, this was no small problem. Second, the support of *efficient* firms was felt to be more in line with the selective and strategic approach being pursued by the Government. The CIASI therefore decided to emphasise this by diversifying its interventions and taking a catalytic role, intervening in and accelerating the expansion of efficient firms. Indeed, the 'hyper-liberal' nature of the procedure as a tool for 'managing the industrial crisis' was emphasised.

Prima facie, this change in the nature of the CIASI's interventions, together with the use of 'participatory loans', suggests an overlap in its activities and those of the IDI. In both cases, the emphasis is on intervening in enterprises expected to be viable in the longer-term — potential industrial winners. The election of a Socialist Government in 1981, however, suggested that this situation would change. Indeed the collapse of Boussac Saint Frères (BSF), France's leading textile group, shortly after the Socialists assumed office, pushed the issue of industrial rescue to the top of the political agenda. The collapse happened just three years after the Willott brothers had taken over the Boussac textile group, saving it from liquidation, with the backing of the Government. Measured by the number of jobs at stake, it was France's biggest post-World War II bankruptcy.[43] BSF was only the first of a long list of firms needing urgent treatment presented to the incoming Government by the CIASI.[44] Some of these (for example Chapelle Darblay, the main newsprint producer, in which IDI had a 49 per cent holding) had apparently only been kept afloat by the extension of credit on a month by month basis.

Although the growing list of casualties and the increasing number of bankruptcies (over 20,000 firms went into liquidation in 1981) can be explained by the continuing economic crisis, they are also a direct consequence of the policies of the previous regime. The strategy of picking and backing industrial winners, designed to remedy some of the structural weaknesses of the economy and accelerate specialisation, inevitably resulted in the disappearance of a large number of firms and, more generally, a contraction of the industrial base. Given the Socialist Government's commitment

to employment creation and softer line on employment maintenance, however, it seems likely that the rescue function of the
CIASI will be strengthened *vis-à-vis* its role as a source of venture
capital.

CIDISE: a Recipe for Success?

The CIDISE was set up in March 1979 to assist the expansion of
small and medium-sized companies, in France and overseas, by
providing risk capital.

The scheme is only available to small, independent firms (that
is, they must not be subsidiaries of a larger industrial group, and
turnover is expected to be below 1 billion francs).[45] While it is
aimed mainly at the manufacturing sector, firms in other sectors,
for example, construction and services, are not excluded (see
Table 7.3 for sectoral analysis).[46] Selection is not determined by
sectoral considerations but by the dynamism and importance of

Table 7.3
Sectoral Analysis of CIDISE Interventions, 1979–80

Sector	Number of interventions	
	1980	Total 1979 & 1980
Mechanical industry, machines	57	69
Heavy engineering, metallurgical goods	25	34
Electronics and informatics	26	45
Agro-food	53	67
Textiles, clothing	25	31
Chemicals & pharmaceuticals, glass	14	23
Plastics	26	28
Wood, furniture	40	50
Printing, paper	15	21
Leisure goods	5	10
Medical instruments, optics, watches	9	15
BTP, off-shore	19	21
Engineering, information services	8	9
Miscellaneous	7	13
Total	329	436

Source: CIDISE, unpublished documents.

the firm. Firms must be financially sound, well structured and 'exceptional', to the extent that they stand out from other firms in the sector by the size of their profits, their organisation and the quality of their product and management. Exposure to international competition is, however, a critical factor. Interventions under the CIDISE procedure take place when such firms wish to undertake long-term investment programmes, either in France, or overseas. When the investment takes place in France, the firm is expected to show that the planned investment will allow it:

(a) to expand its exports and/or increase its share of the domestic market at the expense of imported products;

(b) to redeploy its activities towards new products and markets; and

(c) to develop new techniques in an advanced technology sector.

Interventions take the form of 'participatory loans' with a loan ceiling of 25 per cent of the cost of the investment programme.[47] Assistance is not available where investment programmes are already under way, nor is it available as an *alternative* to the financing obtained through the capital market. Current (or future) shareholders of the firm are expected to match the amount of capital applied for in the participatory loan during the term of the investment programme, that is, the venture is a *joint venture* between public and private capital, with the state taking a share of the risk and of the eventual rewards.

The contract authorising the participatory loan spells out the details of the investment programme and the sources and amounts of additional finance. It may also specify 'industrial' targets (that is, import substitution and export targets, the number of jobs to be created and so on).

The CIDISE is clearly another mechanism for picking and promoting actual and potential 'winners' in both the domestic and overseas market. How successful it has been in this respect is rather more difficult to determine. Certainly, in the first twenty-one months of its operation, the results seemed quite impressive. It contributed to the financing of 436 investment projects with a total value of 4.3 billion francs at a cost, in terms of public funds, of 626 million francs. (The average participatory loan granted in

Table 7.4
Analysis of CIDISE Interventions, 1979–80

	1979[a]	1980	Total
Number of cases	107	329	436
Planned investment (million francs)	970	3 309	4 279
Participatory loans authorised (million francs)	107	519	626
Capital subscribed by shareholders (million francs)	141	498	639

Source: CIDISE, unpublished documents.
[a] Nine-month period.

1980 was 1.6 million francs for an average investment of 10 million francs — see Table 7.4).

In 1980, investment programmes undertaken to the tune of 3.3 billion francs produced 10,400 jobs, at a cost to the state considerably below that of other job support schemes (estimated at equivalent to a subsidy of 5000 francs per job). The scheme was not specifically designed to create jobs; rather the aim was to reinforce the financial structure of the firms thus allowing them to consolidate, and eventually expand their workforce. The fact that, under the terms of the partnership agreement, private capital assumes the lion's share of financing both the investment *and* the job creation, is clearly an attractive feature (in both political and public expenditure terms).

Other Para-public Agencies

A number of 'participation institutes' (*instituts de participation*) have grown up, quite spontaneously, over the last two or three years, at the regional level as a result of the failure of the existing agencies to meet the demand for equity capital. They differ in respect of both their judicial status and the scale of their operations. In some cases, local firms have collaborated with the local chamber of commerce and industry (Siparex at Lyons and Participex at Lille, for example), in other cases they are linked to existing financial institutions (Sofinnova provides funds for innovatory firms and Battinova provides assistance for firms in the construction industry), while others are linked to the big industrial groups, (for example Sofirem [Charbonnage de France] and Afinaq [Elf Aquitain]). They are para-public agencies, set up to deal with a specific problem (the shortage of equity capital) and enjoying some state support (often in the form of guarantees). They tend to operate on a relatively small scale, (Siparex's issued capital, for example, is only 100 million francs) and, to the extent that they specialise sectorally, complement the role of IDI and its SDRs.

INTERNATIONAL TRADE PROMOTION

In spite of the French Government's commitment to free trade, at least at the level of political rhetoric, there is little evidence of any attempt to eradicate protectionist practices. Indeed, since 1974 the French authorities have extended even further the battery of mechanisms specifically designed to distort competition in their bid to secure a greater share of world markets.[48] Although a number of the new measures are inspired by the same 'philosophy' as more traditional export promotion tools (that is, the provision of subsidised finance over very long periods of time), a notable feature of several of them is that they are inspired by and are an extension of the Government's broader industrial strategy.[49]

That the provision of export credit has, in many cases, become another form of selective financial assistance (thus blurring even further the borderline between industrial and exports policy) is underlined by the proliferation of contractual schemes which include explicit export promotion targets.[50]

The IDI has also become involved in the promotion of international trade, [51] in three main ways. First, the IDI is a shareholder in Sofinimdex, an investment company linked to the Crédit National which takes shares in the capital of exporting firms. Second, as a result of a study of the structural problems affecting French exports in 1975, the IDI decided to set up a number of international trading companies. A number of these were set up in 1977 and 1978 and it extended its interest to South-east Asia by subscribing 10 million francs to SCOA's issue of convertible bonds.[52] More recently, IDI's foreign holdings were regrouped in a wholly-owned subsidiary, the Société de Développement International (SODI), to allow it to create trading companies and distribute French products in North America as well as the Middle and Far East. At the same time, it launched a joint venture with a Chinese group based in Hong Kong. The main aim of this subsidiary, the Société Commerciale pour l'Extrême Orient (SCEO), is to promote exports in this part of the world. Third, the IDI has begun to assist the process of relocating manufacturing plant in low-wage, low-cost countries in a bid to improve competitiveness. In 1979, it took a holding in Bataan Optical (a subsidiary of Essilor International) in the Philippines. It has also signed an agreement with the China International Trust and Investment Corporation (CITIC — a sort of Chinese IDI) with the object of promoting and coordinating investment in China.

During the 1970s, French governments pursued their main and unambiguous ambition — to secure a French presence in international markets in certain 'strategic' sectors — with an extraordinary singlemindedness. As I have shown elsewhere, the Barre Government did not hesitate, in spite of its liberal pretensions, to overrule market forces and throw its free-trade principles out of the window in the pursuit of these ends. Protectionism and aggressive export promotion (using subsidies, procurement and a policy of marrying foreign policy and international trade) are just two examples of the extent to which the state is involved in French industrial and commercial development. The extension of the IDI's activities into the area of international trade is therefore not unexpected. In this area it is clearly acting within the framework of the Government's industrial policies and alongside the other institutions (public and para-public) involved in the expansion of French international trade — that is, it is simply one of a number of policy tools deployed in this area. The extent to which it is an arm of the state raises, however, a number of worrying questions about the *nature* of its activities here.

PERFORMANCE OF THE IDI

The hybrid nature of the IDI, which makes it difficult to determine to what extent it is a private-sector investment company operating according to commercial criteria or a tool of the Government's industrial policy, complicates any assessment of its performance. It is not immediately obvious which performance criteria should be adopted. Given the insistence by the Institute that it is a strictly commercial operation, the profitability of its operations would at first sight appear to be a useful measuring rod of its success. In practice, however, the nature of the firms in which it invests means that, in many cases, the return on its investments is minimal. Relatively few of the companies in its portfolio are quoted companies. It is therefore not possible to undertake a systematic analysis of changing levels of profitability as measured by stock market performance. Information about performance, especially that of the smallest and family-owned firms, is sketchy and there are clearly dangers in relying too heavily on the IDI's annual reports. Within these constraints, it is perhaps possible to say something about the Institute's performance in the light of the objectives set for it by the Government.

During the ten years it has been in existence, more than 1,500 companies have approached the Institute for finance. Conversely, the IDI has invested about 1.6 thousand million francs in French industry (see Figures 7.1 and 7.2), mainly in the form of equity capital but also in convertible bonds, loans and advances, and it currently has a portfolio of seventy-eight companies. How success-

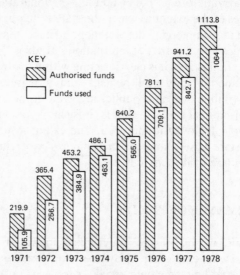

Figure 7.1
Evolution of IDI's Investments, 1971–78 (Fr.F million)

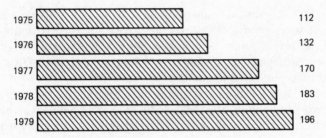

1975 112
1976 132
1977 170
1978 183
1979 196

(a) Cumulative total of firms in which investment has been made (Fr.F million)

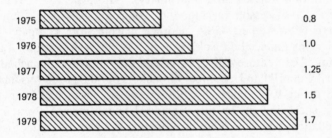

1975 0.8
1976 1.0
1977 1.25
1978 1.5
1979 1.7

(b) Cumulative total of authorised funding (Fr.F billion)

Figure 7.2
The IDI's Investments, 1975–79

ful has it been in achieving the objectives set for it by the French authorities?

At a general level, the IDI's remit was to participate in the financial restructuring of small and medium-sized companies as a prerequisite to underwriting their expansion as well as promoting restructuring at the sectoral level in order to create industrial 'poles' and/or oligopolies large enough to be competitive in world markets. In spite of its claim to be a private sector investment company, it was not intended that it compete with private capital. It should intervene only when private capital failed to detect or chose not to accept the risk of potentially profitable investment projects. At the same time, it was expected to behave as if it were a private sector institution (in spite of its hybrid nature), that is, to undertake investments only when there was a reasonable expectation of some return. (Whatever the expectations, it is rumoured that the *actual* return is considerably lower than that of other agencies carrying out a similar function, notably the SDRs. No figures are published to confirm or refute this.)

An analysis of its interventions over time shows a mixture of successes and failures. Broadly, some of its worst failures involved investments in the early stages of its operation, especially where the firms were in industries in structural decline (such as textile, leather and wood) or where French presence has traditionally been weak (such as machine tools) and/or exposed to high import penetration (agricultural machinery). Thus, in 1977, Ratier-Forest, a successful machine-tool company, was persuaded to merge with Ateliers GSP, another machine-tool company experiencing financial difficulties, as part of the restructuring of this sector. The venture failed. A rescue operation was launched in 1978 by the IDI and a number of bankers but the group was finally split up in 1979. Ironically, Ratier-Forest, which had been the most successful of the firms involved in the merger, went into liquidation, while the other firms were taken over by competitors.

Similarly, in the agricultural machinery sector, three of the companies currently in the IDI's portfolio are clearly failures. Indeed, despite asserting that it is not in the game of industrial rescue, the Institute clearly bailed out two of these firms, Braud and Benac, taking majority holdings in them (99.9 per cent and 91.1 per cent, respectively) with a view to eventually merging them as part of the rationalisation of this sector.[53] Similarly, despite its intervention in CMMC (a group formed as a result of a merger in 1975 between firms making a range of products from glass-fibre pipes for the oil industry to wine presses), one of the main subsidiaries, COQ SE, went into liquidation in 1979. The only 'success' in this sector is Gouvy, an old established agricultural machinery firm in which the IDI took a 20 per cent holding in 1975 when demand collapsed dramatically.[54] The injection of funds allowed the company to diversify into garden tools, a growth area for a number of years, and in 1979 the company's turnover increased by 15 per cent while exports increased by 21 per cent.

A number of the Institute's investments have, however, been very successful. Interestingly, not all the successes have been in growth sectors. The case of Leonard Danel, the printing company sold to Gaz et Eaux, has already been mentioned. Other successes can be found in sectors which are generally regarded as problematical (for example, footwear, furniture and publishing). Thus, a 25 per cent holding in the GEP-Pasquier footwear company in 1977 enabled this family firm to pursue an ambitious expansion programme, centered on a narrow range of modestly priced shoes, and to increase its share of the domestic market (in the face of keen competition from cheaper imports) and exports (exports of children's shoes grew by 31 per cent in 1978). Similarly, the Institute's intervention in the Gautier company (a family-owned firm specialising in children's furniture), in 1972, allowed it to undertake important investment programmes both in France and overseas.[55] Its turnover increased from 260 million francs to 366 million francs from 1978–79.

In many cases where firms opted for internal growth, the IDI's intervention has been relatively modest.[56] In those cases where expansion has been based on a take-over or merger strategy, underwritten (if not prompted) by the IDI's intervention, the investment has tended to be more substantial and the results have been more uneven. Thus, whereas the Institute's intervention in the motor components' sector (assisting the restructuring of this sector around Ferodo) can be counted as one of its successes, its interventions in the machine tools' sector, (sponsoring the restructuring of this sector around Ratier-Forest) was, as indicated above, a complete disaster. It may be significant that in the first of these examples, the actions of the IDI were backed by the state. Indeed, the subsequent attempt by Ferodo to complete the restructuring exercise by taking over Ducellier (the electrical components company, jointly owned by the Bendix company of the United States and Lucas of the United Kingdom) sparked off a take-over battle which provided a classic and justly notorious example of the French Government's protectionism in action.[57] Similarly, the IDI's success in the case of the Benson company was clearly assisted by direct state support in the shape of a 'growth contract' designed to help Benson expand its range of products and strengthen its investment overseas to increase exports. Yet, paradoxically, even state support is not a guarantee of success, as can be seen from the venture with Logabax, another company in the mini-informatics area. Despite important state or state-engineered contracts (with the PTT, the Banque Nationale de

Paris and the Crédit Lyonnais), the company has experienced continuous financial difficulties and has recently gone into liquidation. (IDI wisely sold off its holding in Logabax in 1979.) The unevenness of its performance therefore casts doubt on the assumption that the IDI is any better than the state (or the market) at picking industrial winners. It also underlines the very problematical nature of the Institute's relationship with the state.

CONCLUDING REMARKS

No definitive conclusions about the IDI's performance can be drawn from this superficial analysis. A number of points can, however, be made in respect of the problems it has faced in attempting to carry out its aims.

Broadly speaking, the Institute appears to have both an economic and a political function. Its economic function is to strengthen the financial structure of small and medium-sized firms. The progressive deterioration of the corporate sector's financial position — both large corporations and smaller firms — had been a matter of concern to the French Government for some time. The rate of self-financing had deteriorated progressively and corporate growth was largely financed through bank credit.

The creation of IDI was one of a series of moves initiated by the Government to reverse this trend. How successful the Institute has been in achieving this objective is rather difficult to assess, not least because it is difficult to distinguish the impact of its activities from that of other measures. That it was inadequate to tackle the problem is indicated, perhaps, by the government's introduction of *additional* institutions (notably the CIASI) with broadly the same purpose. Indeed, the deterioration of corporate financing has continued during the period of the IDI's existence. This can be seen in the increasing burden of debt, together with a substantial increase in financial liabilities, which have almost doubled in ten years (5.5 to 9.3 per cent of value added).[58] The deterioration was not, in fact, halted until the government introduced a package of reforms under the 'Monory Law'.

At the same time, the IDI was clearly created for political reasons to the extent that its second main function is to promote and accelerate the growth of French industry within the framework of the Government's industrial policies. This has had a number of consequences. First, it has been active in promoting and underwriting a number of restructuring exercises, the industrial logic of which is not greatly in evidence. The failure of some of these exercises (such as the Ratier-Forest venture described above) not only constrains the Institute's ability to demonstrate its viability as a profit-making concern, it also casts doubt on some of the industrial and economic assumptions behind its actions; thus, for example, increased firm size may be a necessary condition of competitiveness in world markets but is not a sufficient condition. Furthermore, to assign a 'motor' role to an efficient company in such a restructuring operation is to increase the risk of the viable parts of the business being dragged down by the inefficient. At the same time, pressure from the Government (overtly or covertly) to engage in some of the more politically motivated restructuring exercises (Ferodo for example) has reinforced the suspicion that the IDI is simply the secular arm of the state. Its independence should become rather more credible as it reduces its financial dependence on the state and becomes fully self-sufficient. Real autonomy is not possible, however, while the state retains a majority share in the Institute's capital, bolstered by control at the board level.

One of the main weaknesses of the French financial system is its centralised and compartmentalised nature. The specialised nature of the various institutions, reinforced by the tendency of the state to allocate responsibility for funding individual financial regimes to specifically nominated institutions, means that each enjoys a substantial amount of monopoly power, increasing the inefficiency of the system. The creation of the IDI, an investment company with an arms-length relationship with the state, could be seen as a well-intentioned attempt to introduce an element of competition into the financial system. If this is indeed the case, the initiative has clearly failed. As was indicated earlier, the Institute has sought to present itself not as a competitor to the banks and financial institutions but as a partner. Moreover, as this chapter has shown, the IDI has become yet another specialised agency, financing the expansion plans of small and medium-sized companies in return for a participation in share capital (and any subsequent profits). It only competes with other institutions to the extent that the requirement to make profitable investments leads it to invest in companies in which risk is minimal (that is, it is not interested in high-risk ventures which it leaves to other, specialised, agencies).

Finally, the importance of the IDI should not be exaggerated. The scale of its activities means that its role in the economy is modest, both relatively and absolutely. Even if its independence is doubted and it is seen as an arm of the state, as such it is simply one of a battery of mechanisms used by the French Government to intervene directly in industry and direct structural change. In other words, the extent to which its operations are buttressed by more radical and extensive forms of intervention is much more worrying than the impact of its actual operations. Any attempt to reverse this trend is likely to be blocked by the tradition of *dirigisme* which is so deeply entrenched and that is both expected and looked for by French industrialists.

The French authorities are confronted by a dilemma. On the one hand, the size of the domestic market means that they are 'condemned' to specialise: specialisation is the logical strategy for a small open economy. In the French case, however, protectionism is a deeply rooted tradition, as is manifested by the continuing belief in a rather outmoded, but politically potent, form of industrial nationalism (visible, *inter alia*, in the most recent derivative of the 'national champions' strategy, that is, the designation of 'strategic' technologies). Moreover, there is a limit to how far this strategy can be pursued. Although it has clearly produced companies or groups with a considerable amount of monopoly power, they are essentially *national* champions rather than world leaders. The construction of European champions, which seems the next logical step, appears to be an option available only in a limited number of instances (Airbus Industries, for example).

This chapter has examined the role and the performance of the French Industrial Development Institute during the 1970s. Does the election of a socialist president to office in 1981 mean that its role, and French industrial policy, are likely to be changed in the near future? Since the extent of government intervention is likely to increase under the socialists (in addition to the nationalisation programme), *prima facie* the essentials of past policy are likely to be maintained.

There are, however, a number of factors which make predictions about policy changes particularly difficult. First, the ranking of priorities in the economic policy area is not at all clear. Recent statements do seem to indicate a marginally greater concern for preserving and expanding the domestic industrial base (for example, a softer line on 'lame ducks', the extension of loans at ever more favourable rates to ease the financial position of the corporate sector in the face of escalating interest rates, *et cetera*) and creating jobs. Nevertheless, the balance-of-payments problem is likely to persist, at least while France continues to be so heavily dependent on imports for her energy needs (the more so if the nuclear energy programme is slowed down or cut back).

Given these constraints and the adjustment problems that French industry still has to confront, the feasibility of a more liberal stance must therefore remain open to question.

NOTES AND REFERENCES

1. It was felt that the general technological level of French industry was too low. A comparative analysis of international competitiveness carried out by the Ministry of Industry in 1976, based on the utilisation of factors of production, shows that France had specialised in industries which are relatively capital intensive but which utilise a low-skilled labour force (for example, volume car production which relies heavily on unskilled immigrants).

2. 'Le Développement des Initiatives Financières Locales et Regionales', Rapport de Groupe de Réflexion des Initiatives Financières Locales et Régionales (Rapport Mayoux), *La Documentation Française*, Paris, 1979.

3. Its holdings tend to fall within a range of 10 to 34 per cent although in a number of cases it does have a majority share. It can, exceptionally, set up companies; it has, for example, set up wholly owned trading companies.

4. Interventions are technically supposed to be for a maximum of five years.

5. Crédit National is a joint-stock company, established under private law, but controlled by the state. It is the main channel for public assistance to private industry, provides direct long-term loans and rediscounts medium-term credit granted by the banks.

6. The operation was part of the government's plan to restructure the computer industry, the '*Plan Calcul*'. The IDI's interven-

tion involved a 23.8 per cent share in the company and the issue of short-term convertible bonds to the value of 43 million francs. The interest was sold to Thomson in 1976.

7.   The Lip watch manufacturing company became a *cause célèbre* when it was taken over by the employees in a bid to avoid liquidation.

8.   The initial 333 million francs proved hopelessly inadequate. A number of banks with shares in the Institute refused to participate in the rescue operation and the state was forced to intervene. The crisis was, apparently, at least partly engineered by the government as a means of changing the management team. The chairman, a banker (ex-Crédit Lyonnais), 'resigned' under pressure from the Finance Minister, Valéry Giscard d'Estaing. The incoming board members were predominantly industrialists.

9.   Relations with the Crédit Agricole, whose vice chairman became the first Director-General of the IDI, were good.

10.   At 31 December 1979, the main shareholders were: the state (49.9 per cent); Crédit Agricole (13.3 per cent); Crédit National (11.2 per cent); the three nationalised banks (approximately 4.5 per cent each); SDRs (1.58 per cent); Banques Populaires (1.71 per cent); Paribas (1.37 per cent); Groupe Compagnie Bancaire (0.63 per cent); Crédit du Nord (0.45 per cent); Groupe CIC (1.02 per cent); Crédit Commerciale de France (0.74 per cent); CNME (0.57 per cent); BFCE (0.45 per cent); Crédit Mutuel (0.13 per cent); Crédit Cooperatif (0.13 per cent).

11.   Letter of Intent from the Ministers of Finance and Industry to the board of the IDI spelling out its new terms of reference, 20 February 1976.

12.   Many of the sectoral plans which appeared under the umbrella of the Strategy in fact predated its launching. Many of them, especially those relating to the industries in structural decline, were essentially a protectionist response designed to slow down/postpone indefinitely essential adjustment in order to save jobs.

13.   Lettre de Mission from the Ministers of Finance and Industry to the board of the IDI, September 1976.

14.   Unlike most other lame-duck agencies in Western Europe, its terms of reference were quite tightly drawn. Interventions only took place in healthy (that is efficient) firms which were experiencing temporary difficulties. Rescues are joint ventures, involving

public *and* private capital, underlining the longer-term viability of the rescued firms.

15. In 1979, 63 per cent of its affiliated companies had an annual turnover of over 100 million francs. Seven of these had a turnover of over 1,000 million francs.

16. Loans to French firms at subsidised rates of interest are a key feature of French industrial policy. According to the Banque de France, about 44 per cent of all loans and credits granted in 1979 were at preferential rates.

17. In July 1980, the members of the Management Council were: Chairman, A. Temkine (Editions Mondiales); Vice Chairmen, A. de Lattré (Crédit National) and G. Chabanes (Leroy-Somer); B. Deconimck (Sommer-Allibert), J.-C. Garret (Secemia), P. Giffard (CIO), J. Lallement (Crédit Agricole), G. de Massacre (Hutchinson Mapa), A. d'Oiron (Union Nationale de la PMI), P. Schmitt (Le Creuset), A. de Tavernost (Expanso) and J. Verspieren (Legrand).

18. A senior official from the *Trésor* (Economics Ministry) and the Director-General of the Industry Division in the Ministry of Industry.

19. The government representatives (*censeurs*) have no veto over the management council's decisions, but are there 'to make the views of the Government known'.

20. Each *chargé de mission* is expected to be well-briefed about the firms in his sector (their investment plans, financial needs, management competence *et cetera*), so that the IDI can step in at the appropriate moment.

21. In 1979, Benson acquired a division of Mountview (California) Inc., a move which increased its share of the world market in automated design equipment.

22. See Diana Green, 'Promoting the Industries of the Future: the Search for an Industrial Strategy in Britain and France', *Journal of Public Policy*, Cambridge, August 1981.

23. For example, Promecam, the machine tools producer, has been in IDI's portfolio since 1972.

24. In 1979, Sopromec-IDI undertook investments to the tune of 12 million francs, 9.2 million francs of which was in the form of convertible bonds, the rest in shares. The official explanation of the preference for bonds is that 'it allows the two partners [that is, IDI and the Banks] to get to know each other better before the

latter commit themselves to a share in the capital of the firm'; see *Annual Report* (Paris: IDI, 1979).

25.   The Director-General of IDI is an administrator of Siparex.

26.   The move was seen as a means of tapping the unused resources of the insurance companies which, being risk averse, have shown little interest in industrial investment. It also opens up the way for IDI's entry into real estate.

27.   Other shareholders include: Société Centrale d'Etudes Marcel Dassault (10 per cent); Groupe Crédit Mutuel (9.5 per cent); Sofipa, Elf-Aquitaine Group (8.3 per cent); Mutuelles Générales Françaises (6.3 per cent). It became a holding company in 1977, managing holdings in France and overseas.

28.   The transaction was effected through the acquisition by Gaz et Eaux of 80 per cent of the capital of Sidechar, a subsidiary owned jointly by the French steel producers and Charbonnages de France. IDI then acquired 51 per cent of this.

29.   Those operations involving a state subsidy (for example, certain loans and share capital operations benefiting from a special *prime*) are subject to the approval of the sponsoring ministry.

30.   All the employees are shareholders in the SDRs and profits are distributed. Dividends are generally around 10 per cent — that is, the SDRs are considerably more successful than the IDI.

31.   In a bid to encourage the SDRs to deploy a greater proportion of their funding in equity operations, assisting firms in the small business sector, the government decided, in 1976, to provide a system of *primes* by means of which *up to 50 per cent of the cost* of share acquisition in certain firms is covered by the state. This allows the SDRs to spread risk and increase the number of their acquisitions. Their loan operations are also subsidised. In addition to equity capital, the SDRs provide long-term loans (up to fifteen years, and a special twelve-year loan scheme, heavily subsidised by the state (*prêts super-bonifiés*) for investment programmes which create jobs, save energy and raw materials or increase exports), 'participatory loans', convertible bonds, long-term loaning operations and management services.

32.   In September 1980, the Government announced that, in future, SDRs would be able to raise capital through ordinary share issues. Their capital was doubled (to 880 million francs) and they

were to be given much greater scope in these operations. 'Participatory loans' could be extended to firms in the services sector as well as to local authorities for industrial and tourist projects.

33.   The number of bankruptcies increased from under 10,000 a year in 1973 to 13,000 a year between 1973 and 1977 making France 'the biggest graveyard for companies in Western Europe'; see Veronique Maurus, 'S.O.S. Canards Boiteux', *Le Monde*, Paris, 22 March 1979.

34.   The Committee is actually a sub-committee of the Economic and Social Development Fund (FDES) which provides soft loans for industry. The initial allocation to the Fund was 3,000 million francs. It is clear that it is the least successful of these schemes. Unfortunately the French government attempted to marry two conflicting aims: creating new jobs in the regions most severely affected by the restructuring of industries in structural decline (coal mining, textiles, steel and shipbuilding) and attracting 'footloose' capital investment (French or foreign). The scheme broke new ground as far as traditional regional policy tools are concerned in that it dropped the strict job creation stipulations: the only requirement is that at least fifty jobs should be created as a result of the investment over a three-year period. The scheme was revised in September 1981 as part of the new socialist government's overall review of regional development schemes.

35.   The CODIS was created to underpin the 'new' industrial strategy launched by the government in 1980. The main thrust of the 'strategic reinforcement' approach centres on the promotion of certain key industries, that is, those which are felt to be strategically important to the extent that failure to develop an effective *French* presence in them will have serious consequences for the French economy in the years ahead. The role of the CODIS is to *select* these strategic areas and *coordinate* state intervention (primarily, but not exclusively, financial intervention) *in order to increase the international competitiveness* of the firms concerned. The strategy is based, then, on the rapid development of French technology and particular French products (underlining the extent to which the French have embraced the Japanese model). For details see Green, *op. cit.*

36.   Participatory loans were first introduced under the 1978 'Loi Monory' and were first used in the 1978 Steel Plan. They are fifteen- to seventeen-year unsecured loans with repayment on

capital deferred for two to three years. Repayment is the sum of fixed and variable amounts (a fixed amount, 8-9 per cent, payable at the end of the first year and a variable amount payable at the end of the deferred payment period and indexed to the ratio of the gross self-financing margin to turnover before tax) and are subject to a maximum interest rate.

37.   Director of the Treasury, Director-General of the key policy division of the Industry Ministry, Director-General of Social Affairs, Director of the Foreign Trade division of the Economics Ministry, Delegate of DATAR and the Planning Commissioner.

38.   *21st Report of the Management Council of the Economic and Social Development Fund*, Report for 1975/76 (Paris: FDES, 1976) p. 114.

39.   *Report to Parliament on State Assistance to Industry*, Appendix to 1975 Finance law (Budget) (Paris: Imprimerie Nationale, 1977).

40.   Between the launching of the scheme in November 1974 and the end of June 1977, 434 firms had been given assistance, involving 201,000 jobs at a cost to the state (excluding private capital) of almost 450,000 francs. About 90 per cent of the cases examined received some state aid.

41.   By 1979 the number of firms going into bankruptcy had risen to about 1,500 per month.

42.   The manufacturer of sporting firearms, bicycles and sewing machines, based at St Etienne. It also published the sporting paper, *Chasseur Français*, and was one of France's largest mail-order houses. After being considered by the CIASI, the government decided not to rescue the company, largely because the banks refused to join in the rescue, being doubtful of the company's longer-term viability, at a cost of 2,000 jobs.

43.   BSF, the manufacturing arm of the Agache-Willot textile and retail group collapsed with debts of about 2,000 million francs and losses of 10-15 million francs per month at the end of June 1981. It employed 20,000 people in eighty factories, mainly in two regions (the Nord and the Somme). Its collapse also threatened the viability of a number of sub-contractors, many of which were located in the same regions. A rescue plan has been worked out within the framework of the overall plan for the troubled textiles sector. Interestingly, Anatole Temkine, the Chairman of the IDI,

is in charge of the rescue plan. Whether the rescue will involve the participation of IDI is a matter for speculation. See Green, 'France', in K. Dyson and S. Wilks (eds), *The Management of Industrial Crisis* (Oxford: Martin Robertson, 1983).

44. The CIASI informed the government that fifteen firms needed immediate rescue. Some time later, one of the unions (the CFDT) drew up its own list, including more than 700 firms.

45. During the first twenty-one months of its operation, intervention has taken place in firms of all sizes (that is, with an annual turnover ranging from 3 million francs to 950 million francs). The *average* turnover of assisted firms was 30 million francs.

46. Separate procedures, under the general umbrella of the CIDISE, have been set up for firms in the textiles and agro-food industries. In the case of the former (introduced in November 1980), the criteria determining eligibility are relaxed. The principle that the firm should be basically 'healthy' still holds but 'the criteria determining future prospects are less rigorously applied'.

47. It is also possible to combine the participatory loan with other forms of assistance up to a ceiling of 40 per cent of the programme cost.

48. See Green, 'The Export Imperative: French Policies to Promote Overseas Trade', prepared for the Department of Industry, May 1981, unpublished.

49. This is particularly evident in the area of export finance. Thus, export credits may be provided for specific types of *firm* (small or medium-sized firms which are rapidly expanding [the CIDISE] or those which already export a substantial part of their output but wish to expand [Concours IX, the CIDISE, Sofinimdex]) or for specific *sectors* (for example, long-term credit for capital goods exports, the 'plans professionels à l'exportation' and the money directed to increasing exports in sectors like aviation), or for specific *products* (the CODIS) or to encourage firms to export/to invest in specific geographical areas (DIE, Ufinex).

50. For example, the 'development contracts' used by the CODIS (which provide for the mobilising and coordination of whatever state action is deemed to be necessary from financial assistance to import controls).

51. The 1976 Letter of Intent (see note 11 above) opened the way for this development by allowing the IDI to intervene

'exceptionally' in services related to manufacturing 'especially those which contribute to the development of exports'.

52.   SCOA is one of the most important of France's trading companies. Originally based in Africa, it has now diversified its activities geographically to include the Far East and the South Pacific.

53.   IDI took control of Braud (which manufactures harvesters) in 1972 and took a majority holding in Benac (which makes corn-pickers) in 1973.

54.   Gouvy's annual growth rate (by volume) had averaged 12.5 per cent since 1971 but slumped dramatically in 1975 as a result of the crisis affecting this sector. Its output fell in that year by 14 per cent.

55.   Since 1978 it has taken over a furniture manufacturing plant in Canada, set up a subsidiary supplying wood in the Ivory Coast and taken over a plant in France.

56.   For example, it holds 9.35 per cent of Gautier, 8.62 per cent of Robert Laffont and 25 per cent of GEP.

57.   See Green, *Managing Industrial Change?* (London: H.M. Stationery Office, 1981).

58.   This is also, and perhaps especially, true of rapidly expanding firms. According to a study of the 200 fastest growing firms in France, financial liabilities grew from 6.3 per cent of valued added in 1970 to 7.3 per cent in 1976 (Ministère de l'Industrie, 'Les Entreprises en très Forte Croissance', in *La Documentation Françaises*, Paris, 1981).

CHAPTER EIGHT

West Germany: Managing Without a State Investment Company

Karl Heinz Jüttemeier and Klaus-Werner Schatz

Economic activity in the Federal Republic of Germany is subject to more numerous government interventions than is generally believed. For instance, large parts of the private sector are directly or indirectly regulated, through subsidies and tax allowances and, also, incentives for capital formation in specific industries and branches. Moreover, state investment companies exist.

This chapter focusses on these state investment companies and on the actual role they play. First, the historical background is related in order to help explain the specific way in which state investment companies have developed in the Federal Republic. Then the current activities of state investment companies are investigated in more detail. Next, an attempt is made to analyse the degree to which Federal Governments have used their industrial property as a substitute for state investment companies and whether Federal research and development policies are designed to serve the same purposes as state investment companies in other countries. Finally, an effort is made to judge the role of state investment companies within the framework of other, competing, policy measures and to assess the role which could be assigned to investment companies in the Federal Republic.

HISTORICAL BACKGROUND

The Berliner Industriebank AG, founded in 1948, was the first to pursue the aims of a state investment company in West Germany. In 1953, in addition to its traditional activities, the Bank, owned 90 per cent by the Federal Government, was enabled to buy, with public funds, equity holdings in private enterprises. The activities of the Bank were limited to West Berlin. Nevertheless, it is important in the broader context because its structure governed the debate about state investment companies in West Germany later on.

In 1953, rapid economic development had already been achieved in the Federal Republic. Investment had been high, and unemployment had been reduced from its 10 per cent peak in 1950 to 6 per cent, although the labour force had increased rapidly as a result of the influx of refugees. But in West Berlin unemployment, though lower than its 1950 peak of 27 per cent, was still 24 per cent in 1953. The economic achievements of the city were poor in spite of substantial Federal Government assistance and capital formation was insufficient to provide for faster growth and for rapid creation of jobs. Under these circumstances the Federal Government commissioned an institute in the United States to investigate the causes of the poor development record and to suggest means of improving aid to West Berlin. The institute's report placed emphasis on the difficulties of West Berlin enterprises in obtaining equity capital.[1] For obvious reasons, investment in Berlin was at this time thought to be very risky.

In response, the United States Administration granted 100 million German marks to the Federal Republic in order to buy equity capital from Berlin enterprises. The Berliner Industriebank AG was the agent for allocating the funds. Under the guidelines laid down for it the Bank was to:

(a) improve the financial structure of private enterprises by increasing equity capital;

(b) restrict its participation to a form of silent equity holding, although exceptions were possible, and

(c) to limit the time period of its engagement; but,

(d) the Bank was not allowed to withdraw from its participation save in extraordinary circumstances, while the private company could repurchase the Bank's share at any time.

In the case of a silent equity holding, the Bank received a fixed return on its capital, though at a rate substantially lower than market rates for long-term investment funds, but shared — to a limited degree — in the profits of the business. In the case of an active engagement, the bank was not allowed to make use of more than 49 per cent of the voting power in a company, even if the equity holdings it acquired would allow for more, and it fully participated in losses and profits without any fixed returns to investment.[2]

The guidelines highlight that the primary purpose was to generally strengthen private business activities: the equity holdings were not a vehicle for pursuing specific economic policy goals, such as nationalisation or promotion of selected industries. Moreover, the guidelines indicate the care which was taken in order to overcome private enterprises' particularly strong distrust of holdings of equity capital by public authorities. For, although capital markets were tight in the 1950s — and there were complaints about the difficulty of financing new investment — there were, also, strong fears of losing independence in decision making. As mentioned above, however, in creating the first German state investment company, governments were far from pretending to intervene in managerial autonomy. On the contrary, the official philosophy was that governments should refrain from selective economic policy interventions, at least through direct engagement in private enterprises. The activities of the Berliner Industriebank AG have to be seen in the context of the economic situation of the city of West Berlin in the early 1950s; and even despite this situation, the then prevailing thinking was so unsympathetic that the newly established state investment company branch of the Bank probably would not have been called into existence if it were not for an American initiative.

There were no limits on the size of the enterprises in which equity holdings could be acquired by the Berliner Industriebank. Later on, with respect to state investment companies to be founded outside West Berlin, it was argued that only small and medium-size enterprises should be recipients, to counter discrimination against them elsewhere.

From the very beginning, a remarkable discrepancy often existed between official doctrines and the outcome of actual policies in the Federal Republic. Thus, it was the official doctrine that competition would prove best for growth and that, for maintaining competition, the existence and emergence of small and medium-size enterprises was essential. Anti-monopoly and anti-cartel legislation was implemented immediately before and after the foundation of the Federal Republic. This met Allied requests and substituted for already existing Allied laws; it corresponded as well to independent German conceptions for restricting market power and concentration and for ensuing competition.[3] Nevertheless, the first years of the Federal Republic saw rather a strengthening of, and assistance to, large enterprises, mainly due to the effects of policies aiming at fast growth and at rapid job creation.[4] Nearly any price was thought appropriate for these goals, including the sacrifice of part of official doctrine.

Small and medium-size enterprises could not draw the same advantages as large enterprises from the incentive system — including the tax system — as privileges granted were, in particular, favourable to the more capital-intensive enterprises which were also often large. And as small and medium-size enterprises, due to their legal construction, mostly have no access to the capital markets, they could not profit from the tax advantages provided for outside financing. Moreover, these enterprises suffered particularly from tight markets for long-term investment funds, as banks often seem to prefer serving larger enterprises and to ask for unduly high interest rates. Only since 1960, has it ceased to be a major complaint of small and medium-size enterprises that they could not borrow. This, at least, was stated by the Federal Ministry of Economics in a report concerning the financing of this type of enterprises.[5]

Of course, given the official doctrines propagating the beneficial role of small and medium-size enterprises, the fact that actual policies often favoured big enterprises and little hindered the emergence of giant industrial trusts[6] could not be completely ignored and so a number of measures aimed at supporting smaller producers in the framework of 'Mittelstandspolitik' (small business promotion policy) were introduced. But this is a loose bundle of vague ideas concerning preferential treatment of small and medium-size enterprises rather than an elaborated concept for economic policies. The measures, which were taken from the existence of the Federal Republic onwards, were of a minor financial order, as a Federal Government report, concerning the situation and the development of small and medium-size enterprises and the Federal aids provided to them, reveals.[7]

With the spectacular economic performance of the 1950s, the growth target lost its largely unchallenged priority. Moreover, there was increasing complaint that the unfettered growth policies of this decade had led to over-concentration, to decreasing competition, to the decline of small and medium-size enterprises and, thereby, to a shortage of the entrepreneurship required for stimulating future growth. Such complaints led to a Federal law requiring an investigation into concentration in the German economy and this was completed and published in 1964.[8] Although the report reached no clear cut conclusions for the whole economy, either with respect to changes in, or the impact of, concentration or with respect to the causes of concentration,[9] the Federal Government's statement on the report announced some policy changes. In particular, new and additional measures, enabling small and medium-size enterprises to increase self-financing through equity capital from the capital market, were to be introduced.

Support for this idea had been given, for instance, by recommendations from the Scientific Council to the Ministry of Economics in 1963 and from the Council of Economic Advisers as early as its first report in 1964.[10] It was the Council of Economic Advisers, in particular, which stressed the necessity to help small and medium-size enterprises, given a spectacular decrease in the relative importance of self-financing of German enterprises which, it argued, was largely due to obstacles to outside-financing. In the period following this, it became an increasing Federal Government concern to decide how equity capital could best be allocated to small and medium-size enterprises.[11] However, there were neither Federal nor other government plans to establish state investment companies nor significant requests from industry organisations for their creation: a strong feeling still existed that governments should refrain from engaging in private enterprise by means as direct as state investment companies.[12] Instead, at that time the idea was to further strengthen the so-called Kreditgarantiegemeinschaften which, since the end of the 1950s, had emerged with the organisational and financial aid of the Federal and Länder Governments and of which about thirty already existed around 1965. The Kreditgarantiegemeinschaften are private non-profit organisations, established by associations of various types, mostly on a regional basis and for specific production sectors, which grant guarantees for long-term investment credits of small and medium-size enterprises. The role of the Federal Government was seen in supplementing funds raised by the Kreditgarantiegemeinschaften from other sources, so that part of the investment risk was taken by government.[13] Another approach was to persuade private corporations, in particular from the banking sector, that equity capital investment was a promising field for new activities and to give them incentives to undertake these.[14]

It took another couple of years to overcome fundamental doubts with respect to state investment companies which existed both within governments and in the private sector of the economy. Concrete efforts to establish a Federal state investment company were made in 1969 by a conservative minister of the then conservative/social democrat coalition (CDU/CSU; SPD) government with the social democrats as junior partner. The efforts even led to an announcement of the planning of such an institution in the official bulletin of the Federal Government.[15] The idea was to found a Federal institution following the guidelines given to the Berliner Industriebank AG in 1953. It was stressed, in particular, that the planned state investment company should not influence the decision making of private enterprises. By contrast to the Berlin model, and in line with the then ongoing discussion of aids to small businesses, the state investment company was to restrict its activities to small and medium-size enterprises.

The proposed Federal German state investment company, however, was not founded. The proposal was made before the Federal parliamentary elections of 1969, which replaced the CDU/CSU- and SPD- supported Government by a government which relied on a coalition of the social democratic party with the liberal party (FDP) as junior partner. In its programmatic proclamation of 28 October 1969, the new Government declared that the conditions of financing should be improved for small and medium-size enterprises. Half a year later, the social democrat Minister of Economics, Professor Karl Schiller, explained what the Government thought about capital investment companies in this context: 'We ... affirm and promote the idea of capital investment companies. But we say no to public or semi-public companies. The capital investment company should not and must not become an instrument of state capital control.'[16] As a matter of fact, during the life of the social democrat/liberal government, a Federal state investment company never was established. Instead, a number of state investment companies have emerged on the level of the German Federal states in the 1970s, playing a particular role in states with conservative governments.

ACTIVITIES OF STATE INVESTMENT COMPANIES IN THE 1970s

In the second half of the 1960s, a number of privately financed capital investment companies had been founded which, however, concentrated their efforts on large enterprises and taking equity capital shares usually only from 500,000 German marks upwards. Small and medium-size enterprises, for which the Federal Government had seen most need for strengthening equity capital, were still neglected. While the Government refrained from the establishment of a state investment company of its own, in the summer of 1970 it introduced a programme aiming at providing equity capital in an indirect way through the European Recovery Programme (ERP) Fund.[17] As a result:

(a) loans were made available to private capital investment companies for refinancing equity capital outlays; and

(b) guarantee funds were put at the disposal of the credit guarantee associations (Beteiligungsgarantiegemeinschaften).[18] For the same purpose, the associations could rely on additional funds from the Federal budget.

The term 'private' capital investment company is not restricted to privately owned companies, rather, it covers enterprises operating under commercial law irrespective of private or public (state) ownership.

The guidelines for the Federal Government programme provide for a two-stage procedure. Small and medium-size enterprises can apply for equity capital to the capital investment companies, in cases of projects involving (i) cooperation with other enterprises, (ii) innovation, (iii) adjustment to structural change, (iv) building up, enlargement, basic rationalisation or reorganisation of plants and (v) new undertakings of young entrepreneurs. According to the guidelines, participation in the enterprise has a maximum of 750,000 German marks and is limited to ten years (generally) and the maximum financial burden on the equity capital must not exceed 12 per cent of the amount invested (all conditions as valid at present).[19] The capital investment company is not allowed to participate in the management of the enterprise, except during the initial start-up phase of newly established undertakings or during major changes in lines of business.

In the second stage, the capital investment companies can apply to the ERP-Fund for refinancing on the following conditions for credits: (i) interest rate 5 per cent annually; (ii) credit period ten years; (iii) payments in full and (iv) maximum credit 75 per cent of the equity capital investment — that is, 562,000 German marks.

The programme does not relate to capital investment companies in West Berlin for which the programme mentioned earlier already existed.[20] It aims at a balance of conflicting requirements.

First, it provided Federal Government aid for facilitating equity investment in small and medium-size enterprises. Second, it avoided any direct interference by the Federal Government in private decision making through the use of private investment companies. Third, it did not require the establishment of a new and, given the large number of potential addressee enterprises, a potentially huge Federal bureaucratic apparatus. Fourth, it could be carried out on a decentralised basis, meeting best the requirements of the individual enterprises.

One of the most important properties of the programme was that it corresponded to the political system of West Germany as a federation. As a general rule, the constitution of the Federal Republic assigns legislation to the member states of the federation, the Länder, except for some important fields comprising the uniformity of legal and economic conditions. Moreover, the execution of Federal law is as far as possible a matter for the Länder. While, over time, Federal Governments have increasingly taken over responsibilities and developed legislative regulations, the Länder have always insisted on, and maintained, their own competences in economic policies (among important other cases) in order to promote regional development. The Federal capital investment programme takes care of these sensibilities in as far as it is a Federal offer for financial aid; it was open to the Länder to use already existing institutions or to create new ones in order to raise funds from the programme for equity capital formation. As a matter of fact, since the introduction of the programme, investment companies have emerged under private law in all Länder. No company under private (majority) ownership, however, has been established in response to this programme, as, given its conditions, it is rather unattractive to profit-oriented private business. The returns on investment are limited to only 12 per cent, of which 3 per cent is normally profit sharing, and the companies are not allowed to engage in managing the enterprises (except in certain specific cases). Also, of course, the companies do not share in any hidden assets of the enterprises.

Two types of investment company emerged (see Appendix 8.1). The first type comprises ten investment companies fully owned by Landesbanks.[21] The Landesbanks are central credit institutes for the saving banks systems of the Länder; mostly the Länder hold a 50 per cent share in the Landesbank, while the rest of the shares are held (indirectly) by municipalities in the respective Länder. While the companies of the first type make use of the Federal programme, independently from that programme, they also engaged with their own funds from bank resources in providing equity capital to private enterprises. The companies are profit oriented. The second type comprises five companies, in which Landesbanks, various public utilities and also private banks hold shares. Majority shares, however, seem to lie directly or indirectly with the states, either by holdings of the Landesbanks or other state-owned banks, or even through direct state shareholding (as in Bavaria and Hesse). This is a presumption which cannot be substantiated as detailed information is available only on the names of the partners in the capital investment companies, but not on the size of their share. Even if the label 'state investment company' could not be justified for public majority holding in these companies, it would be justified by their financing and by their policies. The companies operate within the framework of the Federal programme only, not making any independent equity capital investment, although in addition to Federal funds the companies can draw on public funds from other sources. Their business policy is non-profit oriented.

Companies of the first type exist in all Länder save Hamburg and Berlin (in the case of Baden-Württemberg, a separate company has been established for both regions). At the end of 1979, these state investment companies, under control of the Landesbanks, held equity capital in 119 enterprises. Roughly 50 per cent of these equity capital holdings accounted for less than

750,000 German marks, thus meeting the limits of the Federal Government programme. In only 50 per cent of these cases, however, were funds from the programme taken for refinancing. This is to say that three quarters of the equity capital holding cases were engagements due to independent Landesbanks' initiatives for which limits, with respect to the amount of equity capital acquisition, seem not to exist. Information about the volume of this additional equity capital holding is not available.[22] The average size of the 119 enterprises in which the investment companies hold equity capital was 39 million German marks turnover and 260 persons employed. Thus small companies (accounting for less than 100 employees according to usual definitions) seem to constitute a minority of investment cases. Given that the intended addressees of the Federal programme are small businesses, this is presumably due to the independent engagement of the state investment companies with equity capital holding in enterprises far above average size. The Federal programme is an offer open to any enterprise meeting the requirements but it is possible that the state investment companies or their shareholders pursue specific aims. It is not clear why and in what way enterprises are singled out for equity capital investment by them.[23] Presumably, one purpose of the share taking is to avoid bankruptcies of private enterprises and to secure jobs. As has been intimated to the authors, it is no rare case that equity capital investment is made in order to prevent losses of credits which had earlier been provided by banks holding shares in the equity capital investment companies.

The second type of state investment company exists in the Federal states of Bavaria, Baden-Württemberg, North-Rhine-Westphalia, Hamburg and Hesse. In contrast to companies of the first type, which have made use of the Federal programme in roughly thirty cases only, these companies have engaged in a much larger number of private enterprises by equity capital investment. This can be explained by the fact that the companies, which buy shares from small and medium-size firms exclusively, strictly following the Federal programme, can draw on supplementary funds provided by additional equity capital programmes in their respective states. Up to 75 per cent of the refinancing of capital investment is provided by the Federal programme. The state programmes offer the remaining refinancing, either directly by offering credits from the budget at lower interest rates than those of the Federal programmes, or by cheap loans from public banks, or by relying on the capital market. In the latter case, public subsidies are granted in order to decrease the interest burden.

In the case of Hamburg, no additional state programme has been introduced. The Hamburg capital investment company, however, has refrained since 1975 from further equity capital investment as risks seem to be too high and persistent losses inevitable. Its 1979 business report announced the liquidation of still existing engagements and its complete withdrawal from the Federal programme.[24] This supports the view that the Federal programme alone is not an efficient means for achieving its assigned purpose. Since the addressee of the Federal programme is a small business, which cannot obtain or increase equity capital or credits from private sources on tolerable terms, the programme is directed at a high risk clientèle. Apparently, however, the risks are not met by the financial assistance offered to the capital investment companies within the framework of the Federal programmes. Moreover, the participation of private profit-oriented banks in these non-profit-oriented investment companies presumably has to be seen in close connection with the enterprises covered by the Federal programme. Potentially, it can provide opportunities to channel public funds to enterprises which may default on bank credits granted earlier. Another rationale behind the shareholding of privately owned banks and of public utilities is that the number of potential addressees for the programmes is thereby increased and selection of investee companies exclusively by state-owned banks avoided.

As Table 8.1 reveals, there were at the end of 1978 about 230 cases of equity capital holding by the five companies. Obviously the companies in Bavaria and in Baden-Württemberg have been most active in granting equity capital. This is largely due to the favourable conditions they can offer which, in turn, is due to state programmes. Thus, the introduction of a state programme aimed at giving incentives to the creation of new establishments coincided with a sharp rise in the number of equity capital holdings by the Baden-Württemberg company in 1979.

Taken together, equity capital holding by the five companies can be estimated at roughly 100 million marks at present. The average amount of capital invested per enterprise amounts to 280,000 marks. This is substantially less than in the case of capital

Table 8.1
Equity Capital Holding by Five Small-business-orientated Investment Companies, 1977–79

	Company in:				
	Baden-Württemberg	Bavaria	Hamburg	Hesse	North-Rhine-Westphalia
Number of investee companies					
1977	201	42	120	12	22	5
1978	236	48	144	11	27	6
1979	—	136	—	11	—	—
DM '000 invested per investee company, average					
1977–78	279	225	336	294	309	314

Source: Appendix 8.1.

investment companies of the first type where the average involvement can be roughly estimated to be at least three to five times higher.[25] Also, based on turnover and from employment figures, the presumption is substantiated that the clientèle of the second type of company consists of smaller enterprises than in the first case. For instance, in Bavaria, the average number of persons employed per investee enterprise was seventy in 1978, and the average turnover was 9.5 million marks (Hesse 8 million marks in 1978). This is only a quarter of the respective figures for the first type companies. This provides evidence that the aims of the Federal programme are pursued best by the second type of company. Evidence also exists that the five original small-business-oriented companies try to limit the time horizon for their holdings. All companies mention that repurchase of equity capital by the investee companies takes place to a reasonable degree. With regard to capital losses from bankruptcies of the investee enterprises, only limited information exists. The Hesse company mentions three cases of capital loss amounting to 850,000 marks since the beginning of equity capital investment.[26] The Bavarian company has suffered from five cases of capital loss adding up to 1.27 million marks or 3.9 per cent of a total of 43.2 million marks capital investment up to the end of 1978. The company regards these losses as relatively low, given its aim of providing capital in cases of high investment risk.[27]

As mentioned, both types of the discussed state investment companies make use of the Federal equity capital programme; in addition, type one companies invest in equity capital with their own resources and type two make use of funds provided from state programmes, of which part supplements the Federal programme. Figures concerning all equity capital holdings by the two types of companies are scarce and do not allow for detailed analyses. More comprehensive information is available for the Federal programme as a whole[28] which is not limited to the use of the above mentioned state investment companies. Of the credits granted by the ERP Fund to capital investment companies by the end of 1979, however, 93 per cent have been acquired by these state investment companies; the rest have been granted mostly to cooperative associations and comparable organisations. For this reason it can be claimed that the information provided for the whole Federal programme is likewise characteristic of the capital-investment structures of state investment companies, in so far as they raise funds from the programme. Until the end of 1979, 556 cases of credits granted have been accounted for in the framework of the Federal programme, amounting to a total sum of credits of 108 million marks and a total sum of equity capital investment by the investment companies of 114 million marks (Table 8.2). At the end of 1979 approximately 450 credits were still outstanding, accounting for about 85 million marks with an associated equity capital holding by the capital investment companies of about 115 million marks.

The fact that the overwhelming majority of involvements still exists can be traced to three factors. First, in the initial years of the programme only few equity capital investment cases occurred and, therefore, the number of credits to be repaid for reasons of time is small. Second, with the increase of capital market interest rates over the last few years, the programme has become most attractive. Third, state programmes supplementing the Federal Government programme were introduced only in 1977. Presumably this is a major reason why 35 per cent of all credits were granted by 1980;

Table 8.2
Development of Equity Capital Grants Within the Framework of the Federal Equity Capital Programme, 1971–80[a] (DM million)

Period	Cases	Credits granted to capital investment companies	Equity capital acquired by capital investment companies
1971	11	1.9	2.6
1972	29	4.8	6.3
1973	41	10.6	14.1
1974	61	15.0	20.0
1975	54	13.4	17.9
1976	58	14.4	19.2
1977	46	12.4	16.5
1978	58	12.4	16.5
1979	198	23.3	31.0
1980[b]	147	13.5	18.0

Source: Unpublished information of the Kreditanstalt für Wiederaufbau, Frankfurt (M).
[a] Affirmations of investee enterprises, of which, in a small number of cases, no use has been made.
[b] January to July.

figures for the first seven months of 1980 showed a further significant increase. The average volume of the credits given (108,000 marks) and of equity capital investment (144,000 marks), however, has decreased by roughly half in 1979 and 1980 as compared to earlier years (average 1971–78 credits, 237,000 marks; equity capital acquirement, 316,000 marks) which is also related to the implementation of the state programmes addressing young entrepreneurs starting new small businesses. In more than 90 per cent of all refinancing credits taken from the ERP Fund, capital investment companies have made use of the government subsidies offered within the framework of the programme for obtaining guarantees from guarantee companies (Beteiligungsgarantiegemeinschaften) against the risk of loss of equity capital. As could be expected from the activities of the regional capital investment companies oriented to small businesses in Baden-Württemberg and in Bavaria, these two states, above all, make use of the Federal programme. Bavaria accounts for 30 per cent of all cases and for 45 per cent of the credits provided by the ERP Fund;

Baden-Württemberg for 50 per cent and 30 per cent, again underlining that the programme of this state addresses small enterprises in particular.

Table 8.3 provides a sectoral breakdown of credits granted to equity capital investment companies for refinancing investment. The breakdown shows that about 60 per cent of all cases are manufacturing enterprises, accounting for 60 per cent of the credits as well. Credits per case are highest in the primary and intermediate goods industries, reflecting the above average capital intensity of these branches.

While it is obviously the intention of the Federal programme to give subsidies to small and medium-size enterprises, the whole amount of the equity capital granted to an enterprise cannot be regarded as a subsidy. Rather, the subsidisation consists of differences in costs of equity capital provided by the companies and costs of other ways of providing capital. It is important, too, that in cases of financing by equity capital funds, the investing company has to pay (local) business taxes, while in cases of outside financing these taxes are raised from the investee company. Table 8.3 contains figures for the subsidy equivalent of equity capital provided. These figures have been calculated taking into account both interest rate differences and taxation differences.[29] The calculations reveal a small subsidy equivalent ranging between 2,900 marks and 8,000 marks per case of equity capital holding, making up for less than 2 per cent of equity capital investment. Presumably, however, the actual subsidisation is often substantially higher since the programme in particular addresses (and attracts) those enterprises which cannot obtain bank credits or equity capital from other sources.

Examination of equity capital drawing by manufacturing branches reveals that the programme plays a more important role and, increasingly so, in branches which are above average export oriented, internationally competitive, technology and human capital intensive and little protected by external trade barriers. Also, they are more important in branches which are assisted by above average subsidies for research and development. The results seem to support the view that manufacturing enterprises engaged in more risky and new fields of activity make use of the programme more often. The results should not be overstressed, however, given (i) the relatively small number of enterprises

Table 8.3
ERP-Fund Refinancing Credits for Capital Investment Companies, 1971–79

Sector/industry	Cases (number)	Cases (% of total)	Credit per case (DM '000)	Subsidy equivalent per case[a] (DM '000)
Primary and intermediate goods[b]	41	7.4	252.6	5.1
Non-metallic minerals	9	1.6	264.9	5.9
Iron and steel	11	2.0	164.0	3.6
Non-ferrous metals	2	0.4	187.5	3.8
Foundries	1	0.2	375.0	7.5
Chemicals	9	1.6	318.1	6.6
Sawmills, woodwork	7	1.3	279.4	6.4
Rubber, asbestos	2	0.4	300.0	6.0
Capital goods	121	21.8	190.2	3.8
Structural and light metal engineering	3	0.5	324.7	8.0
Mechanical engineering[c]	40	7.2	243.6	5.2
Tranport equipment	15	2.7	72.5	1.8
Electrical engineering[d]	21	3.8	204.0	4.2
Professional goods	15	2.7	115.0	2.7
Metal products	27	4.9	192.7	4.1
Consumer goods	98	17.6	239.8	4.8
Pottery, chinaware, glass	5	0.9	227.6	5.5
Wood products (furniture)	41	7.4	261.4	5.8
Paper and products	—	—	—	—
Printing and publishing	20	3.6	180.4	4.0
Plastic products	20	3.6	251.1	5.5

covered by the Federal programme, (ii) the regional bias and (iii) the low degree of subsidisation which has been calculated. Moreover, information about the actual situation of the individual investee enterprises is not available.

From the figures provided it can be concluded that until July 1980 about 7.8 million marks, or 5 per cent of equity capital investment, have been lost due to bankruptcy in twenty-six investee enterprises. While these figures seem to indicate a relatively low investment risk, other cases of bankruptcy may have been avoided by granting additional funds (and funds, too, from private banks which are shareholders in the investment companies).

Table 8.3 cont'd

Sector/industry	Cases (number)	Cases (% of total)	Credit per case (DM '000)	Subsidy equivalent per case[a] (DM '000)
Leather and products	3	0.5	317.3	7.9
Textile and wearing apparel	9	1.6	229.9	5.3
Food, beverages and tobacco	28	5.0	199.9	4.3
Construction	39	7.0	134.8	3.0
Wholesale and retail trade	177	31.8	171.4	3.7
Wholesale trade	76	13.7	222.0	4.7
Retail trade	101	18.2	133.4	2.9
Others	52	9.4	191.1	4.1
Forwarding and storage trade	5	0.9	232.4	5.0
Hotels, restaurants	27	4.7	195.4	4.1
Other services	20	3.6	175.0	3.9
Total	556	100.0	194.3	4.2

Source: Unpublished information of the Kreditanstalt für Wiederaufbau, Frankfurt (M). Authors' own calculations.

[a] Cash value.
[b] Mineral oil refining excluded.
[c] Office machinery included.
[d] Data processing machinery included.

STATE INVESTMENT COMPANIES WITHIN A BROADER FRAMEWORK; WHAT ALTERNATIVE?

At present, the Federal Government provides only 15 million marks per annum from the ERP-Fund for refinancing credits within the framework of its equity capital programme and state governments add on approximately the same sum in order to finance equity capital investment by state investment companies which have been mostly created by public banks or in which public banks hold significant shares. The public banks, which are the sole or the majority shareholders in the state investment companies, have to compete in the market and are profit oriented. For this reason, in general, they follow a quite conservative business policy, not differing much from that of other banks. Such policies also have been followed in the activities of their state investment company subsidiaries which either are profit oriented (type one) or plan at least to make no losses (type two). The financial conditions provided within the framework of the Federal equity capital programme are too unattractive to induce strong efforts by the banks to extend their activities. While investee companies often regard the financial burden as too high, from the point of view of the investing company the returns to such investment appear too small to allow any substantial lowering of selection standards for equity capital investment. In addition, the companies and the private enterprises have reservations with regard to each other. From the side of the state investment companies, the management quality of the private enterprises is often put into question and, as the owner of these enterprises is also normally its business manager, it is hardly possible to improve the management quality. On the side of the enterprises, a possible loss of managerial autonomy of decision making is feared which in fact has occurred in some cases concerning important changes in business activities. For this reason the enterprises prefer to apply for funds from various other public sources before turning to the Federal governmental equity capital programme.

Such funds for the use of medium and small-size enterprises only, have become increasingly available and their volume far surpasses that of the equity capital programmes. For instance, in 1979, within the framework of Federal Government programmes financed out of the ERP-Fund, roughly 50 per cent (or 0.1 per cent of the gross national product) was provided for the purposes shown in Table 8.4.

Credits are available at effective interest rates of about 6.8 per cent annually for up to ten years though enterprises are required to provide collateral, as with credits from merchant banks. In addition to such funds from the ERP-Fund, credits are also available within the framework of a joint programme of the Federal and the state Governments (of roughly 1,000 million marks annually) to support economic development in selected regions. These are financed from the Federal budget and are not restricted to small and medium-size enterprises. Also, the Federal Government has recently introduced a programme of wage and salary subsidies

Table 8.4
Projects Within the Framework of the Federal Government Programme Financed out of the ERP-Fund in 1979[a]

	DM million	%
Investment in selected problem regions	625	43.3
Establishment of new enterprises and of new enterprises in new towns; investment to reduce pollution	660	48.9
Intra-enterprise training facilities, cooperation among enterprises	15	1.1
Introduction of electronic data processing	23	1.7
Enterprises of refugees	10	0.7
Small and medium-size press enterprises	15	1.1
Inland shipping enterprises	3	0.2
Total	1351	100.0

Source: 'Gesetz über die Feststellung der Wirtschaftspläne des ERP-Sondervermögens für das Jahr 1979', *Bundesgesetzblatt*, Part 1, Bonn, 1979, p. 1339.
[a] Out of the total sum provided by the ERP-Fund, roughly 50 per cent — or 0.1 per cent of the GNP — was provided for these projects.

which provide up to 500,000 marks per case in West Berlin and up to 400,000 marks elsewhere in the Federal Republic and which is designed to support research and development in small and medium-size enterprises (1979, 300 million marks). In addition, subsidies are available for cooperative research by small and medium-size manufacturing enterprises (67 million marks) or for the introduction of innovations to the market (20 million marks). These programmes, which cover the largest part (60 per cent) of funds available from the Federal Government budget (1979, 510 million marks) — additional state government funds are also provided on a similar scale — make it evident that the equity capital programme is relatively unimportant.

These programmes largely correspond to the traditional West German economic order as a set of rules for the market. But it has been increasingly argued that the market cannot by itself solve West Germany's economic problems and that specific incentives and intervention are needed to tempt capital into promising sectors of production.[30] A comprehensive Federal industrial policy designed to pursue specific government aims has not been developed, however, for the simple reason that such a policy cannot find a majority, given the governing coalition of parties in which opinions on the left wing of the social democrats differ widely from those in the middle and on the right wing of the liberals.

In contrast to what has sometimes been presumed, the Federal Government has not used its own industrial enterprises as an instrument of industrial policy or, at least, there has been no marked change in its attitudes to these enterprises over the last few decades. The Federal industrial property (see Appendix 8.2), inherited from the former German Reich and from the former Prussian state, has never been assigned any clear function. Governments have returned part to private hands and have attempted to do so in other cases in which, however, due to the unattractiveness of their offer they were not very successful.

To a significant degree Federal industrial enterprises are involved in supporting sectors which suffer from severe foreign competition, such as coal mining, iron and steel production or shipbuilding. Very often, moreover, these public enterprises are concentrated in regions which face a high rate of unemployment, below average per capita income or income growth and which lack fast growing modern industries. Government enterprises, for example, are important for regions such as the Saar (iron and steel industry, coal mining), Northern German regions on the border of the German Democratic Republic (brown coal, iron and steel), the Baltic (shipbuilding), the Ruhr area (coal mining) or Berlin (mechanical engineering). Reasons for this concentration in structurally weak sectors and regions are easily found. They are partly attributable to the engagement of pre-World War II governments in specific industrial branches. Some of these branches like iron and steel, which earlier were leaders of growth in the highly developed countries, have, in the course of world economic development, come under competitive pressure from newly industrialising countries. Pre-World War II government engagement in certain branches or regions was also designed to secure material supplies or to provide for employment. Finally, some of the public enterprises suffer from the post-World War II borders, which have created locational disadvantages, cutting down the hinterland (for example, Berlin, or eastern parts of Lower Saxony). If a policy strategy can be associated at all with Federal industrial property, it has to do with regional economic policies. When important enterprises prove to be uncompetitive, they normally are granted subsidies in order to avoid regional unemployment.[31]

Nevertheless, there has recently been criticism of the acquisition, by government owned and controlled enterprises, of equity in small and medium-size private enterprises. It has been argued that the Federal Government could by this means act as an equity capital investor without creating a specific state investment company. Between 1975 and 1979, Federal industrial enterprises have in fact invested about 440 million marks in private companies, of which the VEBA trust alone accounted for roughly two thirds.[32] While these engagements may be criticised as further increasing concentration, they have little to do with Federal policy attempts to strengthen government control over the economy. Rather, they are efforts of the public enterprises to improve competitiveness by diversifying production structures and by acquiring know-how. It is a different question, however, whether the Federal industrial enterprises are an efficient means of providing for economic growth.

Increasing criticism has also been aimed at the activities of the Federal Ministry for Research and Technology. The policies of this Ministry come the closest of any in the Federal Republic to industrial policy. Initially created in 1956 under the same Bundesministerium für Atomfragen (Federal Ministry for Nuclear Questions), in order to stimulate scientific and commercial progress in nuclear power generation, the Ministry in the course of time has subsidised various other new lines of technology regarded as promising for West German economic growth. More recently, it has seemed to claim competence and responsibilities also in the broader field of structural policies[33] and has rapidly increased funds going towards extension of its activities into new fields. Critics are concerned with this extension as such, but above all are concerned that the policies pursued are extremely selective and, moreover, support big business. In 1974, for which a detailed analysis has been carried out, roughly 70 per cent of the research and development (R and D) subsidies to manufacturing enterprises of 734 million marks were granted to only thirteen companies, all of them belonging to the list of the biggest German companies; 28 per cent were allocated to one company.[34] Since

1974 there has been some change, but R and D policies are still biased towards large business.

The reasons for this bias seem to be obvious. Politicians argue that the most promising new lines of technology require such huge amounts of R and D investment and such huge research capacities that they can be provided only by big companies. The argument lacks empirical support, however. Of course, the biggest steps in technological development are sometimes made by the biggest companies. While big companies may carry out the biggest projects which draw much attention to themselves, however — which may partly explain the big business preference of R and D policy makers — this is neither to say that these projects provide the highest overall economic returns to R and D investment nor that they contribute most to technological advance. But, in the view of policy-makers, orienting R and D policies to big business, instead of supporting large numbers of small and medium-size enterprises, has the advantage of avoiding the establishment of a huge bureaucracy. This reasoning is valid, however, only in cases where R and D policies entail project selection and subsidisation. If programme aid were provided by tax cuts or depreciation allowances to all enterprises undertaking R and D efforts, for example, a ministry for research and development would not even be needed.

Recent policy changes have mainly been intended to increase the number of projects and to extend project aid to smaller and medium-size enterprises. This clearly raises the danger that Federal Government interference in the economy, and in the till now sacrosanct small- and medium-size sector of the economy, will become much more intensive, introducing strong elements of investment control. This is the more so as R and D subsidies are far more lucrative than, for instance, the much more expensive equity capital obtained from the Federal programme.

SUMMARY AND CONCLUSIONS

The creation of state investment companies in the Federal Republic has not been motivated by ideas of sharper government control over the private sector: rather, improving the equity capital basis of private enterprises has played the dominant role in the debate. From a very high level at the beginning of the 1950s, self-financed investment in the following decades fell substantially. While this development has drawn much public attention, it was not, as such, really regarded as an economic policy problem. The earlier high degree of self financing was due to artificial measures which had led to a number of disadvantageous side effects. Indeed, it was argued that an increase in outside financing could even be fruitful in so far as it leads to more informed choice among investment projects. It was also argued, however, that economic policies should aim to strengthen the equity capital basis of small and medium-size enterprises which, by their legal construction, hardly have access to capital markets.

When the equity capital programme of the Federal Government, which led to the creation of state investment companies, was finally introduced in 1971, after a long debate, it was mostly for these fundamental economic policy reasons. In the meantime, this (*ordnungspolitische*) reasoning has been supplemented by arguments stemming from the poor economic performance of the West German economy. Adjustment to the structural changes, which have imposed severe pressures on West Germany as on other industrialised countries since the early 1970s, requires, it is said, the mobilisation of ideas and energy from entrepreneurs of small- and medium-size enterprises.

Although these arguments have been increasingly stressed, state investment company activities, with 570 cases of equity capital holding at the end of 1979, have not achieved major importance.[35] The main industrial policy concept has never been developed, defining specific aims and assigning their pursuit to specific institution. Admittedly, in the early 1950s, measures were adopted to promote the growth of some selected industries. This was done on an *ad hoc* basis for alleged practical reasons — it was aimed at rapidly widening 'bottlenecks' to overall economic growth — and not for fundamental doctrinaire convictions which, for instance, might have led governments to engage in the enterprises involved by acquisition of equity capital. That many of the sectors assisted in the 1950s still enjoy public aid is a different matter. The reasons for granting such aid have often changed, at present focussing, for example, on help against international competition (shipbuilding, iron and steel; coal mining).

The lack of and the dislike of the idea of a comprehensive

industrial strategy presumably explains, too, why the sizable Federal industrial property has never been used for any specific purpose, except in some cases for regional policy aims. Equity capital investment by public industrial enterprises, therefore, is motivated by efforts to strengthen competitiveness rather than by any attempt by governments to achieve stronger control over private enterprises and their decision making. Such decision-influencing impacts, however, obviously result from Federal research and development policies which are not designed generally to induce research and development efforts but to promote selected lines of production and selected technologies.

It could be argued, however, that equity capital provision to small and medium-size enterprises should play a stronger role than at present. One major economic argument behind all the programmes of aid mentioned (including state investment companies) is that the social benefits from the activities of these enterprises are higher than the private returns. For this reasons, the equity capital and credits available to such enterprises are less in the absence of intervention than is desirable from a social welfare point of view. This might occur because a similar risk is given greater weight in investment decisions for smaller enterprises; or because the external benefits deriving from the existence of small and medium-size enterprises are not accounted for in private (including bank) decision-making. The efficiency gains stemming from the competition provided by the existence and emergence of large numbers of innovative, small- and medium-size producers is an example of such an external benefit.

Given the attitudes of private agents, it can be argued that governments could induce a better allocation of financial resources between different sized enterprises. This does not require governments themselves to place equity capital or credits or subsidies at the disposal of private enterprises. Rather, governments should reduce the difference between the private and social returns by granting interest subsidies to private capital investment companies to induce them to channel more private venture capital to small and medium-size enterprises.

At present, the conditions attached to the Federal programme are too unfavourable to attract private capital investment companies. This explains why the programme is used almost exclusively by state investment companies. An equity capital programme of the proposed design could largely replace the various credit programmes introduced by Federal and state Governments. With publicly subsidised equity capital costs for the investee company, for instance, comparable to those of the present credit programmes, the equity capital programme presumably would be quite attractive to small- and medium-size enterprises. This would require a selection among the applicants for the programme. A selection has to be made at present with the governmental credit programmes, too. But it makes a difference, whether the selection is by bureaucrats or by those involved in private capital markets. A different question, however, is whether governments should concern themselves with the allocation of funds to small and medium-size enterprises. In so far as capital markets favour investment in bigger companies due to previous government actions (tax laws, laws concerning bank policy, or whatever), the best remedy is to abolish such measures.

NOTES AND REFERENCES

1. The results and the consequences of the report entitled 'Bericht über die Möglichkeit zur Förderung der wirtschaftlichen Entwicklung West-Berlins vom 15. Dezember 1952' (Wood-Bericht) are described in *ERP-Hilfe für Berlin 1948–1958* (Bad Godesberg: Bundesministerium für wirtschaftlichen Besitz des Bundes, 1959) pp. 17 *et seq.*

2. See 'Gesetz über die Feststellung des Wirtschaftsplans des ERP-Sondervermögens für das Rechnungsjahr 1954', *Bundesgesetzblatt*, Bonn, Part II, 1954, pp. 1052–98, and *ERP-Hilfe für Berlin 1948–1958, op. cit.*

3. On 12 February 1948, the United States and British military governments enacted US-Law 56 and British Ordinance 78 for their respective zones forbidding too high an economic concentration. The laws were to be carried out by the military governments. It was intended that these laws should be replaced by a later German anti-monopoly law. On 29 March 1949, the Bipartite Control Office demanded in a letter (BICO Memo 49/30) that the Economic Council for the Joint Economic Zone (Wirtschaftsrat des Vereinigten Wirtschaftsgebietes) provide a draft for a law aimed at strengthening competition. The Council itself had

already decided upon such legislation in connection with the currency reform of 20 June 1948. See *Entwurf zu einem Gesetz zur Sicherung des Leistungswettbewerbes und zu einem Gesetz über das Monopolamt mit Stellungnahme des Sachverständigenausschusses und Minderheitsgutachten* (Frankfurt: Lutzeyer, 1952).

4.   For details of the incentive system, see Harald Jürgensen and Werner Ehrlicher, 'Einkommensbesteuerung und Wirtschaftswachstum', Hamburg, 1964; Dorothea Meyer, *Entwicklung und Motive der nichtfiskalischen (insbesondere der wirtschaftspolitisch orientierten) Besteuerung in Deutschland auf der Ebene des Zentralstaates von 1871 bis 1969* (Münster: Universität Münster, 1977).

5.   See *Bericht der Bundesregierung über die Kreditversorgung der kleinen und mittleren Betriebe in der Wirtschaft vom 29. Juli 1963*, Deutscher Bundestag, 4. Wahlperiode, Drucksache IV/1444 (Bad Godesberg: Dr Hans Heger, 1963) p. 9.

6.   The Federal Government contributed also in a very direct way to the strengthening of big enterprises. With the Investment Aid Law of 1952, business was forced to buy one billion German marks' worth of securities from the so-called bottleneck (to growth) sectors. 132,000 firms had to contribute funds which were transferred to 187 enterprises; thirty-four were coal mining and electricity generation firms and twenty-two firms were in the iron and steel industry. See Wolfgang F. Stolper and Karl W. Roskamp, 'Planning a Free Economy: Germany 1945–1960', *Zeitschrift für die gesamte Staatswissenschaft*, Tübingen, Vol. 135, 1979, pp. 374–404. As early as 1952, large enterprises were to be found in the above-mentioned industries and, in the course of time, the degree of concentration increased substantially, surpassing (by far) the degree of concentration in most other industries.

7.   See *Berichte zur Lage und Entwicklung kleiner und mittlerer Unternehmen in ausgewählten Wirtschaftsbereichen und zur Förderung dieser Unternehmen durch die Bundesregierung, Oktober 1968*, Deutscher Bundestag, 5. Wahlperiode, Drucksache V/3678 (Bad Godesberg: Dr Hans Heger, 1968).

8.   See *Bericht über das Ergebnis einer Untersuchung der Konzentration in der Wirtschaft vom 29. Februar 1964*, Deutscher Bundestag, 4. Wahlperiode, Drucksache IV/2320 (Bad Godesberg: Dr Hans Heger, 1964).

9.   These poor results were mainly traced back to a weak

empirical basis and to legal regulations restricting the availability of material to public authorities.

10. See Wissenschaftlicher Beirat beim Bundeswirtschaftsministerium, *Selbstfinanzierung bei verlangsamtem wirtschaftlichen Wachstum, Gutachten vom 16. Februar 1963* (Göttingen: Vandenhoek und Ruprecht, 1966) pp. 41–5; and Sachverständigenrat zur Begutachtung der gesamtwirtschaftlichen Entwicklung, *Stabiles Geld — Stetiges Wachstum, Jahresgutachten 1964* (Stuttgart: W. Kohlhammer, 1965).

11. In 1967, for instance, a research project carried out on behalf of the Federal Ministry of Economics was completed which investigated national and international experience with various types of investment corporation. The authors suggest that a decentralised system of public utility investment companies be established with companies able to buy equity capital with cheap, government-subsidised credit. See Karl Hax, *Kapitalbeteiligungsgesellschaften zur Finanzierung kleiner und mittlerer Unternehmungen* (Köln and Opladen: Westdeutscher Verlag, 1969).

12. This becomes evident from the various papers delivered, among others, by government officials at the Deutsche Genossenschaftstag 1965 (1965 Meeting of the German Association of Cooperatives), devoted to the financing of small and medium-size enterprises. See especially Franz Coester, 'Finanzierungsprobleme der Klein- und Mittelbetriebe wirtschaftspolitisch gesehen', *Blätter für Genossenschaftswesen*, Bonn, Vol. 111, 1965, pp. 286–91; and papers delivered by other authors in the same volume.

13. In this context, it is interesting to know that the Federal Government refused to grant interest-rate subsidies to the Kreditgarantiegemeinschaften. The argument was that demand for investment funds would be artificially increased, leading to capital market disequililbria and higher interest rates. Therefore, requests for such subsidies were rejected as 'non market conforming' — a term labelling actions contradictory to the official economic philosophy. See Coester, *op. cit.*

14. For 1969, ten privately financed equity capital investment companies are mentioned as operating in the Federal Republic of Germany. Friedrich K. Feldbausch, 'Die Kapitalbeteiligungsgesellschaft in Deutschland', *Zeitschrift für das gesamte Kreditwesen*, Frankfurt (M), Vol. 9, 1969, pp. 353–6.

15. Presse- und Informationsamt der Bundesregierung, 'Vor-

bereitung der Gründung einer ERP-Kapitalbeteiligungsgesell-
schaft', *Bulletin*, Bonn, No. 114, 1969, p. 976.

16.   Karl Schiller, 'Handwerk hat Zukunft', in *Text 7, Reden
zur Wirtschaftspolitik* (Bonn: Bundesministerium für Wirtschaft,
1970).

17.   The ERP-Fund is a special property of the Federal Government. Its assets originally stem from grants awarded to the
West German economy by the United States government under
the Appropriations for Relief in Occupied Areas programme
(1,700 million dollars) in 1946 and by the European Recovery
Programme (1,300 million dollars) in 1948. While the German
Federal Government had to repay one billion dollars, which it did
in 1961, German importers had to make payments in German
marks to the German Federal Government for deliveries from the
United States in the framework of the aid programmes mentioned
above; thus, the ERP-Fund represents the German mark equivalent of American deliveries and since the end of the programmes
the fund has been totally financed from credit repayments and
interest payments for credits granted. The assets of the ERP-Fund
accounted for about 5,000 million marks in 1952 and about 10,000
million marks in 1981. The fund is at the disposal of the Federal
Government which uses it mostly for structural adjustment policies.

18.   To clarify the different activities of the institutions mentioned, the following should be said: (i) the term Kapitalbeteiligungsgesellschaften (capital investment companies) refers to companies directly investing in equity capital; (ii) the term Beteiligungsgarantiegemeinschaften (equity capital guarantee company)
applies to companies granting guarantees to capital investment
companies; (iii) the term Kreditgarantiegemeinschaften (credit
guarantee associations) is restricted to associations providing
credit guarantees and not equity capital or guarantees for equity
capital investment. Despite these differences, the shareholders or
members of the three institutions which belong to the system of
financing small and medium-size enterprises, may often be identical; for instance, state-owned banks.

19.   For more details see Der Bundesminister für Wirtschaft,
'Bekanntmachung der Allgemeinen Bedingungen für die Vergabe
von ERP-Mitteln sowie der Richtlinien zur Gewährung von ERP-
Darlehen vom 21. Juli 1976', *Bundesanzeiger*, Bonn, 1976, Vol.
28, No. 139, pp. 1–5 and in particular Anlage 6 (Annex 6).

20.   As mentioned, the Berlin programme extends also to large enterprises and in general provides for more favourable conditions (see Der Bundesminister für Wirtschaft, *ibid.*, in particular Anlage 23). In Berlin, in the case of a silent partnership, for instance, the rates of fixed return on investment vary between 3.5 per cent and 4.5 per cent annually and additional profit sharing is limited to 3 per cent. In the programme for West Germany no regulations with regard to the split of returns on the investment have been made but, as a rule, apart from a limitation of profit sharing to 3 per cent, the fixed returns on investment are 8 per cent. See, for instance, *Geschäftsbericht für 1978/79* (Dusseldorf: Kapitalbeteiligungsgesellschaft für die mittelständische Wirtschaft in Nordrhein-Westfalen GmbH, January 1980). Moreover, the available funds of the Berlin programme are significantly larger. In 1979, out of the ERP, 120 million marks were granted for equity capital purposes in Berlin, which compares with 15 million marks in West Germany. It is true that 100 million marks of the Berlin programme were for strengthening the capital base of the Deutsche Industrieanlagen GmbH (DIAG) which had suffered severe losses. This is a company originally formed by four Berlin mechanical engineering enterprises which, for different reasons, were acquired by the Federal Government in the aftermath of World War II. Through earlier equity capital investment, approximately 99 per cent of the DIAG shares are held by the ERP-Fund, that is, the Federal Government. Even leaving aside the funds allocated to the DIAG, however, the Berlin programme nevertheless exceeds the programme for other Federal areas and, of course, its impact is the more significant as its regional coverage is much smaller. On 31 August 1978, thirty-five cases of existing equity capital holding were accounted for within the framework of the Berlin programme making a total of 217 million marks in equity capital shares; fifteen out of the thirty–five cases had been acquired in 1978.

21.   In the case of the Saarland, another public bank holds shares in the state's investment company and in private banks, in addition to the Landesbank. Landesbanks are operated independently of state governments, although, effectively, political influence can be substantial; this is the more so as both the supervisory board and the executive board mostly consist of (former) eminent persons from the political scene.

22.   The Landesbank-owned capital investment companies are

rather secretive about their activities. Most companies, as well as their shareholders, refused to give information other than scattered hints in their annual reports.

23. As has been mentioned by a member of the board of managing directors of the Landesbank of the Rhineland-Palatinate, the companies subordinate their own policies for capital acquisition when higher ranking state policies play a role. See Paul Skonieczny, 'Grundsätze und Probleme der Beteiligungs-politik der Girozentralen — dargestellt am Beispiel der Landesbank Rheinland-Pfalz', *Beiträge zu aktuellen Problemen des deutschen Kreditwesens*, Mainz, Vol. 6, 1975, pp. 83–95.

24. See *Geschäftsbericht 1979* (Hamburg: BG Hamburg, Beteiligungsgesellschaft für Industrie, Handwerk, Handel und Verkehr GmbH, 1980) p. 6 *et seq.*

25. Exact figures for equity capital holdings by the type one companies in the 119 cases mentioned are not available. Presumably, they account for significantly more than the 100 million marks' holdings of the type two companies.

26. *Bericht über das Geschäftsjahr vom 1. Januar bis 31. Dezember 1978* (Wiesbaden: MBG, Mittelständische Beteiligungs-gesellschaft Hessen GmbH, 1979) p. 11.

27. *Geschäftsbericht 1978* (Munich: Kapitalbeteiligungs-gesellschaft für die mittelständische Wirtschaft Bayerns GmbH und Bayerische Garantiegesellschaft GmbH für mittelständische Beteiligungen, 1979) p. 16.

28. Much of this information was made available in an unbureaucratic manner by the Kreditanstalt für Wiederaufbau to whom the authors owe thanks.

29. The calculations were done in the following way: annual differences between capital market interest rates and costs of equity capital plus 2 per cent of the sum invested stemming from tax advantages, both discounted for the period of the equity capital investment.

30. This argument has been supported, for instance, by the Federal Minister of the Treasury, Hans Matthöfer. According to the *Frankfurter Allgemeine Zeitung*, Frankfurt, 10 August 1978, he stated frankly: 'I want to control investment'. He believed he personally knew what future structures would be necessary in order for West Germany to remain internationally competitive.

31. Besides manufacturing, a number of other important

Federal — and also state or local — enterprises exist, which enjoy either monopolies or advantageous regulations and mostly receive large subsidies (Federal railway system, postal services). Structural policy aims are formulated and pursued specifically for these enterprises. Mostly, however, these aims concern social or regional policy (for example, the railway system) and sometimes it is claimed that public monopolies are necessary in order to avoid private monopolies (postal services, electricity distribution). See Klaus-Werner Schatz, 'La Experiencia Nacionalizadora En Alemania Federal', in James M. Buchanan, Enrique F. Quintana, Herbert Giersch *et al.* (eds), *El Sector Publico En Las Economias De Mercado* (Madrid: Espasa-Calpe, 1979) pp. 344–54.

32. *Antwort der Bundesregierung auf die Kleine Anfrage von fünf Abgeordneten und der Fraktion der CDU/CSU: Aufkäufe privater Unternehmen durch Bundesunternehmen*, Deutscher Bundestag, 8. Wahlperiode, Drucksache VIII/3284, 18 October 1978 (Bonn: Dr Hans Heger, 1979).

33. For instance, the ministry has strongly supported the results of a research project carried out on its behalf demanding a 100,000 million marks Federal programme (which means an annual GNP quota of roughly 1 per cent for 1980–85) to overcome present and future adjustment requirements and to provide full employment.

34. The term subsidy refers to direct financial assistance (excluding tax privileges) without any material equivalent from the subsidised enterprise. For details of the comprehensive study covering subsidies of various sorts in the Federal Republic of Germany, see Karl Heinz Jüttemeier *et al.*, *Auswirkungen der öffentlichen Haushalte auf sektorale Investitionsentscheidungen im Industrie und Dienstleistungsbereich*, Forschungsauftrag des Bundesministers für Wirtschaft, Endbericht (Kiel: Institut für Weltwirtschaft, 1977); Karl Heinz Jüttemeier and Konrad Lammers, *Subventionen in der Bundesrepublik Deutschland*, Kiel Discussion Paper No. 63/64 (Kiel: Institut für Weltwirtschaft, 1979).

35. In roughly 80 per cent of the 570 cases equity capital is provided within the framework of the Federal programme by the ERP-Fund, another 6 per cent are concerned with the specific Berlin programme. In the other cases, equity capital is held independently of Federal programmes by state banks out of their own funds.

Appendix 8.1
List of Investment Companies with Public Capital Shares

1. Companies Of The Regional Banking Sector (Landesbanken)

In 1979 the equity capital of ten investment companies was held by regional banks with state and/or local ownership. All together, these ten investor companies held capital shares in 119 investee enterprises which mostly belong to the industrial sector.

Schleswig-Holsteinische Kapitalbeteilingungsgesellschaft GmbH, Kiel
Sole owner is the Landesbank of Schleswig-Holstein. Partnership interests exist in about ten investee companies.

Norddeutsche Kapitalbeteiligungsgesellschaft GmbH, Hannover
Sole owner is the Landesbank of Lower Saxony. Partnership interests exist only in a few investee companies.

Nordwestdeutsche Kapitalbeteiligungsgesellschaft GmbH KG, Bremen
Partners are the Landesbank of Bremen and various savings banks of that region. The company has stated its partnership interests are very few.

Westdeutsche Kapitalbeteiligungsgesellschaft GmbH, Düsseldorf
Sole owner is the Landesbank of North-Rhine-Westphalia. Since its foundation the company has taken up capital shares in twenty-nine enterprises representing an ownership capital of about DM 40 million. In 1979 there still existed partnership interests in seventeen investee companies.

Anlagen- und Verwaltungsgesellschaft GmbH, Frankfurt (M)
Sole owner is the Landesbank of Hesse. Partnership interests exist in eleven investee companies.

Kapitalbeteiligungsgesellschaft Rheinland-Pfalz GmbH, Mainz
Sole owner is the Landesbank of Rhineland-Palatinate. Partnership interests exist in nineteen investee companies representing an ownership capital of DM 19 million.

Saarländische Kapitalbeteiligungsgesellschaft GmbH, Saarbrücken
Partners are the Landesbank of Saarland, the Saarländische Investitionskreditbank AG — in which the Saar Government has a controlling majority interest — and some other credit institutions. Partnership interests exist in four investee companies.

Leasing- und Beteiligungsgesellschaft GmbH, Mannheim
Sole owner is the Landesbank of Baden. According to information from

the bank there exist only a few partnership interests representing an ownership capital of DM 6 million.

Württembergische Kapitalbeteiligungsgessellschaft GmbH, Stuttgart
Sole owner is the Landesbank of Württemberg. Number and amount of partnership interest are unknown.

Bayerische Kapitalbeteiligungsgesellschaft GmbH, München
Sole owner is the Landesbank of Bavaria. Number and amount of partnership interests are unknown.

2. Small-Business Oriented Investment Companies

Beteiligungsgesellschaft für Industrie, Handwerk, Handel und Verkehr GmbH, Hamburg
Partners are various public and private regional banks and some national banking houses. Parts of the equity capital are held by the Landesbank of Hamburg and the Hamburg Savings Bank. The investor company operates only in the field of small and medium sized enterprises. In 1979, there existed partnership interests in eleven investee companies representing an ownership capital of DM 3.2 million. Because it lacks rentability the company does not acquire any further partnerships.

Kapitalbeteiligungsgessellschaft für die mittelständische Wirtschaft in Nordrhein-Westfalen GmbH Düsseldorf
Partners are the Landesbank of North-Rhine-Westphalia, some private banks and regional chambers of commerce. Like the Hamburg institution the company operates only in the field of publicly promoted partnership financing. The state government has granted a loan at a low rate of interest; a loss of the company can be charged up against the state loan. In 1979, there existed partnership interests in six enterprises representing an ownership capital of DM 1.7 million.

Mittelständische Beteiligungsgesellschaft Hessen GmbH, Wiesbaden
Partners are the Landesbank of Hesse, the Federal State of Hesse, private banks and regional chambers of commerce. The office routine is done by the Hessische Landesentwicklungs- und Treuhandgesellschaft GmbH, Wiesbaden, which is a state-owned bank with specific functions. The Land of Hesse grants subsidies for interests. In 1978 the investor company held partnership interests in twenty-seven enterprises representing an ownership capital of DM 7.7 million.

Mittelständische Beteiligungsgesellschaft Baden-Württemberg GmbH, Stuttgart
The majority ownership falls upon the Bürgschäftsbank Baden-Württemberg, a guaranty bank which is formed by a variety of public and private institutions. Other partners of the investor company are two Landesbanks of Baden-Württemberg, the Landeskreditanstalt of Baden-

Württemberg which is a state-owned bank with specific functions, and private banks. Apart from Federal programmes the company also has access to refinancing credits at a low interest rate from the Landeskreditbank; additionally, the state government has placed the execution of a supplementary programme for new establishments with the company. In 1979 there existed 136 partnership interests representing an ownership capital of DM 24.4 million.

Kapitalbeteiligungsgesellschaft für die mittelständische Wirtschaft Bayerns GmbH, München
Partners are the Landesbank of Bavaria, the Federal State of Bavaria, the Bayerische Landesanstalt für Aufbaufinanzierung which is a state-owned bank with specific functions, and a variety of private banks and institutions. The office routine is done by the Landesanstalt. Apart from Federal programmes the investor company has access to refinancing credits at a low rate of interest with the Landesanstalt, too. In 1978 there existed 144 partnership interests representing an ownership capital of DM 48.4 million.

3. *Berliner Industriebank AG, Berlin*
The Berlin Industry Bank, which operates only in specific fields, is a publicly-controlled bank; most of the shares are held by institutions of the Federal Government (ERP-Fund 68 per cent, Kreditanstalt für Wiederaufbau 20 per cent). The bank has a special branch for acquiring partnerships with credit instruments supplied by the ERP-Fund. In 1978 there existed thirty-five partnership interests representing an ownership capital of DM 217 million.

Appendix 8.2
Industrial Holdings of the Federal Government

Salzgitter AG, Berlin and Salzgitter
This is a holding at 100 per cent under Federal Governmental ownership with a workforce of about 54,000 persons and holding shares in 134 other companies (at least 25 per cent of the shares of these companies). Main activities of the Salzgitter AG concern production of and trade with steel and steel products, shipbuilding, railway transport equipment and machinery. The Salzgitter AG can be described as a conglomerate of production activities ranking around some involvements of the former German Reich in the 1930s in iron ore mining and processing which would not have been profitable from a private investor's point of view.

Vereinigte Industrie-Unternehmungen AG, Berlin and Bonn (VIAG)
In the VIAG-holding, Federal Government directly accounts for 84 per cent of the shares, the rest of the shares held by the Kreditanstalt für Wiederaufbau, a bank which belongs to the Federal and regional govern-

ments; the VIAG employs 22,000 persons and is engaged in a further seventy-nine companies. VIAG mainly produces and processes aluminium, generates electricity and supplies chemicals. VIAG was founded in the 1920s in order to organise in one holding all government involvement in industrial production which then existed; to an important extent this involvement stemmed from governmental investment in the production of aluminium and of electrical power plants complementary to the production of aluminium which had been made for military purposes during World War I. Post World War II, there was a reorganisation of governmental activities which brought about the present concentration of VIAG in the activities named above.

Saarbergwerke AG, Saarbrücken

This holding which employs 29,000 persons (Federal governmental share, 74 per cent; the Saarland, 26 per cent), holds shares in another fifty companies. The activities of the Saarbergwerke AG, mainly engaged in coal mining and processing, in electricity and in trade with coal, coal products and mineral oil, are regionally concentrated in the area near to the French border. In the Saarbergwerke AG a number of productions is organised, which came under governmental control in the aftermath of World War II mainly due to lacking private rentability.

Industrieverwaltungsgesellschaft GmbH, Bonn (IVG)

This is a smaller holding with about 4,000 employees; it is wholly owned by the Federal government and holds shares in eight other companies. The IVG administers governmental industrial properties and real estate; it is also engaged in mineral oil transport and storage and in leasing of railway transport equipment.

Vereinigte Elektrizitäts- und Bergwerks AG (VEBA), Bonn and Berlin

The share of the Federal government accounts for 43.75 per cent; the rest falls upon 1m shareholders. The VEBA holding is engaged in 365 companies and employs altogether 80,000 persons. Main fields of operation are electricity, mineral oil, chemicals, trade and transportation. VEBA is the biggest individual shareholder in the Ruhrkohle AG (27.2 per cent), a company which accounts for nearly all of the coal mining in the Ruhr area. VEBA was founded in 1920 by the then Prussian state in order to concentrate various industrial enterprises in one holding. In the 1960s more than 50 per cent of the shares were sold to private persons.

Volkswagenwerk AG, Wolfsburg

The Federal Government and the Federal state of Lower Saxony each hold 20 per cent of the capital; 60 per cent are held by mostly private shareholders. In 1978 Volkswagen employed roughly 200,000 persons in more than fifty different companies. Main fields of operation are all sorts of activities concerning production and distribution of cars. However, in recent years the company has put a lot of emphasis on diversifying production. Volkswagen was founded in the late 1930s as a public enterprise by the then German Reich; in the late 1950s 60 per cent of the capital was sold to private persons.

Deutsche Industrieanlagen GmbH (DIAG), Berlin
DIAG belongs to the ERP-Fund (98.8 per cent) which is itself controlled by the Federal Government. The holding mainly consists of four Berlin mechanical engineering companies that came under Federal control after World War II. In 1978 DIAG employed 5,500 persons; main fields of operation are production and distribution of machines, tools and all kinds of fabricating parts.

CHAPTER NINE

United Kingdom: Pulling Dragon's Teeth — the National Enterprise Board

Brian Hindley and Ray Richardson

The National Enterprise Board (NEB) is a symbol in a political debate as well as an economic institution. Probably it has more significance in the former capacity than in the latter and, certainly, its true importance might be missed by any purely economic evaluation of its purposes and performance.

When a government loses office in Britain, at least one section of the out-going party is likely to hold an inquest on the reasons for the loss. When Labour Governments lose office, the inquest is typically held by the left wing of the Party and usually results in the verdict that the defeat was caused by an inadequate application of the party's fundamental programme.

The ensuing debate does not usually end in clear victory for any faction: the normal outcome is an ambiguous compromise. Following the election defeat of the Labour Government in 1970, however, the left wing won a clear victory, albeit one that was limited to certain policy areas. The most important of those was industrial intervention and the NEB was first conceived as a central instrument of the Party's planned new policies in this area.

In 1974, however, with the return of a Labour Government, it became apparent that the left's victory was empty of practical consequence. The Party's novel industrial proposals were not translated into the necessary legislative forms. In particular, the NEB emerged as a modest and limited organisation, bearing little relationship to the NEB that had been planned while the Party was in opposition.

One consequence of this political reversal is that, following the general election defeat of the Labour Government in 1979, the left wing embarked on a more urgent and far more comprehensive attempt to control both the Labour Party and any future Labour Government. This attempt goes far beyond industrial and economic policy and involves constitutional questions affecting traditional Parliamentary processes as well as the Labour Party itself.

In the following sections, the post-1970 debate and its denouement is followed in some detail — in part because of its intrinsic interest but in larger part because it serves as an illustration of the elasticity inherent in the notion of a state investment company. We then turn to an assessment of the performance of the NEB as it actually emerged in 1974.

BACKGROUND TO THE NEB

The major industrial policy innovation of the 1964–70 Labour Governments was the Industrial Reorganisation Corporation. This, as we have suggested in Chapter 5, was a product of the Party's right wing and was clearly intended to strengthen the privately-owned sectors of manufacturing industry. The IRC never aroused the enthusiasm or the affection of the left wing of the Party: nor was its record seen elsewhere to supply a basis for a claim that it should be reconstituted after the Conservative Government had dismantled it in 1970. Instead, the Labour Party's industrial policy intentions went in a very different direction. If the key word of the Labour Party's industrial policy of 1964 was 'modernisation', its counterpart ten years later was 'planning'. The twin centres of this planning experiment were to be a proposed network of planning agreements and the establishment of a powerful NEB.

Planning agreements were seen as a system of individual tripartite agreements involving the Government, the relevant trade unions and at least the largest 100 private manufacturing firms, as well as all the major public corporations. The system was intended to diffuse up-to-date information among the participants and to assist the Government in meeting its planning objectives, whatever they were. There was considerable discussion on whether the system should be voluntary or compulsory (the contradictions involved in the notion of 'compulsory agreements' revealed themselves only to those with a taste for irony — a taste sometimes not well-developed in parts of the Labour Party).

The role of the NEB was originally seen to be more complex. It was officially described in 1973 as 'a new and more flexible instrument of national and regional planning'. Its potential tasks were then seen to be: (i) job creation, especially in areas of high unemployment; (ii) investment promotion; (iii) technological development; (iv) growth of exports; (v) promoting government price policies; (vi) tackling the spread of multi-national companies; (vii) the spread of industrial democracy; and (viii) import substitution.[1]

It was natural for the Labour Party to have policy goals in all of these areas. The regional problem, low rates of investment, slow technological advance and balance of trade difficulties had provided staple policy targets for many years. The other areas were of more recent interest but it was not surprising that they should have been matters of concern. The novelty, then, lay not in the ends but in the means.

Most of the above goals had been the focus of policy initiatives by all British Governments for many years. What the NEB represented in 1973 was a belief in Labour Party circles that such initiatives should no longer be confined to providing financial incentives to the private sector for their achievement. The NEB implied that henceforth there would be *command* and *direction*. It was seen to provide an instrument for exercising direct control over profitable manufacturing industry. This was to be done by the compulsory acquisition of a controlling state interest in a range of large private manufacturing companies. The controlling interest was seen to provide the means by which the choices of the market would be short-circuited and the Government's planning goals implemented by direct instruction.

Implicitly or explicitly, the supporters of this version of the NEB were making large claims to have identified some of the institutional reasons for previous economic failure. It might be thought that such claims had been the focus of widespread and searching debate before they had become integrated into the platform of a prospective government party. This, however, was not the case.

Within the Labour Party, perhaps the initial stimulus to establish an NEB type organisation was made in 1969 in the document *Labour's Economic Strategy*.[2] There the proposal was for a state holding company along the lines of the Italian organisation IRI; its principal purpose was to promote new public enterprise in an attempt to assist in the solution of the regional problem. By 1972, it was seen as 'the instrument for integrating industries and firms into the public sector'[3] and was no longer confined to regional problems. In 1973, with the publication of an opposition 'green paper', *The National Enterprise Board*,[4] the proposal was nearer full development. This document was the report of a Labour Party study group, later described by Sir Harold Wilson, who was in 1973 leader of the Labour Party, as a sub-committee of a sub-committee.[5] It argued that the extension of public ownership into 'the areas of manufacturing and profitability' was appropriate for two reasons.[6]

First, it was seen to be necessary in order to achieve a fundamental change in 'power relations' or, more specifically, to attack at their roots the causes of inequality. This objective might seem inconsistent with paying compensation to existing private shareholders. Expropriation, however, was not explicitly advocated for these transactions and would have been contrary to the Party's traditions. It seems possible, therefore, that this aspect of the assault on inequality was either bogus or insufficiently analysed.

The second stated reason for extending the public sector in this way was to seek to prevent the 'arbitrary exercise of economic power' from frustrating the 'national will for full employment, regional justice and success in exports'. It was 'plainly evident that private and public interests do not by any means always coincide, and that only direct control through ownership' would allow a future Labour Government 'to achieve its essential planning objectives'. In this connection it was seen to be essential that the NEB would have a substantial involvement in what were termed the 'growth sectors of industry'.

This diagnosis raises a number of problems. First there is the problem of what is meant by the phrase 'arbitrary exercise of economic power' and why such acts might lead to economic failure. For example, economic failure was usually identified by comparing the United Kingdom with other West European countries where similar 'arbitrary' decisions were presumably common. Of course, attempts to maximise profits (which might be one meaning of 'arbitrary') by no means necessarily maximise social well-being. It does not automatically follow, however, that the resulting failure can be avoided by public ownership, still less that it can only be avoided by public ownership.

The second problem concerns the difficulties which face the authorities when they seek to ensure that their chosen instruments of control actually carry out policy goals. There is certainly no shortage of evidence that nationalised industries have not always carried out government wishes. In many areas, in fact, the problem of controlling the nationalised industries has become central for recent governments. Of course, even if effective control over a policy instrument can be achieved, it does not follow that the policy goals can be achieved.

A third problem is that even if a programme works, in the sense, for example, of providing some net new jobs or investment, the cost of these may be too high — the programme may use too many resources. Investment can be raised but will it provide an adequate return? For many of the prospective goals of the early versions of the NEB what was at issue here was whether the organisation could identify growth sectors. This provides a consistent theme for many experiments in the field of industrial policy. The IRC was supposed to confine itself to commercially profitable areas, the original NEB was supposed to identify future success stories, the actual NEB was required to aim for (and implicitly to hit) a target rate of return of 15 to 20 per cent. The big question is how was this to be achieved?

This discussion on the early versions of an NEB organisation, and the range of tasks assigned to it, is largely of academic interest. When they returned to power in 1974, the senior Labour politicians were deeply sceptical of the case made out and they began to water down the proposals. The process is well captured in the titles of two government White Papers. The first, issued in August 1974 was rather bold: *The Regeneration of British Industry*.[7] The second, fifteen months later, was more humble: *An Approach to Industrial Strategy*.[8]

The first draft of the earlier of these two documents was later described by the then Prime Minister as being 'sloppy and half-baked ... polemical, even menacing, in tone'. After redrafting, the 'role and powers of the NEB were strictly defined; above all it was to have no marauding role'.[9] Evidently, considerable infighting accompanied this redrafting and one outcome of this was the replacement of Anthony Benn, a prominent left winger, as chairman of the ministerial committee by the Prime Minister himself and subsequently the substitution of Eric Varley for Mr

Benn as Secretary of State for Industry.

One of those who left office in this process was Eric Heffer. He had had responsibility for piloting the relevant legislation (the Industry Act 1975) through Parliament and occupied (and still does) an influential position on the left of the Party. *The Times* report of his contribution to the debate on the bill conveys some of the tensions and issues:[10]

'Mr Heffer said the private enterprise system had let the British people down over the years. They needed to extend public ownership to get the necessary investment in productive industry. They needed to extend it because the whole structure of Britain's class-ridden society, one of the worst class-ridden societies in the world, was based upon private ownership of the means of production, distribution, and so on.

'This Bill [he said] is only a tiny step towards the type of public ownership I would want to see. If we are to get full employment back and guarantee our people a constant rise in their standard of living we need to extend public ownership on a much greater scale.

'They were not pushing forward a great octopus for taking over every industry in the country.

'His complaint was that the Bill had been weakened in a number of directions. It was not precisely the Bill they had envisaged originally in the Labour Party and the party programme had not been carried out to the full. It was an emasculated Bill, but it could still be a useful instrument, and the disclosure of information to trade unionists could be one of the most important methods of involving the workforce in the running of their country.

'However, the Bill was at least a step in the direction he wanted to go, a step along the line of building the type of egalitarian society where the working people would come into their own and benefit by the labours they put into industry.'

In the same report, a Conservative back-bencher expressed succinctly the views and concerns of many on his side of the House:

'Mr Crouch said the Bill had started off fiercely as a wolf ready to devour any prey. The Prime Minister had dressed it up in sheep's clothing but it was still the same wolf underneath and deceived nobody.'

ROLE OF THE NEB

The NEB, even in the form that emerged in legislation, retained a wider scope than the IRC. The NEB was intended to take over the rationalising and restructuring role of the IRC but, in addition, it had three other functions which the IRC had not had, or had not had to the same extent. These required it to act:

(a) as a state holding company for shares passed to it by the government as well as for those that it might itself acquire in the course of its own operations:

(b) as a provider of finance for industrial investment; and

(c) as a channel for funds which the Government would put into industry for reasons of national policy, regional development and so on. The NEB was, however, to exercise this function only when explicitly directed by the Government to do so.

To perform these functions, the NEB came into legal existence on 19 November 1975, equipped with an opening capital of £1,000 million to be used over the period to April 1980. The Board also took over (though the exact details of the transaction were not agreed for several months) government-owned shareholdings in eight companies: British Leyland, Rolls-Royce, Alfred Herbert, Ferranti, ICL, Dunford and Elliott, Brown Boveri Kent, and Cambridge Instrument Co.

The domination of the NEB's finances (and not only its finances) by these companies — and by two of them in particular, British Leyland and Rolls-Royce — is a major fact of its history. Thus, at 31 January 1979, just prior to the arrival of a Conservative Government, the NEB had made loans totalling £240 million to twenty-four companies; but of this amount, £160 million had gone to British Leyland and £62 million to Rolls-Royce. The other twenty-two companies had received £18 million between them and, of that, Alfred Herbert had received £5 million.

Similarly, at the same date, the Board held shares in fifty companies, the acquisition of which had cost if £1,023 million. Of this amount, £696 million had been used to purchase British Leyland shares and £203 million to purchase Rolls-Royce shares. Its other opening acquisitions from the Government had cost £67 million. Thus, despite the size of the book figures, the NEB had spent only £57 million on its shareholdings in the other forty-two companies.

It could be argued that the book figures on the cost of shares exaggerate the proportion of NEB funds spent on British Leyland and Rolls-Royce. Negotiations between the NEB and the Department of Industry on the price at which government-owned shares should be transferred to the Board continued for several months after its formation. At the root of these negotiations was the fact that the shareholdings which the Government wanted to transfer to the Board were worth less than the Government (or its agencies, such as the IRC) had paid for them. At issue for the NEB was the disposition of its opening capital and the extent to which this would be absorbed by these acquisitions of what were, for the most part, potentially unpromising enterprises. Moreover, the Board had a statutory obligation to aim for a target of a 15 to 20 per cent rate of return on capital employed and the price at which the transfers took place would obviously affect its ability to achieve this. For the Government, a major issue apparently was an unwillingness to focus public attention on the extent to which its holding in British Leyland had lost value since its purchase by the Government. In the event, the NEB 'paid' £246.5 million for the Government's Leyland shares in contrast to their market value of roughly £64 million.

Whatever the element of exaggeration from this source, however, the outstanding fact is that in financial terms the NEB, under the Labour Government that created it, was largely a holding company for assets that were already under government ownership. Its financial commitments elsewhere were small, even trivial, when compared with investment flows in the British economy or, perhaps more pertinently, when compared with the ambitions and intentions of those on the left wing of the Labour Party when they initially advocated its formation. However appropriate the concern of Mr Crouch, as quoted above, and others of like views, with the principle of the NEB, he was wrong in his assessment of the NEB in practice; Mr Heffer was right, and the Prime Minister had indeed changed the NEB from something that could have been a wolf into something very much like a sheep.

The same process is visible in, for example, the progress of the *Guidelines* for the NEB (eventually published on 1 March 1976).[11] In the version of these prepared when Mr Benn was Secretary of State for Industry, the following direction appeared for NEB-controlled enterprises: 'There should be worker's democracy at all levels'. This was later modified into an instruction that the NEB should ensure 'the full involvement of employees in decision making at all levels'. In the published version of the *Guidelines*, the NEB was to ensure that 'management is playing its part in furthering government policies in this field'.

Such matters of political management are of less interest in the present context than is an assessment of the NEB as it actually emerged from this process — that is, as an organisation that combined two distinct functions. These functions were (i) to act as a holding company for the eight companies in which the prior government interest was transferred to the Board at its inception and (ii) to provide finance and management skills for a range of small and medium-size companies. They are distinct in the sense that there is no obvious reason for them to be discharged by the same organisation: neither needs the other in order to be effectively performed. The Conservative Government that took office in May 1979 distinguished the two functions and, in effect, gradually moved towards the elimination of the holding company role. A similar distinction will be made here and the two functions will be treated as requiring separate assessment.

ASSESSING THE NEB

There are major problems of assessment under either heading. How can it be known, even in principle, whether British Leyland would have been more or less of a drain on national resources if it had not been under the umbrella of the NEB? With the smaller companies, selected by the NEB itself, on the other hand, the problem is one of time: the first such NEB investment was in July 1976 and if a selected company has not to date been liquidated, or its association with the NEB otherwise terminated, insufficient time has elapsed to make a persuasive judgement of its merits. Particularly in the case of companies engaged in new technologies: a company which has lost money since 1976 or 1977 may still prove to be an excellent investment.

The NEB as a Holding Company

The experiences of the eight companies inherited by the NEB vary. Possibly the most straightforward way of handling this aspect of NEB activity is to summarise the outcomes of the NEB's involvement with each company. British Leyland and Rolls-Royce are treated first: the remaining six follow in alphabetical order.

British Leyland (BL)

British Leyland's record of profits and losses before tax since 1975 can be seen in Table 9.1. The company's net assets have risen rapidly, from £252 million in 1975 to £1060.8 million in 1978 and £1145.4 million in 1979. The NEB has served as a conduit for close to a thousand million pounds of public funds placed in BL during that company's connection with the NEB.

Table 9.1
British Leyland's Profits (and Losses) Before Tax, 1975–79 (£ million)

12 months to 30.9.75	15 months to 31.12.76	12 months to 31.12.77	12 months to 31.12.78	12 months to 31.12.79
(76.1)	70.6	3.2	1.7	(122.2)

Source: *Annual Report* (London: NEB, various issues).

In the 1979 *Report* of the NEB, its new Chairman, Sir Arthur Knight, made the following comment:

'The Government has decided to relieve the NEB of responsibility for Rolls-Royce and, at the time of writing, is still considering whether to take similar action with BL. My board and I made it plain on our appointment that we welcomed the opportunity to serve an NEB which would no longer be involved in either of these major companies. The magnitude of BL, its problems and its financial requirements means that Government must inevitably be closely involved in its major decisions, thus leaving for the NEB only a relatively minor intermediary role. We would gain nothing of substance by having this illusory responsibility.'

Rolls-Royce (1971) Ltd

Rolls-Royce came into public ownership in 1971 as a result of difficulties with its contract to develop and supply the RB211 engine for the Lockheed Tristar. The Government's 100 per cent stake in the company was transferred to the NEB at a 'cost' of £175 million.

The transfer led to a well-publicised clash between the then Chairman of the NEB (Lord Ryder) and the Chairman of Rolls-Royce (Sir Kenneth Keith) over the extent of the NEB's powers to control Rolls-Royce. Sir Kenneth based his position on the fact that there should be only minimal control (if that) on a memorandum agreed between Rolls-Royce and the Department of Industry under the previous Government but not published until Mr Benn became Secretary of State. This memorandum guaranteed Rolls-Royce substantial freedom from official control. The argument between the two chairmen, however, led to a new 'Memorandum of Understanding' such that *The Times* commented that Sir Kenneth appeared 'to have lost on points'.[12] Nevertheless, the same issue arose again in 1979 after the election of a Conservative Government. This clash was if anything more extensively publicised than the first and Sir Kenneth was widely quoted as having described the NEB as 'a bureaucratic contraceptive' or, in some versions, as having the functional merits of a used contraceptive. On this occasion, the Chairman of the NEB (Sir Leslie Murphy) resigned with his entire board. Rolls-Royce, as indicated by the quotation above from the report of his successor, Sir Arthur Knight, was withdrawn from the NEB portfolio in 1980.

Rolls-Royce profits and losses, before tax, in recent years can be seen in Table 9.2. In 1979, the firm had net assets of £331.5 million.

Table 9.2
Rolls-Royce Profits (and Losses) Before Tax, 1973–79 (£ million)

1973	1974	1975	1976	1977	1978	1979
22.8	16.7	4.5	(21.9)	20.3	11.7	(58.4)

Source: *Annual Report* (London: NEB, various issues).

Brown Boveri Kent and Cambridge Instrument

In June 1968, the IRC paid £6,504,874 for 3,017,577 ordinary and 1,244,180 deferred ordinary shares in Geo. Kent. The purchase was designed to assist a Kent offer for Cambridge Instrument, contested by Rank. Kent was successful. In its 1969 *Report*, the IRC states that: 'The IRC intends to retain its shareholding in Kent for a limited period only until the benefits of the merger have been realized.'[13]

In mid-1974, Kent itself was the object of a bid by Brown Boveri (of Switzerland) which, however, by the terms of the bid effectively excluded the assets of Cambridge Instrument. The bid was contested by GEC. The GEC bid was first backed by the Government but was later opposed by it (Mr Benn changing the government's position on the basis of a vote among Kent workers that favoured Brown Boveri, although those who had been employees of Cambridge Instrument favoured GEC). This opposition was successful and the result was Brown Boveri Kent and a new company, Scientific and Medical Instruments, which essentially comprised the assets of Cambridge Instrument and in fact later changed its name to Cambridge Instrument.

The NEB's *Annual Report* of 1979 notes that Cambridge Instrument had been acquired by CIC Investment Holdings Ltd in October 1977. The NEB held 93 per cent of CIC equity. It remarks that: 'Following the reorganization, the NEB has revised the value of its investment in CIC Investment Holdings. It now stands at £2.9m; £12.1m having been written off in the NEB's accounts for 1979.'[14] In addition, the NEB held 10,856.585 ordinary shares in Brown Boveri Kent (representing a 20 per cent share of the equity) acquired by it at a total cost of £3.29 million. The market value of this holding at 6 February 1981 was £2.39 million.

Dunford and Elliott

The NEB disposed of this holding in March 1977. It had been acquired at a total cost of £192,663 and was sold (to Lonrho) for £353,794.

Ferranti

In its 1978 *Report*, the NEB stated that:

> 'The successful recovery of the Group enabled it to seek a quotation for its shares on the London Stock Exchange. In accordance with the terms of the original agreement between Ferranti and HMG [the Government], the NEB offered for sale part of its holding in Ferranti. This reduced to 50% the NEB's share of the equity and Ferranti has thus become an associate instead of a subsidiary of the NEB. The NEB made a profit of £960,000 on the sale.
> 'The market value of the NEB's investment at 31 December 1978 was £37.9 million, compared with a cost on acquisition of £6.9 million.'[15]

The official shareholding in Ferranti dates from 1974, when the company found itself in financial difficulties — described by it as short-term. Ferranti's bankers (National Westminster) nevertheless refused to provide further finance and insisted that the company approach the Government. The Department of Industry provided a loan of £6.3 million and purchased 62.5 per cent of the equity for £8.7 million. This purchase, however, was subject to the condition that the holding would be reduced to 50 per cent by means of an offer to existing shareholders if the company obtained a listing for its stock before 1 October 1978.

In June 1980, the NEB, under pressure from the Government, announced an intention to sell its remaining 50 per cent share. This proposal raised sharp protests from the Ferranti family, who argued that they had gone to the Government in 1974, rather than having sought a private sector solution to their difficulties, in order to maintain their control of the firm; and that to market the NEB's half of the equity would now, in contradiction to their understanding of 1974, make them vulnerable to a takeover and a loss of

control. The NEB announced in July 1980 that it would sell its
Ferranti holdings with a restrictive covenant preventing resale of
the shares for two years.

Herbert

In May 1970 the IRC was directed under Section 2(1)b of the
IRC Act to assist Herbert-Ingersoll. The IRC announced on 20
May 1970 that it had agreed to make available to Herbert-Ingersoll
a total of £2.5 million. An initial £1 million was taken up on 3 June
1970 — £525,000 in exchange for equity and the remainder as a
loan.

In its 1979 *Report*, the NEB stated that: 'In view of the
reorganization [of Herbert], the cost of the NEB investment of
£44.5 million has been written down to £33.4 million being the
book value of net assets at 31 December 1979.'[16] The NEB
announced at the end of 1979 that it would not provide further
funds and, following a refusal by the NEB in June 1980 to provide
£5 million for a new range of machine tools, the effective
liquidation of the company was announced. This was completed in
September 1980.

ICL

The NEB disposed of its entire holding on 17 December 1979.
The 1979 *Report* notes that: 'The proceeds of the disposal
amounted to £37m, giving a profit of £24m on the NEB investment
of £13m.'[17]

This shareholding (25 per cent of the total equity) derived from
financial assistance given in 1972 by the Government. Since the sale
by the NEB of its shares in ICL, it became clear that the company
was once again experiencing difficulties. Large losses were
announced for 1980 and its share price fell sharply. The Government guaranteed a £200 million bond issue.

How Should these Histories be Weighed?

In the first place, for neither British Leyland nor Rolls-Royce is
there any substantial evidence of underlying improvement in

performance, and certainly none of any improvement wrought by NEB involvement. There is also, however, Sir Arthur Knight's comment, quoted above and presumably made with inside knowledge of past events, that the NEB could have, in the case of such large companies '... only a relatively minor intermediary role'. Treating this as a description of what actually occurred, it seems possibly appropriate and certainly generous to give to the performance and non-performance of British Leyland and Rolls-Royce a zero weight in assessing the NEB.

Six companies then remain. The affairs of three of them — Brown Boveri Kent, Cambridge Instrument and Herbert — cannot at the moment compare well with any ambitions the NEB might ever have had for them.

The NEB has had better results, at least financially, with disposals of its holdings in Dunford and Elliott, Ferranti and ICL. The relevant question in these cases, however, from the point of view of assessing the NEB, is whether the involvement of the NEB with these companies produced, or contributed to, the good financial results, in particular, by improving the quality of management decisions. The facts of each case rest between the NEB and the company concerned; but, in each case, there is ground for scepticism that the NEB played a large role. In the case of Dunford and Elliott, the company was associated with the NEB for only a few months prior to the bid from Lonrho. In both this case and that of ICL, the NEB had only a minority holding. Moreover, in each of these cases, those who purchased from the NEB have had some cause to be disgruntled. The decline in ICL's profits and share-price has already been mentioned; in addition, Lonrho, after its takeover of Dunford and Elliott, discovered major discrepancies between forecast and actual profits and considered legal action against the former directors as a result. These post-NEB performances suggest the possibility that in either or both of these cases, the good financial result for the NEB failed to reflect accurately changes in underlying performance which might have been small or non-existent.

In the case of Ferranti, the NEB did have, for something less than three years, a majority holding in Ferranti. But it obtained that holding — or the Department of Industry did so — precisely because the Ferrantis were unwilling to give up control of the company, as might have been required by a private sector solution to the 1974 difficulties of the firm. It might seem implausible, then, that the Ferranti management would be willing to concede much scope to the NEB. Moreover, the Ferrantis always mentioned that their financial difficulties were temporary and that the company would again become profitable as new products were commercially established. These observations cannot disprove, of course, those press reports which, at the time of the first NEB sale of Ferranti stock, claimed for the NEB a major share in Ferranti's recovery. Nevertheless, they suggest that it would be sensible to exercise some caution before accepting such reports at face value.

Regardless of whether the NEB had any hand in restoring any company to profitability, however, the fact remains that — still excluding British Leyland and Rolls-Royce — it made a great deal of money on the shares that it acquired from the Government. Of course, one part of the art of making money in the stock market is to buy at the bottom. A government standing ready to buy shares offered to it by distressed companies is likely to find that its purchases tend to cluster around that point of depression; and if some of these distressed companies recover, such a government will find that it has 'picked' some winners. In December 1979, The *Financial Times* Actuaries 500 Share Index[18] stood at close to twice the value it had had in December 1976, the year in which these companies were transferred from the Department of Industry to the NEB; and this latter value was more than twice the value of the same index in December 1974, the year in which Ferranti sought assistance. Anyone entering the market in 1976 should, with average luck, have roughly doubled his initial stake.

But even if the NEB (or the Department of Industry) did genuinely succeed in making money in the stock market, this could not, in and of itself, be adduced as evidence that it had succeeded in its function — which clearly was to improve the operating efficiency of those companies with whom it was associated. The evidence available does not establish any such effect.

Companies Selected by the NEB

In the 1979 *Report* of the NEB, Sir Arthur Knight notes that, after excluding British Leyland and Rolls-Royce: 'The new Board inherited on 22 November 1979 a continuing business containing

67 shareholdings with a book value of £155 million'.[19] As noted above, while a company continues to survive, it must for present purposes be regarded as a potential source of future profits whatever its past record and this is true *a fortiori* for companies engaged in the development of high technology products, as are several members of the NEB's portfolio. Although just, however, this proposition does not provide a good basis for assessment of the NEB; and it follows that particular interest must focus on those companies that have completed their connection with the NEB, in particular, those which have been liquidated.

At the time of the 1979 NEB *Report* there were ten of these. They are listed below together with the month and year of the initial NEB investment and the loss to the NEB as a result of the liquidation (see Table 9.3).

During 1976, the NEB made a total of five investments. By the end of 1979, one of these had been liquidated and one (Reed and Smith Holdings) had been taken over at a profit to the NEB of £0.76 million. The three investments in which the NEB had a continuing financial interest had received by that date a total of some £16 million of NEB funds. Similarly, the surviving members of the NEB's 1977 investment programme numbered fourteen at the end of 1979 and again contained some £16 million of NEB investments.

Table 9.3
Companies Associated with the NEB and Liquidated

Company	Date of first NEB investment	Loss to NEB (£m)
Sinclair Radionics	11.76	7.8
Pakmet International	4.77	0.36
Thwaites & Reed	5.77	0.45
BTP	5.77	5.56
Hivent	9.77	0.11
Mayflower Packaging	12.77	0.17
Vicort	1.78	0.25
Power Dynamics	1.78	0.3
J and P	7.78	0.2
Technical Resources	12.78	0.33

Source: *Annual Report* (London: NEB, various issues).

The eventual pay-off on these investments may be sufficiently handsome to cover the £7 million already lost on 1976 investments and the £6 million on 1977 investments. Evidently, however, the dice are now loaded against that possibility: in order to compensate for these losses, the remaining investments must earn a rate of return that is some 50 per cent higher than that earned in the economy at large.

CONCLUSIONS

In July 1981, the NEB disappeared through merger with another public body — the National Research Development Council — from which emerged British Technology. This merger may signify the *de facto* end of the NEB's activities. Nothing in the evidence suggests that the British economy would be worse-off as a result.

Nevertheless, the idea lives on. The Trades Union Congress (TUC) Economic Review of 1981 states:[20]

> 'The TUC is calling for the establishment of a new National Investment Bank as an engine for rebuilding the economy. The new NIB would channel £1 billion from the National Oil Fund and £1 billion from the pension and life assurance funds each year into strategic long-term manufacturing investment. Closely linked to this bank would be a body like the National Enterprise Board but with a stronger initiating role.

> 'The NEB and other planning bodies must avoid being over centralized or obsessed with narrowsighted "rationalisation". These problems can be avoided if economic planning is firmly rooted in industrial democracy, extending the influence and activities of workplace union organisation.'

NOTES AND REFERENCES

1.   *Labour's Programme 1973* (London: Labour Party, 1973) p. 33.

2.   *Labour's Economic Strategy* (London: Labour Party, 1969) p. 40.

3. *Labour's Programme for Britain* (London: Labour Party, 1972) p. 29.

4. *The National Enterprise Board*, Report of a Labour Party Study Group (London: Labour Party, 1973).

5. Harold Wilson, *Final Term* (London: Michael Joseph, 1979) p. 30.

6. *The National Enterprise Board, op. cit.*, pp. 9–10.

7. *The Regeneration of British Industry*, Government White Paper (London: H.M. Stationery Office, August 1974).

8. *An Approach to Industrial Strategy*, Government White Paper (London: H.M. Stationery Office, November 1975).

9. Wilson, *op. cit.*, p. 33.

10. *The Times*, London, 4 July 1975.

11. *Guidelines*, Department of Industry, London, 1 March 1976.

12. *The Times*, 27 February 1976.

13. *IRC Report* (London: IRC, 1969) p. 31.

14. *NEB Annual Report* (London: NEB, 1979).

15. *NEB Annual Report* (London: NEB, 1978).

16. *NEB Annual Report*, 1979.

17. *Ibid.*

18. *Financial Times*, London, December 1979.

19. *NEB Annual Report*, 1979.

20. *Trades Union Congress Economic Review* (London: TUC, 1981) pp. 23–24.

Index

In subdivisions throughout this index, names of state investment companies have been abbreviated to their initials. A list of abbreviations can be found on pp. xxiii–xxiv.